Conference of the North American Chapter of the Association for Computational Linguistics: Human Language Technologies (NAACL HLT 2019)

Demonstrations Sessions

Minneapolis, Minnesota, USA
2 – 7 June 2019

ISBN: 978-1-5108-8757-2

NAACL HLT 2019

**The 2019 Conference of the
North American Chapter of the
Association for Computational Linguistics:
Human Language Technologies**

Proceedings of the Demonstrations Session

June 2 - June 7, 2019
Minneapolis, MN

Introduction

Welcome to the system demonstrations track at NAACL-HLT 2019. We received 63 submissions in total, 24 of which were accepted.

We thank all the authors who submitted their work, and our program committee members for their hard work in helping us select an excellent set of demos.

Organizers:

Waleed Ammar, Allen Institute for Artificial Intelligence
Annie Louis, University of Edinburgh
Nasrin Mostafazadeh, Elemental Cognition

Program Committee:

Puneet Agarwal, TCS Research
Tamer Alkhouli, RWTH Aachen University
Omar Alonso, Microsoft
Pepa Atanasova, University of Copenhagen
Tyler Baldwin, IBM Research - Almaden
Guntis Barzdins, University of Latvia
Iz Beltagy, Allen Institute for Artificial Intelligence
Akash Bharadwaj, Elemental Cognition
Mikhail Burtsev, Moscow Institute of Physics and Technology
Miles Crawford, Allen Institute for Artificial Intelligence
Montse Cuadros, Vicomtech
Thierry Declerck, DFKI GmbH
Tim Dettmers, University of Washington
Lipika Dey, TCS
Pradeep Dogga, UCLA
Eduard Dragut, Temple University
Roald Eiselen, South African Centre for Digital Language Resources (SADiLaR)
Emad Elwany, Allen Institute for Artificial Intelligence
Debasis Ganguly, IBM Research Lab, Dublin
Ulrich Germann, University of Edinburgh
Martin Gleize, IBM Research Ireland
Ajda Gokcen, The University of Washington
Maarten van Gompel, Radboud University Nijmegen
Frank Grimm, Semantic Computing Group, CITEC, Bielefeld University
Joel Grus, Allen Institute for Artificial Intelligence
Suchin Gururangan, Allen Institute for AI
Francisco Guzmán, Facebook
Jingguang Han, Accenture Labs
Jer Hayes, Accenture Labs
Ari Holtzman, University of Washington
Charles Jochim, IBM Research
Sujeong Kim, SRI International
Roman Klinger, University of Stuttgart
Sunil Kumar Kopparapu, TCS Research and Innovation - Mumbai
Brigitte Krenn, Austrian Research Institute for Artificial Intelligence
Vishwajeet Kumar, IITB-Monash Research Academy
Ni Lao, mosaix.ai
Chen Li, Tencent
Zuchao Li, Shanghai Jiao Tong University
Yiyun Liang, University of Waterloo
Ying Lin, Rensselaer Polytechnic Institute
Wei Liu, The University of Western Austarlia
Nicholas Lourie, Allen Institute for Artificial Intelligence

Di Lu, Rensselaer Polytechnic Institute
Ayush Maheshwari, IIT Bombay
Yuji Matsumoto, Nara Institute of Science and Technology
Jonathan May, USC Information Sciences Institute
James Mayfield, Johns Hopkins University
Marie-Jean Meurs, Université du Québec à Montréal
Ivan Vladimir Meza Ruiz, Insituto de Investigaciones en Matemáticas Aplicadas y en Sistemas (IIMAS-UNAM)
Pasquale Minervini, UCL
Sebastião Miranda, Priberam Labs
Preslav Nakov, Qatar Computing Research Institute, HBKU
Tsuyoshi Okita, Kyushuu institute of technology university
Girish Palshikar, Tata Consultancy Services Limited
Michael Pust, Information Sciences Institute
Brendan Roof, Allen Institute for Artificial Intelligence
Dan Roth, University of Pennsylvania
Masoud Rouhizadeh, Johns Hopkins University
Irene Russo, ILC CNR
Swapna Somasundaran, Educational Testing Services
Oyvind Tafjord, AI2
Niket Tandon, Allen Institute for Artificial Intelligence
Zhucheng Tu, University of Waterloo
Chuan-Ju Wang, Academia Sinica
Lyndon White, The University of Western Australia
Zhuoran Yu, Google
Boliang Zhang, Rensselaer Polytechnic Institue
Zhuosheng Zhang, Shanghai Jiao Tong University

Table of Contents

Conference Program

Monday, June 3, 2019

15:00–16:30   *Session I*

Abbreviation Explorer - an interactive system for pre-evaluation of Unsupervised Abbreviation Disambiguation
Manuel Ciosici and Ira Assent

ADIDA: Automatic Dialect Identification for Arabic
Ossama Obeid, Mohammad Salameh, Houda Bouamor and Nizar Habash

Enabling Search and Collaborative Assembly of Causal Interactions Extracted from Multilingual and Multi-domain Free Text
George C. G. Barbosa, Zechy Wong, Gus Hahn-Powell, Dane Bell, Rebecca Sharp, Marco A. Valenzuela-Escárcega and Mihai Surdeanu

INS: An Interactive Chinese News Synthesis System
Hui Liu, Wentao Qin and Xiaojun Wan

Learning to Respond to Mixed-code Queries using Bilingual Word Embeddings
Chia-Fang Ho, Jason Chang, Jhih-Jie Chen and Chingyu Yang

Train, Sort, Explain: Learning to Diagnose Translation Models
Robert Schwarzenberg, David Harbecke, Vivien Macketanz, Eleftherios Avramidis and Sebastian Möller

17:00–18:30   *Session II*

compare-mt: A Tool for Holistic Comparison of Language Generation Systems
Graham Neubig, Zi-Yi Dou, Junjie Hu, Paul Michel, Danish Pruthi and Xinyi Wang

Eidos, INDRA, & Delphi: From Free Text to Executable Causal Models
Rebecca Sharp, Adarsh Pyarelal, Benjamin Gyori, Keith Alcock, Egoitz Laparra, Marco A. Valenzuela-Escárcega, Ajay Nagesh, Vikas Yadav, John Bachman, Zheng Tang, Heather Lent, Fan Luo, Mithun Paul, Steven Bethard, Kobus Barnard, Clayton Morrison and Mihai Surdeanu

fairseq: A Fast, Extensible Toolkit for Sequence Modeling
Myle Ott, Sergey Edunov, Alexei Baevski, Angela Fan, Sam Gross, Nathan Ng, David Grangier and Michael Auli

FLAIR: An Easy-to-Use Framework for State-of-the-Art NLP
Alan Akbik, Tanja Bergmann, Duncan Blythe, Kashif Rasul, Stefan Schweter and Roland Vollgraf

Monday, June 3, 2019 (continued)

ChatEval: A Tool for Chatbot Evaluation
Joao Sedoc, Daphne Ippolito, Arun Kirubarajan, Jai Thirani, Lyle Ungar and Chris
Callison-Burch

*LeafNATS: An Open-Source Toolkit and Live Demo System for Neural Abstractive
Text Summarization*
Tian Shi, Ping Wang and Chandan K. Reddy

Tuesday, June 4, 2019

11:00–12:30   *Session III*

End-to-End Open-Domain Question Answering with BERTserini
Wei Yang, Yuqing Xie, Aileen Lin, Xingyu Li, Luchen Tan, Kun Xiong, Ming Li
and Jimmy Lin

FAKTA: An Automatic End-to-End Fact Checking System
Moin Nadeem, Wei Fang, Brian Xu, Mitra Mohtarami and James Glass

iComposer: An Automatic Songwriting System for Chinese Popular Music
Hsin-Pei Lee, Jhih-Sheng Fang and Wei-Yun Ma

Plan, Write, and Revise: an Interactive System for Open-Domain Story Generation
Seraphina Goldfarb-Tarrant, Haining Feng and Nanyun Peng

LT Expertfinder: An Evaluation Framework for Expert Finding Methods
Tim Fischer, Steffen Remus and Chris Biemann

SkillBot: Towards Automatic Skill Development via User Demonstration
Yilin Shen, Avik Ray, Hongxia Jin and Sandeep Nama

15:30–17:00   *Session IV*

Multilingual Entity, Relation, Event and Human Value Extraction
Manling Li, Ying Lin, Joseph Hoover, Spencer Whitehead, Clare Voss, Morteza
Dehghani and Heng Ji

*Litigation Analytics: Extracting and querying motions and orders from US federal
courts*
Thomas Vacek, Dezhao Song, Hugo Molina-Salgado, Ronald Teo, Conner Cowling
and Frank Schilder

Abbreviation Explorer - an interactive system for pre-evaluation of Unsupervised Abbreviation Disambiguation

Manuel R. Ciosici
UNSILO A/S and
Aarhus University
Aarhus, Denmark
manuel@cs.au.dk

Ira Assent
Department of Computer Science
Aarhus University
Aarhus, Denmark
ira@cs.au.dk

Abstract

We present *Abbreviation Explorer*, a system that supports interactive exploration of abbreviations that are challenging for Unsupervised Abbreviation Disambiguation (UAD). *Abbreviation Explorer* helps to identify long-forms that are easily confused, and to pinpoint likely causes such as limitations of normalization, language switching, or inconsistent typing. It can also support determining which long-forms would benefit from additional input text for unsupervised abbreviation disambiguation. The system provides options for creating corrective rules that merge redundant long-forms with identical meaning. The identified rules can be easily applied to the already existing vector spaces used by *UAD* to improve disambiguation performance, while also avoiding the cost of retraining.

1 Introduction

Abbreviations are short forms of concepts that authors employ to avoid repeated typing of long text sequences (e.g. *National Aeronautics and Space Administration* is abbreviated to *NASA*). Because long-forms are represented by shorter sequences of characters (often just two or three), even in the same domain, multiple concepts may map to the same short-form. Such ambiguous abbreviations, i.e., short-forms with several potential meanings, are quite common. A study by Liu et al. (2001) showed that 23.1% of abbreviations in the Unified Medical Language System (UMLS) ontology, a popular resource in the field of medicine, are ambiguous, meaning that they map to more than one long-form.

Abbreviation disambiguation is the task of identifying the intended long-form for an ambiguous short-form, given its use in a sentence. Expansion and disambiguation of abbreviations can make technical text easier to read (Ciosici and As-

sent, 2018). The task of disambiguating abbreviations in context has been included in both the 2013 and 2014 ShAReCLEF eHealth Challenge (Mowery et al., 2016).

Unsupervised Abbreviation Disambiguation (UAD) (Ciosici et al., 2019) is a recent unsupervised approach that identifies ambiguous abbreviations, and makes use of word embeddings to identify the intended long-forms given contextual uses of ambiguous abbreviations. While successfully disambiguating the vast majority of the ambiguous abbreviations, some difficult cases remain. Following an idea of pre-evaluation in suggested by Ciosici et al. (2019), we present a system called *Abbreviation Explorer* that supports investigation and correction of word embedding spaces learned by *UAD*. Highlighting difficult cases, it allows inspection of likely causes and potential resolution through rewrite rules. The rules can either be used to retrain *UAD*, or directly applied to its vector space, thus eliminating the need to retrain the model. *Abbreviation Explorer* does not target simple variations in long-forms such as plurals, hyphenation, or minor text variations as identified by Zhou et al. (2006); Moon et al. (2015). Such noise is eliminated by *UAD*'s pre-processing pipeline. Rather, it focuses on semantically challenging abbreviations, or those where the unstructured text input corpus provided to *UAD* does not provide sufficient context for successful disambiguation. *Abbreviation Explorer* is a general tool for long-form normalization that does not require expert knowledge or domain-specific, human-curated knowledge bases that approaches like Melton et al. (2010) rely on.

Abbreviation Explorer thus supports the user in understanding which abbreviations are difficult to disambiguate, why *UAD* might not have been able to learn how they differ, in issuing corrections that immediately improve the disambiguation perfor-

1

Proceedings of NAACL-HLT 2019: Demonstrations, pages 1–5
Minneapolis, Minnesota, June 2 - June 7, 2019. ©2019 Association for Computational Linguistics

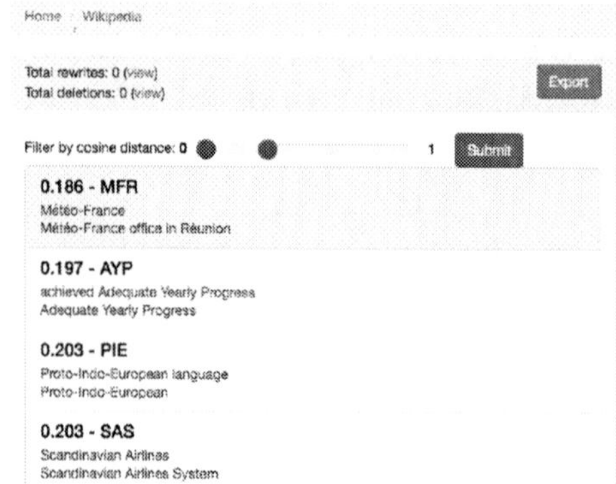

Figure 1: The main screen of *Abbreviation Explorer* listing long-forms that are challenging for disambiguation.

Figure 2: Detail screen with subset of words that appear often in the context of the long-forms *average annual daily traffic* and *annual average daily traffic*. The large frequency of contextual terms indicates that the two long-forms likely denote the same concept.

mance, or in determining where more input text would allow learning of better representations and result in improved disambiguation. All this, without having to conduct expensive, large-scale evaluation on abbreviation disambiguation tasks that require manually labeled data. In fact, *Abbreviation Explorer* takes as input only the vector model trained by *UAD* and the training data that was used to generate the vector model. [1]

2 Pre-evaluation analysis

Long-forms that map into the same short-form and are close to each other in the *UAD* vector space are correlated with low disambiguation performance (Ciosici et al., 2019). Long-forms end up close to each other in the vector space due to incorrect long-form normalization in *UAD*, inconsistent reference by humans (*annual average daily traffic* vs. *average annual daily traffic*), language switching (*Centre National de la Recherche Scientifique* vs. *Centre for Scientific Research*), multi-layer abbreviations (*Voice over IP* vs. *Voice over Internet Protocol*), organization name changes (*Organisation of Islamic Cooperation* vs. *Organisation of the Islamic Conference*), or lack of sufficient examples in the input text for a proper representation.

Abbreviation Explorer identifies these cases using the cosine distance between pairs of long-forms belonging to the same short-form, and presents them to the user for interactive exploration. Figure 1 shows the main screen of *Abbreviation Explorer* displaying a list of long-forms and

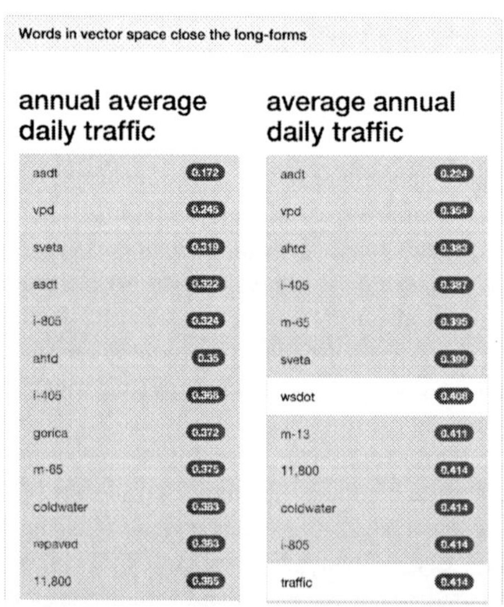

Figure 3: Detail screen with subset of words close to the two challenging long-forms. Red rows indicate words that are close to both long-forms. The large overlap indicates that the two long-forms likely denote the same concept.

---

[1] A presentation video of the system is available at `https://youtu.be/XsBb7QMkDdg`

the cosine distance between them. In some cases, it is obvious even without domain knowledge that the pairs are lexical variations that should be collapsed into a single long-form.

For less obvious cases, *Abbreviation Explorer* provides the user with a page containing information that supports investigation. It provides two indicators for contextual analysis: a list of most common words observed in training examples for both long-forms, and a list of the top 30 words in the word embedding space that are close to each long-form. The list of common words observed in training data for both long-forms helps identify cases where the two long-forms denote the same concept, or where the training data is inconclusive for effective disambiguation. The list of top words in the vector space can be used to pinpoint long-forms that denote the same concept even when the training data does not contain significant word overlap. Figures 2 and 3 show the two views for the abbreviation *AADT* which is expressed in the data as *annual average daily traffic* and *average annual daily traffic*. The view helps users conclude that the two long-forms are term variations of the same concept as they are used in similar contexts. On the other hand, long-forms that denote separate concepts often have little, if any, overlap between the sets of close words. In Figure 4, we can see that for the abbreviation *ABC*, its two correctly identified long-forms *American Broadcasting Company* and *Australian Broadcasting Corporation* have no shared context as they denote separate concepts.

Abbreviation Explorer supports two kinds of actions for pairs of close long-forms that should be corrected. The user can either choose to issue a manual rewrite rule, forcing the system to collapse one long-form into the other, or ask for a long-form to be deleted from the system. The latter action is useful for addressing issues in the input text processing that are not captured in *UAD*'s pre-processing. For example, in the case of the short-form FN, *Front* is picked up as a long-form instead of *Front Nationale* (which is the correct long-form) due to the greedy nature of *UAD*'s normalization which identifies Front as a long-form because it contains both letters F and N.

Rewrite and deletion rules from *Abbreviation Explorer* can be exported as a *JSON* document which can then be used in two ways. It can either be applied to the training data employed by *UAD*,

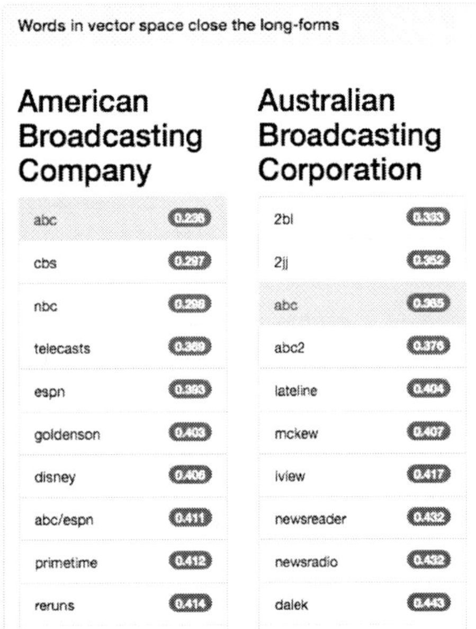

Words in vector space close the long-forms

American Broadcasting Company		Australian Broadcasting Corporation	
abc	0.296	2bl	0.333
cbs	0.297	2jj	0.352
nbc	0.298	abc	0.365
telecasts	0.389	abc2	0.376
espn	0.393	lateline	0.404
goldenson	0.403	mckew	0.407
disney	0.406	iview	0.417
abc/espn	0.411	newsreader	0.432
primetime	0.412	newsradio	0.432
reruns	0.414	dalek	0.443

Figure 4: Detail screen with subset of words in the vector space close to the two challenging long-forms. Red rows indicate words that are close to both long-forms. The lack of vocabulary overlap indicates that the two long-forms denote separate concepts.

and then be used to train another word vector space, or they can be applied directly to the word embedding space to adjust vectors of long-forms. Using the correction rules directly on *UAD*'s vector space avoids the effort required to re-derive word vector spaces. In the next section we discuss the performance benefits of the various ways of applying corrections to *UAD*.

3 Evaluation of Abbreviation Explorer

In order to study the effect of manual corrections created using *Abbreviation Explorer*, we the same Wikipedia data set that was used in the evaluation of *UAD* (Ciosici et al., 2019). For all experiments, we employed $10 - fold$ cross-validation, with the same folds used in the *UAD* evaluation. In experiments requiring *UAD* training, we used the same *word2vec* hyper-parameters as in *UAD* evaluation.

With *Abbreviation Explorer*, we identified 40 pairs of long-forms that denote the same concept. As mentioned earlier, correction rules can either be applied to the data followed by a retraining of *UAD*, or they can be applied directly to already trained *UAD* models. We study two ways to correct preexisting vector spaces: (1) for every pair of long-forms denoting the same concept remove

	Disambiguator	Acc.	Weighted			Macro		
			Prec.	Rec.	F1	Prec.	Rec.	F1
1	UAD with TXT	94.28	96.17	94.28	94.76	90.84	93.29	90.98
2	Removed long-forms	**96.38**	**97.34**	**96.38**	**96.61**	**92.72**	**95.15**	**93.15**
3	Averaged long-form vectors	96.37	97.32	96.37	96.60	92.64	95.12	93.11
4	Retrained UAD with TXT	96.28	97.33	96.28	96.54	92.64	95.13	93.07

Table 1: Comparisons with UAD on data set Wikipedia (no-stopwords).

one long-form from the vector space and (2) for every pair of long-forms denoting the same concept, we replace the two long-form vectors with their average. In Table 1, we provide a comparison of disambiguation performance following the three corrective methods. The first row contains disambiguation performance of *UAD* without any corrections; rows 2 and 3 contain the two vector adjustment methods applied to the vector space from the first row using corrections identified with *Abbreviation Explorer*; and the last row contains the performance of *UAD* retrained on data where we applied corrections identified with *Abbreviation Explorer*.

All three corrective methods outperform *UAD* on the original data, using no corrections, by up to 1.85 weighted F1 points. Both precision and recall are improved after applying the corrective rules. This illustrates the usefulness of *Abbreviation Explorer* in supporting users to issue manual corrections for difficult long-forms. Another important result in Table 1, is that the three correction methods studied result in performances within 0.07 weighted F1 points of each other. Removing a long-form from the vector space, or averaging two long-forms is considerably less costly than a complete re-derivation of the word embedding space utilized by *UAD*. This leads us to conclude that adjusting *UAD*'s vector spaces is preferred as it results in similar performance to retraining *UAD*, but does not incur the time cost of re-deriving word vector spaces.

4   Conclusion

We present *Abbreviation Explorer*, a system that supports interactive exploration of abbreviations that are easily confused by *Unsupervised Abbreviation Disambiguation (UAD)*. *Abbreviation Explorer* works by identifying and understanding long-forms whose learned word embedding representations are close to each other and providing contextual information to help users understand which long-forms denote the same concept. *Abbreviation Explorer* can assist users who are not domain-experts in generating corrective rules that address abbreviation disambiguation difficulties due to incorrect long-form normalization, inconsistent typing, language switching, multi-layer abbreviations, organization name changes, and more. Corrective rules generated using *Abbreviation Explorer* can be used to improve the disambiguation performance of *UAD*, even without performing expensive full-scale evaluation using labeled data. The corrective rules can be applied to the already existing vector spaces used by *UAD* to improve disambiguation performance, while, at the same time, avoiding the cost of retraining *UAD*.

References

Ciosici, Manuel, Sommer, Tobias, Assent, and Ira. 2019. Unsupervised Abbreviation Disambiguation Contextual disambiguation using word embeddings. *arXiv e-prints*, page arXiv:1904.00929.

Manuel Ciosici and Ira Assent. 2018. Abbreviation expander-a web-based system for easy reading of technical documents. In *Proceedings of the 27th International Conference on Computational Linguistics: System Demonstrations*, pages 1–4.

Hongfang Liu, Yves A Lussier, and Carol Friedman. 2001. A study of abbreviations in the UMLS. In *Proc. AMIA Symp.*, page 393.

Genevieve B Melton, SungRim Moon, Bridget McInnes, and Serguei Pakhomov. 2010. Automated identification of synonyms in biomedical acronym sense inventories. In *Proc. Louhi Workshop on Text and Data Mining of Health Documents*, pages 46–52.

Sungrim Moon, Bridget McInnes, and Genevieve B Melton. 2015. Challenges and Practical Approaches with Word Sense Disambiguation of Acronyms and Abbreviations in the Clinical Domain. *Healthc Inform Res*, 21(1):35–42.

Danielle L Mowery, Brett R South, Lee Christensen, Jianwei Leng, Laura-Maria Peltonen, Sanna

Salanterä, Hanna Suominen, David Martinez, Sumithra Velupillai, Noémie Elhadad, Guergana Savova, Sameer Pradhan, and Wendy W Chapman. 2016. Normalizing acronyms and abbreviations to aid patient understanding of clinical texts: ShARe/CLEF eHealth Challenge 2013, Task 2. *Journal of Biomedical Semantics*, 7(1):43.

Wei Zhou, Vetle I. Torvik, and Neil R. Smalheiser. 2006. Adam: another database of abbreviations in medline. *Bioinformatics*, 22(22):2813–2818.

ADIDA: Automatic Dialect Identification for Arabic

Ossama Obeid, Mohammad Salameh,[†] **Houda Bouamor,**[†] **Nizar Habash**
New York University Abu Dhabi, UAE
[†]Carnegie Mellon University in Qatar, Qatar
{oobeid,nizar.habash}@nyu.edu
{msalameh,hbouamor}@cmu.edu

Abstract

This demo paper describes ADIDA, a web-based system for automatic dialect identification for Arabic text. The system distinguishes among the dialects of 25 Arab cities (from Rabat to Muscat) in addition to Modern Standard Arabic. The results are presented with either a point map or a heat map visualizing the automatic identification probabilities over a geographical map of the Arab World.

1 Introduction

The last few years have witnessed an increased interest within the natural language processing (NLP) community in the computational modeling of dialectal and non-standard varieties of languages (Malmasi et al., 2016; Zampieri et al., 2017, 2018). The Arabic language, which is a collection of variants or dialects, has received a decent amount of attention in this regard with a number of efforts focusing on dialect identification, translation and other forms of modeling. In this demo paper, we present ADIDA,[1] a public online interface for visualizing fine-grained dialect identification of Arabic text (Salameh et al., 2018). The dialect identification system produces a vector of probabilities indicating the likelihood an input sentence is from 25 cities (Table 1) and Modern Standard Arabic (MSA). ADIDA displays the results with either a point map or a heat map overlaid on top of a geographical map of the Arab World.

2 Arabic and its Dialects

Although MSA is the official language across the Arab World, it is not the native language of any speakers of Arabic. Dialectal Arabic (DA), on the other hand, is the daily informal spoken variety.

DA is nowadays emerging as the primary language of communication – not just spoken, but also written, particularly in social media. Arabic dialects are often classified in terms of geographical regions, such as Levantine Arabic, Gulf Arabic and Egyptian Arabic (Habash, 2010). However, within each of these regional groups, there is significant variation down to the village, town, and city levels. The demo we present is based on the work of Salameh et al. (2018), who utilize the MADAR Project parallel corpus of 25 Arab cities plus MSA (Table 1) (Bouamor et al., 2018).[2]

Arabic dialects differ in various ways from MSA and from each other. These include phonological, morphological, lexical, and syntactic differences (Haeri, 1991; Holes, 2004; Watson, 2007; Bassiouney, 2009). Despite these differences, distinguishing between Arabic dialects in written form is an arduous task because: (i) dialects use the same writing script and share part of the vocabulary; and (ii) Arabic speakers usually resort to repeated code-switching between their dialect and MSA (Abu-Melhim, 1991; Bassiouney, 2009), creating sentences with different levels of dialectness (Habash et al., 2008).

3 Related Work

3.1 Arabic Dialect Processing

While automatic processing of DA is relatively recent compared to MSA, it has attracted a considerable amount of research in NLP (Shoufan and Al-Ameri, 2015). Most of it focuses on (i) collecting datasets from various sources and at different levels (Zaidan and Callison-Burch, 2011; Khalifa et al., 2016; Abdul-Mageed et al., 2018; Bouamor et al., 2018), (ii) creating processing tools (Habash et al., 2013; Al-Shargi and Rambow, 2015; Obeid et al., 2018) (iii) developing DA to English ma-

---

[1]https://adida.abudhabi.nyu.edu/
The Arabic word عديدة /ʕadida/ means 'numerous'.

[2]https://camel.abudhabi.nyu.edu/madar/

Proceedings of NAACL-HLT 2019: Demonstrations, pages 6–11
Minneapolis, Minnesota, June 2 - June 7, 2019. ©2019 Association for Computational Linguistics

Region	Maghreb				Nile Basin	Levant		Gulf		Yemen
Sub-region	Morocco	Algeria	Tunisia	Libya	Egypt/Sudan	South Levant	North Levant	Iraq	Gulf	Yemen
Cities	Rabat Fes	Algiers	Tunis Sfax	Tripoli Benghazi	Cairo Alexandria Aswan Khartoum	Jerusalem Amman Salt	Beirut Damascus Aleppo	Mosul Baghdad Basra	Doha Muscat Riyadh Jeddah	Sana'a

Table 1: Different city dialects covered in ADIDA and the regions they belong to.

chine translation systems (Zbib et al., 2012; Sajjad et al., 2013), (iv) or performing dialect identification (Zaidan and Callison-Burch, 2014; Huang, 2015; Salameh et al., 2018).

3.2 Dialect Identification

Dialect Identification (DID) is a particularly challenging task compared to Language Identification (Etman and Beex, 2015). Since Arabic dialects use the same script and share part of the vocabulary, it is quite arduous to distinguish between them. Hence, developing an automatic identification system working at different levels of representation and exploring different datasets has attracted increasing attention in recent years. For instance, DID has been the goal of a dedicated shared task (Malmasi et al., 2016; Zampieri et al., 2017, 2018), encouraging researchers to submit systems to recognize the dialect of speech transcripts for dialects of four main regions: Egyptian, Gulf, Levantine and North African, and MSA. Several systems implementing a range of traditional supervised learning (Tillmann et al., 2014) and deep learning methods (Belinkov and Glass, 2016; Michon et al., 2018) were proposed.

In the literature, a number of studies have been exploring DID using several datasets, ranging from user-generated content (i.e., blogs, social media posts) (Sadat et al., 2014), speech transcripts (Biadsy et al., 2009; Bougrine et al., 2017), and other corpora (Elfardy and Diab, 2012, 2013; Zaidan and Callison-Burch, 2014; Salameh et al., 2018; Dinu et al., 2018; Goldman et al., 2018). Shoufan and Al-Ameri (2015) and Al-Ayyoub et al. (2017) present a survey on NLP and deep learning methods for processing Arabic dialectal data with an overview on Arabic DID of text and speech. While most of the proposed approaches targeted regional or country level DID, Salameh et al. (2018) introduced a fine-grained DID system covering the dialects of 25 cities from several countries across the Arab world (from Rabat to Muscat), including some cities in the same country.

3.3 Visualization

Map visualizations are used in multiple fields of study including linguistics, socio-linguistics, and political science to display geographical relations of non-geographic data. Geographical visualizations may include point maps to display individual data points, choropleths and Voronoi tessalation maps that cluster data points by region, and heat maps and surface maps that interpolate data over some geographical area.

In the general context of visualization of language data, one example is the Visualizing Medieval Places project (Wrisley, 2017, 2019), which extracted place names from medieval French texts and overlaid them over their physical locations as a point map with a color ramp to display their frequency. The Linguistic Landscapes of Beirut Project (Wrisley, 2016) visualizes the presence of multilingual written samples within the greater Beirut area using different geographical visualizations to explore different aspects of its data. Specifically in the context of dialectometric visualizations, most relevant to this paper, Scherrer and Stoeckle (2016) provide surface and Voronoi tessalation maps[3] to visualize difference in Swiss German dialects using data extracted from the *Sprachatlas der deutschen Schweiz*. Similarly, data collected from *The Harvard Dialect Survey* (Vaux and Golder, 2003) used point maps to display phrase variation across American English dialects. Katz and Andrews (2013) provide further visualization of *The Harvard Dialect Survey* using heat maps to interpolate data from the survey.

4 Design and Implementation

4.1 Design Considerations

The underlying system we use for dialect identification can work with any number of words (single words, phrases or sentences) and produces probabilities of occurrence in different locales in a one dimensional vector (with 26 values in our case). As such, we want an interface that can visualize

---

[3]`http://dialektkarten.ch/dmviewer`

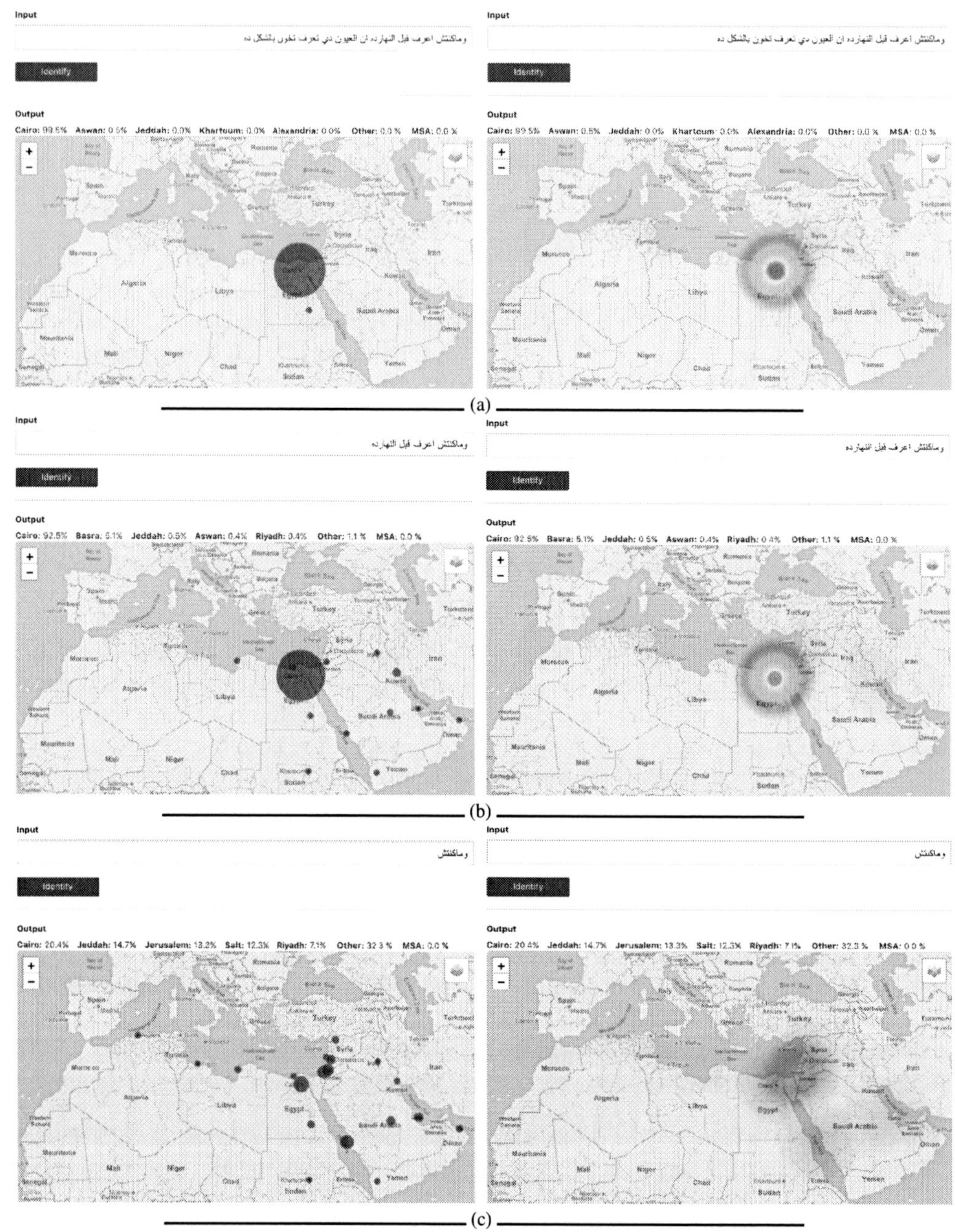

Figure 1: ADIDA Interface showing the output for a verse from an Egyptian Arabic song in the two display modes: point map (right) and heat map (left). The subfigures (a), (b) and (c) correspond to different lengths of the verse: (a) full, (b) first four words, and (c) the first word only.

the probability distribution into a two-dimensional geographical map space allowing us to easily observe and debug connections and patterns relating to dialectal similarities and differences that are harder to catch in the one dimensional output of the system classifier. We also want to visualize aggregations of probabilities of nearby cities that give a sense of regional presence.

Our setup and needs are different from other dialect map visualization efforts discussed in Section 3.3 which mostly focus on specific concepts and their realizations in different forms.

4.2 The ADIDA Interface

The ADIDA interface is publicly available at https://adida.abudhabi.nyu.edu/. Figure 1.(a, *left side*) presents the basic structure of the interface. At the top there is a box to input the Arabic text to dialect identify. The web page automatically fills the box with a randomly selected song verse from a set of well known songs from different dialects. This is intended to make it easy for the user to understand the task of the interface. After the user clicks on the *Identify* button, a geographical map of the Arab world is shown with one of two toggleable overlays: (1) a point map displaying one point per city scaled to the probability of attribution to the city (default mode), or (2) a heat map that plots the probabilities as Gaussians centered on each city with proportional intensities that aggregate any nearby points at a given zoom level. The point map only shows cities that have an attribution probability larger than 0.1% while the heat map displays Gaussians for all cities. Both visualization modes exclude MSA as there is no geographical location that can represent it. The heat map should not be interpreted to make claims about the attribution probabilities of regions between the considered cities. The falloff of each Gaussian and their aggregates are used solely as a high-level visualization aid through allowing aggregation of probabilities of nearby cities. Additionally, the interface presents the top five cities with their probabilities, together with that of MSA and of the remaining probability mass assigned to *Other*. We discuss the rest of the screen shots in Figure 1 in Section 4.4.

4.3 Implementation

Back-end The ADIDA back-end was implemented in Python using Flask[4] to create a Web API wrapper for the dialect ID code. The core dialect ID application is based on the best performing model distinguishing between 26 classes (25 dialects and MSA), described in Salameh et al. (2018). The application makes use of scikit-learn (Pedregosa et al., 2011) to learn a Multinomial Naive Bayes (MNB) classifier using the MADAR corpus (Bouamor et al., 2018), a large-scale collection of parallel sentences built to cover the dialects of 25 cities from the Arab World (Table 1), in addition to MSA. The model is fed with a suite of features covering word unigrams and char-

acter unigrams, bigrams and trigrams weighted by their Term Frequency-Inverse Document Frequency (TF-IDF) scores, combined with language model scores.The output of the MNB model is a set of 26 probability scores referring to the 25 cities and MSA. Results on a test set show that the model can identify the exact city of a speaker at an accuracy of 67.9% for sentences with an average length of 7 words. Salameh et al. (2018) reported on an oracle study showing that accuracy can reach more than 90% with 16-word inputs.

Front-end The front-end was implemented using Vue.js[5] for model view control. We use Leaflet[6] with Mapbox[7] to provide the geographical map display. We also use heatmap.js[8] to generate the heat maps.

4.4 Example

Figure 1 demonstrates the output of ADIDA for a verse from an Egyptian Arabic song (Hafez, 1963). The left side of Figure 1 shows the default point-map mode, while the right side shows the heat-map mode. In Figure 1.(a), the full verse of 11 words is returns a correct preference for Cairo at a high degree of confidence (99.5% probability). In Figure 1.(b) and (c), the length is reduced first to the first four words, and then to the very first word only. In all three cases, Cairo is the top choice, but with decreasing confidence correlating with the length of the input: 99.5% > 92.5% > 20.4%. Additionally we see a great diffusion of the probability score, with the case of one word input resulting with more probability mass in the other 20 cities that are not shown than in the first choice.

5 Conclusion and Future Work

We presented ADIDA, a public online interface for visualizing a system for fine-grained dialect identification. This system produces a vector of probabilities indicating the likelihood an input sentence is from 25 cities and MSA. ADIDA displays the results as a point map or a heat map overlaid on top of a geographical map of the Arab World.

In the future, we plan to continue improving our dialect identification back-end. We also plan to extend the interface in a number of ways: (a) provide

---

[4]http://flask.pocoo.org/

[5]https://vuejs.org/
[6]https://leafletjs.com/
[7]https://www.mapbox.com/
[8]https://www.patrick-wied.at/static/heatmapjs/

a display mode that better serves color-blind individuals, (b) provide a feedback mode that can be used to collect additional data provided by users with their quality judgments, and (c) gamify the interface to allow the use of it as a tool to identify more cities in the Arab World.

The data we use in building the back-end is made available as part of a shared task on Arabic fine-grained dialect identification (Bouamor et al., 2019).

Acknowledgments The work presented was made possible by grant NPRP 7-290-1-047 from the Qatar National Research Fund (a member of the Qatar Foundation). The statements made herein are solely the responsibility of the authors. We would like to thank David Wrisley and Yves Scherrer for their valuable feedback and insights.

References

Muhammad Abdul-Mageed, Hassan Alhuzali, and Mohamed Elaraby. 2018. You tweet what you speak: A city-level dataset of Arabic dialects. In *Proceedings of the Language Resources and Evaluation Conference (LREC)*, Miyazaki, Japan.

Abdel-Rahman Abu-Melhim. 1991. Code-switching and linguistic accommodation in Arabic. In *Proceedings of the Annual Symposium on Arabic Linguistics*, volume 80, pages 231–250.

Mahmoud Al-Ayyoub, Aya Nuseir, Kholoud Alsmearat, Yaser Jararweh, and Brij Gupta. 2017. Deep learning for Arabic nlp: A survey. *Journal of Computational Science*.

Faisal Al-Shargi and Owen Rambow. 2015. Diwan: A dialectal word annotation tool for Arabic. In *Proceedings of the Workshop for Arabic Natural Language Processing (WANLP)*, pages 49–58, Beijing, China.

Reem Bassiouney. 2009. *Arabic Sociolinguistics: Topics in Diglossia, Gender, Identity, and Politics*. Georgetown University Press.

Yonatan Belinkov and James Glass. 2016. A Character-level Convolutional Neural Network for Distinguishing Similar Languages and Dialects. In *Proceedings of the Workshop on NLP for Similar Languages, Varieties and Dialects (VarDial)*, pages 145–152, Osaka, Japan.

Fadi Biadsy, Julia Hirschberg, and Nizar Habash. 2009. Spoken Arabic Dialect Identification Using Phonotactic Modeling. In *Proceedings of the Workshop on Computational Approaches to Semitic Languages (CASL)*, pages 53–61, Athens, Greece.

Houda Bouamor, Nizar Habash, Mohammad Salameh, Wajdi Zaghouani, Owen Rambow, Dana Abdulrahim, Ossama Obeid, Salam Khalifa, Fadhl Eryani, Alexander Erdmann, and Kemal Oflazer. 2018. The MADAR Arabic Dialect Corpus and Lexicon. In *Proceedings of the Language Resources and Evaluation Conference (LREC)*, Miyazaki, Japan.

Houda Bouamor, Sabit Hassan, Nizar Habash, and Kemal Oflazer. 2019. The MADAR shared task on Arabic fine-grained dialect identification. In *Proceedings of the Fourth Arabic Natural Language Processing Workshop (WANLP)*, Florence, Italy.

Soumia Bougrine, Hadda Cherroun, and Djelloul Ziadi. 2017. Hierarchical Classification for Spoken Arabic Dialect Identification using Prosody: Case of Algerian Dialects. *CoRR*, abs/1703.10065.

Liviu P. Dinu, Alina Maria Ciobanu, Marcos Zampieri, and Shervin Malmasi. 2018. Classifier ensembles for dialect and language variety identification. *CoRR*, abs/1808.04800.

Heba Elfardy and Mona Diab. 2012. Token level identification of linguistic code switching. In *Proceedings of the International Conference on Computational Linguistics (COLING)*, Mumbai, India.

Heba Elfardy and Mona Diab. 2013. Sentence Level Dialect Identification in Arabic. In *Proceedings of the Conference of the Association for Computational Linguistics (ACL)*, pages 456–461, Sofia, Bulgaria.

Asma Etman and Louis Beex. 2015. Language and Dialect Identification: A Survey. In *Proceedings of the Intelligent Systems Conference (IntelliSys)*, London, UK.

Jean-Philippe Goldman, Yves Scherrer, Julie Glikman, Mathieu Avanzi, Christophe Benzitoun, and Philippe Boula de Mareil. 2018. Crowdsourcing Regional Variation Data and Automatic Geolocalisation of Speakers of European French. In *Proceedings of the Eleventh International Conference on Language Resources and Evaluation (LREC 2018)*, Miyazaki, Japan. European Language Resources Association (ELRA).

Nizar Habash, Owen Rambow, Mona Diab, and Reem Kanjawi-Faraj. 2008. Guidelines for Annotation of Arabic Dialectness. In *Proceedings of the Workshop on HLT & NLP within the Arabic World*, Marrakech, Morocco.

Nizar Habash, Ryan Roth, Owen Rambow, Ramy Eskander, and Nadi Tomeh. 2013. Morphological Analysis and Disambiguation for Dialectal Arabic. In *Proceedings of the Conference of the North American Chapter of the Association for Computational Linguistics (NAACL)*, Atlanta, Georgia.

Nizar Y Habash. 2010. *Introduction to Arabic natural language processing*, volume 3. Morgan & Claypool Publishers.

Niloofar Haeri. 1991. Sociolinguistic Variation in Cairene Arabic: Palatalization and the qaf in the Speech of Men and Women.

Abdel Halim Hafez. 1963. Gabbar (Arrogant). Lyrics by Hessien El Sayed.

Clive Holes. 2004. *Modern Arabic: Structures, Functions, and Varieties*. Georgetown Classics in Arabic Language and Linguistics. Georgetown University Press.

Fei Huang. 2015. Improved Arabic Dialect Classification with Social Media Data. In *Proceedings of the Conference on Empirical Methods in Natural Language Processing (EMNLP)*, pages 2118–2126, Lisbon, Portugal.

Josh Katz and Wilson Andrews. 2013. How Yall, Youse and You Guys Talk. https://www.nytimes.com/interactive/2014/upshot/dialect-quiz-map.html.

Salam Khalifa, Nizar Habash, Dana Abdulrahim, and Sara Hassan. 2016. A Large Scale Corpus of Gulf Arabic. In *Proceedings of the Language Resources and Evaluation Conference (LREC)*, Portorož, Slovenia.

Shervin Malmasi, Marcos Zampieri, Nikola Ljubešić, Preslav Nakov, Ahmed Ali, and Jörg Tiedemann. 2016. Discriminating between Similar Languages and Arabic Dialect Identification: A Report on the Third DSL Shared Task. In *Proceedings of the Workshop on NLP for Similar Languages, Varieties and Dialects (VarDial)*, pages 1–14, Osaka, Japan.

Elise Michon, Minh Quang Pham, Josep Crego, and Jean Senellart. 2018. Neural network architectures for Arabic dialect identification. In *Proceedings of the Fifth Workshop on NLP for Similar Languages, Varieties and Dialects (VarDial 2018)*, pages 128–136.

Ossama Obeid, Salam Khalifa, Nizar Habash, Houda Bouamor, Wajdi Zaghouani, and Kemal Oflazer. 2018. MADARi: A Web Interface for Joint Arabic Morphological Annotation and Spelling Correction. In *Proceedings of the Language Resources and Evaluation Conference (LREC)*, Miyazaki, Japan.

Fabian Pedregosa, Gaël Varoquaux, Alexandre Gramfort, Vincent Michel, Bertrand Thirion, Olivier Grisel, Mathieu Blondel, Peter Prettenhofer, Ron Weiss, Vincent Dubourg, Jake Vanderplas, Alexandre Passos, David Cournapeau, Matthieu Brucher, Matthieu Perrot, and Édouard Duchesnay. 2011. Scikit-learn: Machine learning in python. *Journal of Machine Learning Research*, 12:2825–2830.

Fatiha Sadat, Farnazeh Kazemi, and Atefeh Farzindar. 2014. Automatic Identification of Arabic Dialects in Social Media. In *Proceedings of the Workshop on Natural Language Processing for Social Media (SocialNLP)*, pages 22–27, Dublin, Ireland.

Hassan Sajjad, Kareem Darwish, and Yonatan Belinkov. 2013. Translating dialectal Arabic to English. In *Proceedings of the Conference of the Association for Computational Linguistics (ACL)*, pages 1–6, Sofia, Bulgaria.

Mohammad Salameh, Houda Bouamor, and Nizar Habash. 2018. Fine-grained arabic dialect identification. In *Proceedings of the International Conference on Computational Linguistics (COLING)*, pages 1332–1344, Santa Fe, New Mexico, USA.

Yves Scherrer and Philipp Stoeckle. 2016. A quantitative approach to Swiss German dialectometric analyses and comparisons of linguistic levels. *Dialectologia et Geolinguistica*, 24(1):92–125.

Abdulhadi Shoufan and Sumaya Al-Ameri. 2015. Natural language processing for dialectical Arabic: A survey. In *Proceedings of the Workshop for Arabic Natural Language Processing (WANLP)*, page 36, Beijing, China.

Christoph Tillmann, Saab Mansour, and Yaser Al-Onaizan. 2014. Improved Sentence-Level Arabic Dialect Classification. In *Proceedings of the Workshop on Applying NLP Tools to Similar Languages, Varieties and Dialects*, pages 110–119, Dublin, Ireland.

Bert Vaux and Scott Golder. 2003. The Harvard Dialect Survey. *Cambridge, MA: Harvard University Linguistics Department*.

Janet CE Watson. 2007. *The Phonology and Morphology of Arabic*. Oxford University Press.

David Joseph Wrisley. 2016. Linguistic Landscapes of Beirut Project. http://llbeirut.org.

David Joseph Wrisley. 2017. Locating medieval French, or why we collect and visualize the geographic information of texts. *Speculum*, 92(S1):S145–S169.

David Joseph Wrisley. 2019. "Aggregate map." Visualizing Medieval Places. http://vmp.djwrisley.com/map/.

Omar Zaidan and Chris Callison-Burch. 2014. Arabic dialect identification. *Computational Linguistics*, 40(1):171–202.

Omar F Zaidan and Chris Callison-Burch. 2011. The Arabic Online Commentary Dataset: an Annotated Dataset of Informal Arabic With High Dialectal Content. In *Proceedings of the Conference of the Association for Computational Linguistics (ACL)*, pages 37–41.

Marcos Zampieri, Shervin Malmasi, Nikola Ljubešić, Preslav Nakov, Ahmed Ali, Jörg Tiedemann, Yves Scherrer, and Noëmi Aepli. 2017. Findings of the VarDial Evaluation Campaign 2017. In *Proceedings of the Workshop on NLP for Similar Languages, Varieties and Dialects (VarDial)*, pages 1–15, Valencia, Spain.

Marcos Zampieri, Shervin Malmasi, Preslav Nakov, Ahmed Ali, Suwon Shon, James Glass, Yves Scherrer, Tanja Samardžić, Nikola Ljubešić, Jörg Tiedemann, Chris van der Lee, Stefan Grondelaers, Nelleke Oostdijk, Antal van den Bosch, Ritesh Kumar, Bornini Lahiri, and Mayank Jain. 2018. Language identification and morphosyntactic tagging: The second VarDial evaluation campaign. In *Proceedings of the Fifth Workshop on NLP for Similar Languages, Varieties and Dialects (VarDial)*, Santa Fe, USA.

Rabih Zbib, Erika Malchiodi, Jacob Devlin, David Stallard, Spyros Matsoukas, Richard Schwartz, John Makhoul, Omar F. Zaidan, and Chris Callison-Burch. 2012. Machine Translation of Arabic Dialects. In *Proceedings of the Conference of the North American Chapter of the Association for Computational Linguistics (NAACL)*, pages 49–59, Montréal, Canada.

Enabling Search and Collaborative Assembly of Causal Interactions Extracted from Multilingual and Multi-domain Free Text

[†]**George C. G. Barbosa**, [‡]**Zechy Wong**, [♀]**Gus Hahn-Powell**, [♀]**Dane Bell**,
[‡]**Rebecca Sharp**, [‡♀]**Marco A. Valenzuela-Escárcega**, [‡♀]**Mihai Surdeanu**
[†]Centre for Data and Knowledge Integration for Health (CIDACS), Salvador, Brazil
[‡]University of Arizona, Tucson, Arizona, USA
[♀]LUM.AI, Tucson, Arizona, USA
{gcgbarbosa,zechy,bsharp,marcov,msurdeanu}@email.arizona.edu
{ghp,dane}@lum.ai

Abstract

Many of the most pressing current research
problems (e.g., public health, food security, or
climate change) require multi-disciplinary collaborations. In order to facilitate this process,
we propose a system that incorporates multi-
domain extractions of causal interactions into
a single searchable knowledge graph. Our system enables users to search iteratively over direct and indirect connections in this knowledge graph, and collaboratively build causal
models in real time. To enable the aggregation of causal information from multiple languages, we extend an open-domain machine
reader to Portuguese. The new Portuguese
reader extracts over 600 thousand causal statements from 120 thousand Portuguese publications with a precision of 62%, which demonstrates the value of mining multilingual scientific information.

1 Introduction

The number of scientific publications has increased dramatically in the past few years. For
example, PubMed[1], a repository of biomedical papers, now indexes more than one million publications per year, for a total of over 29 million publications processed to date[2].

Given this vast amount of information, it is
clear that search must be a key part of the scientific research process. However, we argue that
search tools today do not support this process
properly. We see at least three limitations. First,
most search tools tend to be relatively shallow
(i.e., relying on keywords or topics), while information needs in science often require *semantics*. For example, scientific hypotheses in many
sciences can be represented as causal statements,
e.g., "what causes malnutrition?", or "what are
the effects of pollution?". Such queries are not
easily supported by current tools. Second, many
sciences are becoming increasingly *multilingual*,
as key scientific analyses are published in non-
English venues. For example, Brazil has reduced
the under-5 mortality rate resulting from poverty-
related causes through its *Bolsa Familia* program
(BFP), a widespread conditional money transfer to
poor households (Rasella et al., 2013). However,
most of the data collected in the BFP and the resulting analyses are only made available through
scientific reports in Portuguese. For example,
SciELO[3], an electronic repository of papers published in South America, now indexes 234,596
publications in Brazilian Portuguese[4]. Lastly, research is *iterative* and *collaborative*, whereas most
search is stateless and private. For example, understanding children's health requires collaborations
across multiple disciplines, e.g., biology, economy, education.

We propose a system for the search of scientific
literature that addresses these three limitations. In
particular, the contributions of our work are:

(1) An approach for the search of causal statements that can be both direct and indirect. Our
approach relies on a novel approach for open-
domain information extraction (OpenIE) that is
unsupervised and domain agnostic. The proposed
OpenIE method relies on syntax, and performs extractions using a top-down grammar, which first
extracts relevant events, followed by event arguments, whose boundaries are determined by the
syntactic constraints of the event predicate. The
extractions are assembled into a graph knowledge
base (KB), which supports both direct and indirect
searches across causal pathways.

---

[1]https://www.ncbi.nlm.nih.gov/PubMed

[2]As of February 4, 2019. See the Advanced search tab on
the PubMed website.

[3]http://www.SciELO.br

[4]As of February 4, 2019. See SciELO analytics: https:
//analytics.SciELO.org

Proceedings of NAACL-HLT 2019: Demonstrations, pages 12–17
Minneapolis, Minnesota, June 2 - June 7, 2019. ©2019 Association for Computational Linguistics

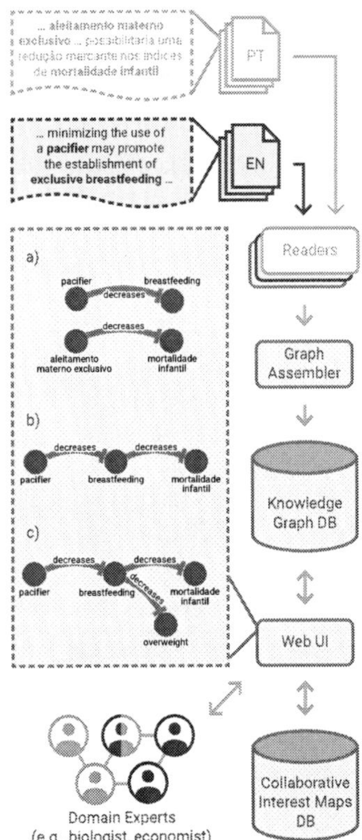

Figure 1: System architecture and example. Causal relations from sentences about breastfeeding in English (Maastrup et al., 2014) and Portuguese (Cavalcanti et al., 2015) are extracted and used by domain experts to collaboratively build a shared causal model of the task of interest, called an interest map, through a web UI. (a) A user searches for causes of *breastfeeding* and effects of *aleitamento materno exclusivo* (exclusive breastfeeding), and adds two interesting links to a shared interest map. (b) A second user merges *aleitamento materno exclusivo* and *breastfeeding*. (c) A third user adds an additional link (to *overweight*) from a new search to the shared interest map. The constructed interest maps are stored in a separate database, where they can be edited in real-time by collaborators.

(2) A multilingual search platform. We provide OpenIE grammars for English and Portuguese, and demonstrate their utility in searching PubMed and SciELO.

(3) A framework for collaborative model building. The proposed system allows end users to save the results of their semantic searches into an editable graph knowledge base, which can be shared and edited in real time by multiple collaborators. The underlying functionality for this collaborative component relies on Operational Transformations (OT), which is a conflict-free and non-blocking change propagation algorithm that allows individual users to edit a shared knowledge base in real time (Sun and Ellis, 1998).

2 Architecture

Our approach for information aggregation combines the output of machine readers into a knowledge graph which can be efficiently queried, stored, filtered, and edited by multiple users in real-time.

Specifically, given a collection of documents, we first extract relevant relations using a set of rule-based machine readers. This approach can use the output of any reader (e.g., the biomedical relation extraction framework of Valenzuela-Escárcega et al. (2018) or the open-domain framework of Hahn-Powell et al. (2017)), but here we focus on the Eidos reader (Section 3) which we extend to Portuguese (Section 3.2) in order to increase the coverage of the knowledge graph by including scientific publications in Portuguese.

The extracted concepts are unified using the deduplication approach of Hahn-Powell et al. (2017), which uses an $\mathcal{O}(n)$ hash-based approach to fingerprint relation and concept attributes paired with a set of normalized terms filtered against a series of linguistic constraints. A graph database is then populated with the unified concepts and the relations linking them. During this process, we preserve all evidence for the extractions, along with information about whether relations were hedged or negated. We employ two Lucene[5] indexes, one for indexing the content of the papers (for use in filtering the knowledge graph based on a specified context), and another for the concepts in the knowledge base (to allow for faster querying).

An important component of this system is a web-based user interface (UI) which allows users to query the graph easily and incrementally select results in order to construct a qualitative influence model, which we refer to as an *interest map* (Section 4). This UI features a real-time collaborative graph editor that is conflict-free and non-blocking, allowing multiple users to work together on a shared interest map.

3 Reader

In the context of OpenIE (Banko et al., 2007), determining the fixed set of relevant entities and events, and aggregating this information across domains and languages is likely impossible. For this reason, we use the Eidos reader (Sharp et al.,

---

[5]`https://lucene.apache.org`

2019), which is a taxonomy-free OpenIE system that uses a top-down information extraction pipeline. This pipeline begins by finding relations of interest such as causal statements (through the use of specific trigger words), and continues by extracting the concepts that participate in these relations from the syntactic context.

3.1 Reading with Eidos

To understand the individual steps of Eidos's top-down approach, consider the example sentence, *According to two studies, breast milk with omega-3 LCPUFA reduced allergic manifestations.*

First, the Eidos system finds causal and correlation relations, using a set of trigger words with a grammar of rules written in the Odin information extraction framework (Valenzuela-Escárcega et al., 2016). Odin consists of a declarative language, capable of describing patterns over surface and syntax, coupled with a runtime engine that applies these rules in a cascade, making the previous matches available for subsequent rules. In the sentence above, a Causal relation would be triggered by the predicate *reduced*, with an initial cause of *milk* and an initial effect of *allergic manifestations.* Using the approach of Hahn-Powell et al. (2017), Eidos then expands these initial arguments by traversing outgoing dependency links (with some exceptions such as conjunctions). For example, here *milk* is expanded to *breast milk with omega-3 LCPUFA.* The final system output of the Eidos system for the sentence above is shown in Figure 2.

3.2 Extension to Portuguese

We adapted the English-based Eidos system to extract causal relations from Portuguese text by first translating the trigger words and words related to filtering, negation, and hedging. We compared the syntactic preprocessing of a sample of causal sentences in English with their Portuguese translations, writing additional rules to account for differences. Rules were also written to capture lexicalized causal patterns in Portuguese. During rule development, we ran the reader over a 1K article sample of SciELO multiple times, evaluating the accuracy of each rule and adjusting them to remove incorrect extractions.

Since the grammars that Eidos uses operate over universal dependency (UD) syntax (Nivre et al., 2016), and are largely unlexicalized (with the exception of certain prominent causal forms, e.g.,

due to), we anticipated that minimal adjustments to the grammars would be needed. However, the Portuguese UD dataset used v2 of UD, while the grammar for English was written for UD v1[6]. Thus, some relations were tagged differently between the two languages, for example, `nmod` relations for English were split into `nmod` and `obl` in Portuguese. Because the Portuguese training data for UD was considerably smaller than for English, we also had to deal with the lower accuracy of the dependency parser[7], which represented a challenge when porting the grammars.

In total, we ported eight high-yield rules to Portuguese. An analysis of the extractions from the 1K article sample showed that approximately 65% of the extractions were made by a single active voice rule whose arguments are matched by traversing `nsubj` and `obj` dependencies. The next most frequently used rule, which matches causal events where the trigger is followed by the token *por*, e.g., *diminuído por* [reduced by], accounted for 15% of the extractions. No other rule accounted for more than 5% of the extractions.

Note that the Portuguese extractions are currently kept separate from the English ones. That is, the user must explicitly search for causal pathways by language. However, these results may be manually aggregated in the collaborative model workspace, described below. We describe possible strategies for the automated integration of cross-language results in Section 6.

4 Collaborative model builder

The causal graphs built from the extractions are useful for finding direct and indirect relations between concepts. However, in order to truly support the scientific research process, we argue that the resulting system must implement the following additional functionality:

(1) It must support *iterative* and *stateful* search. It is unlikely that any single search query solves a real-world research problem. It is thus necessary to allow multiple searches whose outputs are saved in the same state or model. For example, Jensen et al. (2017) showed that understanding children's health requires information from biology, psychology, economy, and environmental science.

---

[6]`https://universaldependencies.org/`

[7]The parser used for this component was an ensemble of Malt parsers (`http://www.maltparser.org`), as introduced in Surdeanu and Manning (2010).

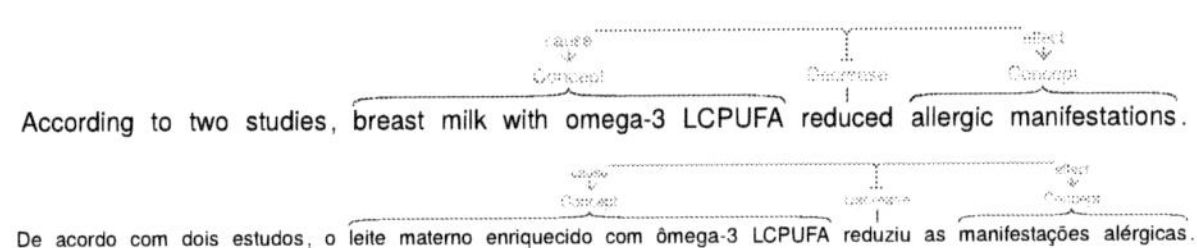

Figure 2: TAG (Forbes et al., 2018) visualization of the multilingual reader's output for one sentence in English and Portuguese.

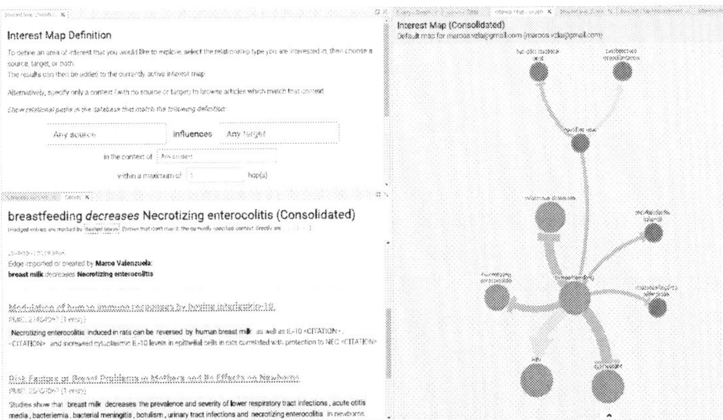

Figure 3: Screenshot showing some key functionality of our system's user interface. In the upper left panel, users can search for direct or indirect causal statements found in the literature. The right panel has the multilingual interest map, collaboratively built by different users from multiple search results. The bottom left panel has the evidence for a selected causal interaction.

(2) It must allow the addition of *background knowledge* that is known to the domain experts, but is not published in literature.

(3) Most importantly, the above operations must be performed in a *collaborative* environment that allows multiple experts to contribute to the same model, or interest map, in real time. The National Science Foundation has recognized that inter-disciplinary collaborations have become a fundamental aspect of science and has called for "growing convergence research" in its "10 big ideas".[8]

To implement the above functionality, we added a module for collaborative model building, which incorporates: (a) the ability to incrementally save the results of causal searches in a user's *interest map*, thus accumulating (a subset of) search results that capture the problem of interest; (b) operations to edit this interest map such as adding causal relations (to account for the user's background knowledge) and deleting them (to account for machine errors); and (c) real-time collaborative functionality, which allows users to share their interest maps, and edit them in parallel, in real time.

The real-time collaborative functionality is implemented using Operational Transformations (OT), which is a conflict-free and non-blocking change propagation algorithm that allows individual users be able to edit without waiting on others even under high-latency (Sun and Ellis, 1998). Typically OT is applied to documents (e.g., as with Google Docs), but here we apply it to our interest maps that are represented as directed causal graphs.

Briefly, each client has a local copy of the shared interest map, which they are free to edit. The edits are represented as *operations* (e.g., deletion of a node, or addition of a relation link). Operations generated by different clients are each transformed according to the operations of the other clients in order to synchronize the interest maps. The result is an intuitively-built unified interest map that incorporates the input from all expert users, without requiring them to be concerned with manual synchronization or conflict resolution.

5 Discussion

As shown in Figure 3, the collaborative model builder summarized in the previous section enables users to aggregate influence statements from multiple searches, multiple domains, and multiple languages. This allows end users to make full use of any information complementarity (i.e., between different domains or different languages) that is inherent in inter-disciplinary research.

Table 1 shows overall statistics for the two document collections currently processed. The table indicates that both collections contain approx-

---

[8]https://www.nsf.gov/news/special_reports/big_ideas/

	English	Portuguese
Documents	94,684	121,801
Concepts in causal interactions	1,550,912	772,470
Causal interactions	2,121,574	631,965
Precision	54%	62%

Table 1: Statistics of English and Portuguese document collections, including number of causal interactions, and number of concepts participating in such interactions. Precision was computed over a sample of 50 statements in each language. We considered an interaction to be correct if the sentence supports the interaction, the polarity (promotes/inhibits) and direction of the interaction are both correct, and the spans of the two arguments overlap with the correct spans.

imately 100K documents (more for Portuguese, less for English), and the readers extracted 2.1M causal statements from the English documents with a precision of 54%, and 631K causal statements in Portuguese with a precision of 62%, which demonstrates the value of mining multilingual scientific information. In this evaluation, extracted causal relation arguments were considered correct if the argument extracted overlapped with the correct argument. For example, in the sentence "IL-10 decreases epsilon transcript expression," the strictly correct extraction would be: (IL-10; decreases; epsilon transcript expression). Based on our evaluation criteria, the following extraction would be also considered correct (IL-10; decreases; epsilon transcript), as the span of the second argument overlaps with the strictly correct argument.

The difference in precision between Portuguese and English might be due to the fact that the Portuguese reader uses a smaller set rules that extracts approximately 4 times fewer causal statements than the English reader. Additionally, the evaluation was performed on a sample of 50 extractions, and so the difference may not be statisticaly significant.

6 Future work

Our future work efforts will focus on extending the multi-linguality of the proposed system. Given the architecture currently in place, we predict that extending it to other languages will not be too costly. We plan to use the corpora from the Universal Dependencies effort[9] to train part-of-speech taggers and syntactic parsers for additional languages. Our semantic causal grammars are mostly unlexicalized; most of the effort required to adapt them to other languages will be on translating the

causal triggers.

In order to merge knowledge graphs constructed using corpora from different languages, we will need to align of multilingual terminology. Some domains may already provide manually translated vocabularies, for example, within the medical domain, UMLS (Bodenreider, 2004) provides translations of the controlled vocabulary MeSH (Lipscomb, 2000) for several languages. For domains in which manual translations are not available, we can take advantage of recent developments in unsupervised bilingual dictionary induction (Conneau et al., 2017; Kementchedjhieva et al., 2018) to learn alignments.

Lastly, we will work on methods to minimize the spreading of accidental misinformation, which may be introduced by incorrect extraction or statements that are not factual. To mitigate the former issue, we found that extraction redundancy provides a strong signal, i.e., statements extracted multiple times from different publications are more likely to be correct. For the latter, we will employ recently-proposed methods for factuality detection (Rudinger et al., 2018).

7 Conclusion

We introduced a novel system[10] that facilitates the search for multilingual and multi-domain causal interactions that are either direct or indirect. Further, the proposed system includes a framework for collaborative model building, which allows multiple domain experts to collaborate in real time on the construction of a causal model for a given problem, which aggregates the results of multiple searches as well as background knowledge manually added by the experts.

Acknowledgments

This work was funded by the Bill and Melinda Gates Foundation HBGDki Initiative. Marco Valenzuela-Escárcega and Mihai Surdeanu declare a financial interest in LUM.AI. This interest has been properly disclosed to the University of Arizona Institutional Review Committee and is managed in accordance with its conflict of interest policies.

---

[9]https://universaldependencies.org

[10]https://multiling.demos.clulab.org

References

Michele Banko, Michael J Cafarella, Stephen Soderland, Matthew Broadhead, and Oren Etzioni. 2007. Open information extraction from the web. In *IJCAI*, volume 7, pages 2670–2676.

Olivier Bodenreider. 2004. The Unified Medical Language System (UMLS): integrating biomedical terminology. *Nucleic Acids Research*, 32(suppl_1):D267–D270.

Sandra Hipólito Cavalcanti, Maria de Fátima Costa Caminha, José Natal Figueiroa, Vilneide Maria Santos Braga Diegues Serva, Rachel de Sá Barreto Luna Cruz, Pedro Israel Cabral de Lira, Malaquias Batista Filho, et al. 2015. Fatores associados à prática do aleitamento materno exclusivo por pelo menos seis meses no estado de pernambuco. *Revista Brasileira de Epidemiologia*, 18:208–219.

Alexis Conneau, Guillaume Lample, Marc'Aurelio Ranzato, Ludovic Denoyer, and Hervé Jégou. 2017. Word translation without parallel data. *arXiv preprint arXiv:1710.04087*.

Angus Graeme Forbes, Kristine Lee, Gus Hahn-Powell, Marco Antonio Valenzuela-Escárcega, and Mihai Surdeanu. 2018. Text annotation graphs: Annotating complex natural language phenomena. In *Proceedings of the Eleventh International Conference on Language Resources and Evaluation (LREC-2018)*. European Language Resources Association (ELRA).

Gus Hahn-Powell, Marco A. Valenzuela-Escárcega, and Mihai Surdeanu. 2017. Swanson linking revisited: Accelerating literature-based discovery across domains using a conceptual influence graph. *Proceedings of ACL 2017, System Demonstrations*, pages 103–108.

Sarah KG Jensen, Anne E Berens, and Charles A Nelson 3rd. 2017. Effects of poverty on interacting biological systems underlying child development. *The Lancet Child & Adolescent Health*, 1(3):225–239.

Yova Kementchedjhieva, Sebastian Ruder, Ryan Cotterell, and Anders Søgaard. 2018. Generalizing procrustes analysis for better bilingual dictionary induction. In *CoNLL*.

Carolyn E Lipscomb. 2000. Medical subject headings (mesh). *Bulletin of the Medical Library Association*, 88(3):265.

Ragnhild Maastrup, Bo Moelholm Hansen, Hanne Kronborg, Susanne Norby Bojesen, Karin Hallum, Annemi Frandsen, Anne Kyhnaeb, Inge Svarer, and Inger Hallström. 2014. Factors associated with exclusive breastfeeding of preterm infants. results from a prospective national cohort study. *PloS one*, 9(2):e89077.

Joakim Nivre, Marie-Catherine de Marneffe, Filip Ginter, Yoav Goldberg, Jan Hajic, Christopher D. Manning, Ryan McDonald, Slav Petrov, Sampo Pyysalo, Natalia Silveira, Reut Tsarfaty, and Daniel Zeman. 2016. Universal dependencies v1: A multilingual treebank collection. In *Proceedings of the Tenth International Conference on Language Resources and Evaluation (LREC 2016)*, Paris, France. European Language Resources Association (ELRA).

Davide Rasella, Rosana Aquino, Carlos A. T. Santos, Romulo Paes-Sousa, and Mauricio L. Barreto. 2013. Effect of a conditional cash transfer programme on childhood mortality: a nationwide analysis of brazilian municipalities. *The Lancet*, 382:57–64.

Rachel Rudinger, Aaron Steven White, and Benjamin Van Durme. 2018. Neural models of factuality. In *Proceedings of the 2018 Conference of the North American Chapter of the Association for Computational Linguistics: Human Language Technologies, Volume 1 (Long Papers)*, volume 1, pages 731–744.

Rebecca Sharp, Adarsh Pyarelal, Benjamin M. Gyori, Keith Alcock, Egoitz Laparra, Marco A. Valenzuela-Escárcega, Ajay Nagesh, Vikas Yadav, John A. Bachman, Zheng Tang, Heather Lent, Fan Luo, Mithun Paul, Steven Bethard, Kobus Barnard, Clayton Morrison, and Mihai Surdeanu. 2019. Eidos, INDRA, & Delphi: From free text to executable causal models. In *Proceedings of the 2019 Conference of the North American Chapter of the Association for Computational Linguistics: Demonstrations*. Association for Computational Linguistics.

Chengzheng Sun and Clarence Ellis. 1998. Operational transformation in real-time group editors: Issues, algorithms, and achievements. In *Proceedings of the 1998 ACM Conference on Computer Supported Cooperative Work*, CSCW '98, pages 59–68, New York, NY, USA. ACM.

Mihai Surdeanu and Christopher D. Manning. 2010. Ensemble models for dependency parsing: Cheap and good? In *Proceedings of the North American Chapter of the Association for Computational Linguistics Conference (NAACL-2010)*, Los Angeles, CA.

Marco A. Valenzuela-Escárcega, Özgün Babur, Gus Hahn-Powell, Dane Bell, Thomas Hicks, Enrique Noriega-Atala, Xia Wang, Mihai Surdeanu, Emek Demir, and Clayton T. Morrison. 2018. Large-scale automated machine reading discovers new cancer driving mechanisms. *Database: The Journal of Biological Databases and Curation*.

Marco A. Valenzuela-Escárcega, Gustave Hahn-Powell, and Mihai Surdeanu. 2016. Odin's runes: A rule language for information extraction. In *LREC*.

INS: An Interactive Chinese News Synthesis System

Hui Liu and **Wentao Qin** and **Xiaojun Wan**

Institute of Computer Science and Technology, Peking University
The MOE Key Laboratory of Computational Linguistics, Peking University
`{xinkeliuhui,qinwentao,wanxiaojun}@pku.edu.cn`

Abstract

Nowadays, we are surrounded by more and more online news articles. Tens or hundreds of news articles need to be read if we wish to explore a hot news event or topic. So it is of vital importance to automatically synthesize a batch of news articles related to the event or topic into a new synthesis article (or overview article) for reader's convenience. It is so challenging to make news synthesis fully automatic that there is no successful solution by now. In this paper, we put forward a novel Interactive News Synthesis system (i.e. INS), which can help generate news overview articles automatically or by interacting with users. More importantly, INS can serve as a tool for editors to help them finish their jobs. In our experiments, INS performs well on both topic representation and synthesis article generation. A user study also demonstrates the usefulness and users' satisfaction with the INS tool. A demo video is available at `https://youtu.be/7ItteKW3GEk`.

1 INTRODUCTION

In the last decade, news websites and apps become more and more popular, which can provide us an extremely large volume of news articles. Even for a single news event, there are usually tens or hundreds of related news articles published online. In order to have a complete image of a news event, we have to look through all of the related news articles, which is very time-consuming and inefficient. With a large amount of time spent, what we get is just fragmented information scattered in different news articles.

Ideally, if there exists an overview article about an event, we will fully and efficiently understand the event by reading it. However, such overview articles are not easy to write, even for professional editors, and the writing of them is

very time-consuming. Though existing multi-document summarization systems can produce short summaries by selecting several representative sentences, they cannot produce long overview articles with good structure and high quality. So it is of vital importance to design a system to help editors or users to efficiently synthesize a batch of related news articles into a long news overview article, either in a fully automatic way or in a semi-automatic way.

To achieve the above goal, we put forward a novel Interactive News Synthesis system (i.e. INS), which can help generate Chinese news overview articles automatically or by interacting with users. Given a news event or topic, INS first crawls news articles from major Chinese news websites, detects different subtopics and represents them with easy-to-understand labels. Afterward, a span of text for each subtopic will be generated and the news synthesis article will be organized accordingly. It is noteworthy that INS can interact with users in different stages.

We automatically evaluate the key component of the INS system, i.e., subtopic detection and representation, and evaluation results demonstrate its efficacy. Human evaluation is employed and a user study is performed to demonstrate the usefulness and users' satisfaction of the INS tool.

2 Related Work

One of the related fields is document summarization. The methods can be divided into extractive methods (Gillick and Favre, 2009; Lin and Bilmes, 2010; Berg-Kirkpatrick et al., 2011; Sipos et al., 2012; Woodsend and Lapata, 2012; Wan and Zhang, 2014; Nallapati et al., 2017; Ren et al., 2017) and abstractive methods (Rush et al., 2015; Nallapati et al., 2016; Tan et al., 2017).

There are several pilot studies on producing

18

Proceedings of NAACL-HLT 2019: Demonstrations, pages 18–23
Minneapolis, Minnesota, June 2 - June 7, 2019. ©2019 Association for Computational Linguistics

long articles from a batch of news articles or web pages(Yao et al., 2011; Zhang and Wan, 2017; Liu et al., 2018). However, the generated overview articles do not have good structures and there are no interaction functions.

There are some attempts of adding interaction functions into the traditional document summarization tasks (Jones et al., 2002; Leuski et al., 2003). However, the above work focuses on producing short summaries and the generation of long news overview articles is more challenging. Moreover, in the above work, the keyphrases to represent salient information are extracted based on some heuristic rules or simple clues, and they are usually not good subtopic representations.

3 System Overview and User Interaction

Our INS system aims to produce a long overview article for a specific news event by synthesizing a number of existing Chinese news articles. It consists of the following components:

News Fetcher: According to the input news event, INS first crawls relevant news articles by using a popular Chinese news search engine (e.g. Baidu News), and extracts the title and body text for each news article. The number of news articles can be set by users and it is set to 100 by default.

Subtopic Finder: This component aims to discover the subtopics in the news articles and represent them with some informative labels. We extract n-grams that meet some demands as candidate labels and leverage a regression model to predict a score for each candidate label. Top 20 labels will be chosen and merged, after which each label represents a specific subtopic.

Article Synthesizer: This component aims to produce a span of text with moderate length for each subtopic, and then assemble the texts of selected subtopics to form the final news overview article. We first split the original news articles into coherent text blocks. The text blocks are then matched with the subtopic label and ranked by using the topic-sensitive TextRank algorithm and the MMR redundancy removal method. We select one or several top-ranked text blocks to describe each subtopic. Finally, all the selected text blocks are assembled to form the final overview article, with the subtopic labels used as the subtitles of the blocks.

The graphic user interface of INS is shown in Figure 1 with the input topic of '俄罗斯世界杯/2018 FIFA World Cup Russia'.

INS can interact with users in different stages: Users can choose and re-order some of the labels according to their preferences; Users can choose and edit the text blocks for each chosen subtopic; Users can edit on the final news synthesis result to get a more excellent article. Note that the interactions are optional. For 'lazy' users, INS can generate the final synthesis article with just one click.

4 Subtopic Finder

There are some existing unsupervised methods for detecting subtopics from documents, for example, text clustering and topic models. They have some drawbacks in common: (1) The number of subtopics (clusters) needs to be manually set beforehand and inappropriate subtopic number will affect the final results significantly. (2) It is hard to represent each subtopic, which is very important for users' understanding and selection of the subtopics.

Different from the above methods which first detect the subtopics or clusters and then extract labels for each subtopic, we decide to directly find subtopic labels by using supervised learning, and the labels are informative and easy to understand. We first extract candidate labels from the news articles and then use a regression model to assign a rating score to each candidate. After that, we merge the top labels to obtain the final subtopic labels.

Candidate Label Extraction: We extract n-grams from the original news articles as our candidate labels, where n ranges from 1 to 3. We employ pyltp for Chinese word segmentation and POS tagging. An n-gram will be a candidate if it meets the following requirements: (1) Its term frequency is higher than a min-count threshold. We set min-count to 25 for unigrams and 10 for bigrams and trigrams. (2) It is not a substring of the input topic name, which is too general to be a subtopic label. (3) It does not include time words and adverbs. (4) A candidate label of unigram is limited to only nouns and verbs. We use these rules to filter out the n-grams that are not suitable for representing subtopics.

Label Score Prediction: We adopt regression models to predict a score for each candidate label. We choose 12 features to describe each label and each feature is expected to indicate whether a

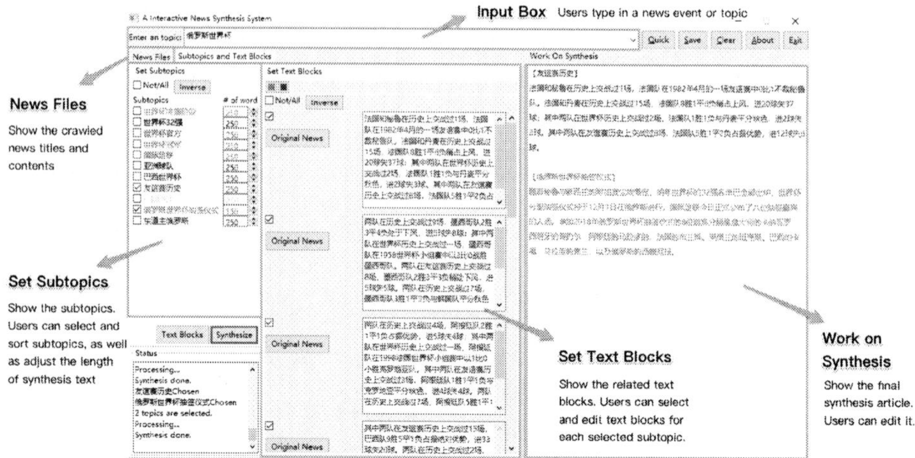

Figure 1: The GUI of our INS system. (Select two subtopics: '俄罗斯世界杯抽签仪式' (The Russian World Cup draw ceremony) and '友谊赛历史' (History of friendly match), and change the order of the two subtopics. Select the text blocks for each subtopic and make some edits on the text blocks. Then click on the synthesize button to obtain the final synthesis article for editing.)

candidate is good or not from some aspect. These features include Term Frequency-Inverse Document Frequency, Document Frequency, Number of words in the label, Number of Chinese characters in the label, Intra-Cluster Similarity, Cluster Entropy, Independence Entropy, Frequency of the label in news titles, Syntactic continuity, Number of nouns in the label, and topic model information.

In the training data, each candidate label is manually assigned with a score of 0~3, and a higher score indicates a better label. We then train regression models for label score prediction. We explore and compare different regression models, and finally choose support vector regression (SVR).

Label Merging: After label score prediction, the candidate labels are sorted by their predicted scores and the top 20 labels are reserved. We will merge similar labels according to the following rules: (1) If two n-grams share a common part which is more than one word, we will merge them into one label. (2) If one label is a substring of another, we only reserve the label with a higher score. (3) If two labels' cosine similarity is greater than a threshold (0.65 in this study), we only reserve the label with a higher score. After merged, labels are shown to users and each label stands for a subtopic.

5 Article Synthesizer

In this step, we need to produce a span of text with moderate length to describe each subtopic and then combine all the texts into the final synthesis article. We first segment the news articles into coherent text blocks and then rank the relevant text blocks for each subtopic. One or more salient text blocks can be chosen to describe the corresponding subtopic.

Text Segmentation: Most of the methods for document summarization use sentences as the basic unit, which is not appropriate for long article generation. Synthesis articles using the sentence as the basic unit tend to be fragmented and hard to read. As a result, we use the text block as our basic unit. A text block is a set of several continuous sentences and it can cover a relative complete idea. We use our proposed SenTiling algorithm (Zhang and Wan, 2017) to segment texts, which is a variant of Hearst's TextTiling algorithm (Hearst, 1997). After text segmentation, news articles are divided into text blocks, which include 2.3 sentences on average.

Text Block Ranking and Selection: For each subtopic, INS system first selects candidate text blocks using exact match. A text block that contains a subtopic label is assigned to the subtopic. Then INS uses a topic sensitive TextRank algorithm to rank candidate text blocks for each subtopic where TextRank((Mihalcea and Tarau, 2004)) is a typical graph-based ranking algorithm applied in document summarization. We build a graph with the candidate text blocks as vertexes and the similarity between text blocks as the weight of the edge. We can determine the importance $WS(V_i)$ of every vertex through a random walk with a restart. In our case, the restart probability of every vertex is set to the normalized similarity between each text block and the subtopic label so that the top text blocks are both important and relevant to the subtopic.

After ranking, the top text blocks may be similar and this leads to redundancy. We try to solve this problem by using the MMR criterion (Carbonell and Goldstein, 1998).

Now we have chosen the text blocks to describe each subtopic. Then we rearrange the text blocks according to the following strategies: (1) If two text blocks are extracted from one article, we sort them by the original order. (2) If two text blocks are extracted from different articles, we put the text blocks written earlier in the front. Because news event usually changes over time, this strategy can partly reconstruct the event process.

Synthesis Article Construction: Now we have labels for different subtopics and the corresponding text for each subtopic. INS then constructs the final news synthesis article. If users choose and rank the labels, INS will use their preferred order. If users choose and edit the text blocks, INS will use them instead of the default ones. Otherwise, INS chooses several labels with the highest scores and use the highly ranked text blocks of the subtopic labels for news synthesis. In this way, INS produces the final news synthesis article. Users can fix it to get their own article.

6 EVALUATION

Data Set: We chose 20 news topics and crawled about 100 Chinese news articles for each news topic, 1969 articles in total. The news topics cover a wide range of fields, including politics(e.g., 萨德系统/THAAD Missile System), technology(e.g., 百度无人驾驶汽车/Baidu Self-driving Car), society(e.g., 江歌刘鑫案/The Case of Jiangge and Liuxin), entertainment(e.g., 绝地求生/PLAYERUNKNOWN'S BATTLEGROUND), and sports(e.g., 俄罗斯世界杯/2018 FIFA World Cup Russia).

In order to train and test the regression models for detecting subtopic labels, we extracted all the n-grams that meet the previously-mentioned requirements and got about 220 candidate labels for each topic on average. Then we tagged them manually, with each label assigned with a score from 0 to 3. A higher score means a better label. The majority of n-grams are assigned with 0 and the labels with nonzero scores account for 26.3% in total. The labels with nonzero scores are considered acceptable subtopic labels.

Evaluation on Subtopic Labels: We leverage all 12 features to train the SVR model, and use 20-fold cross-validation, with 19 news topics for training and the rest one for validation in turn. The values of P@5, P@10 and P@20 for SVR are 0.722, 0.693 and 0.619, respectively. The results indicate the majority of top 20 labels can represent subtopics. Other inappropriate labels can be filtered out by interaction with users.

Evaluation on News Synthesis Articles: There are no gold reference synthesis articles for each news topic, and it is also hard to manually write a few reference articles. Thus we choose to conduct a manual evaluation of the final news synthesis articles. We use the multi-document summarization methods implemented in PKUSUMSUM (Zhang et al., 2016) as baselines.

The summarization methods we choose include Lead, Coverage, Centroid, and TextRank. Centroid and TextRank can work on either the sentence unit (i.e., Centroid-sen, TextRank-sen) or the text block unit (i.e., Centroid-blk, TextRank-blk). Thus we have six baselines. The baselines are compared with INS that does not involve user interaction. Each baseline and INS generate a synthesis article with 1000 words for each news event and 10 news topics will be manually evaluated. We employ 16 Chinese college students as judges. Each student evaluates one or two news topics. We make sure each student judge all the 7 articles for each news topic and each news topic is evaluated by 3 students. The judges are asked to give a rating score between 1 and 6 from the following aspects: readability, structure, topic diversity, redundancy removal, and overall responsiveness. The average results are shown in Table 1. From the table, we can see that INS achieves the best performance in every aspect, which proves the effectiveness of our INS system. We also perform pairwise t-tests when comparing our system with baselines, and find that INS significantly outperforms sentence-based methods in every aspect and block-based methods in almost all aspects (p-value < 0.05).

Note that in the above comparison, INS does not involve any user interaction. We believe after the interaction with users at different stages, the quality of the synthesis articles will be much improved.

Method	Read.	Struc.	Topic.	Redun.	Overall
Lead-sen	4.214	3.500	4.107	3.964	3.964
Coverage-sen	3.250	2.714	4.179	3.179	3.107
Centroid-sen	4.179	3.714	3.964	4.250	4.036
TextRank-sen	3.929	3.464	3.929	3.929	3.786
Centroid-blk	5.036	4.857	4.179	4.571	4.929
TextRank-blk	4.893	4.536	4.393	4.643	4.679
INS	**5.321**	**5.179**	**5.286**	**5.214**	**5.179**

Table 1: Manual evaluation results

User Study on INS: We further performed a user study on INS by employing 10 users to experience it and give their judgments. The rating scores given by users on various aspects (e.g., usefulness, GUI, satisfaction, assistance) are generally high. This indicates that the INS system is useful and users are satisfied with the system.

In addition to scoring, we asked them to give their comments on INS. The majority consider it as an excellent helper. They said subtopics are helpful to know about the given topic clearly, and INS can filter redundant information out. Besides, they think INS provide them with enough and useful interactions to produce synthesis articles. One user pointed out that the GUI of INS can be further improved.

In the future, we will concentrate on improving the performance and beautifying the user interface. We also plan to deploy the system in several Chinese news media.

Acknowledgment

This work was supported by National Natural Science Foundation of China (61772036) and Key Laboratory of Science, Technology and Standard in Press Industry (Key Laboratory of Intelligent Press Media Technology). We appreciate the anonymous reviewers for their helpful comments. Xiaojun Wan is the corresponding author.

References

Taylor Berg-Kirkpatrick, Dan Gillick, and Dan Klein. 2011. Jointly learning to extract and compress. In *Proceedings of the 49th Annual Meeting of the Association for Computational Linguistics: Human Language Technologies-Volume 1*, pages 481–490. Association for Computational Linguistics.

Jaime Carbonell and Jade Goldstein. 1998. The use of mmr, diversity-based reranking for reordering documents and producing summaries. In *Proceedings of the 21st annual international ACM SIGIR conference on Research and development in information retrieval*, pages 335–336. ACM.

Dan Gillick and Benoit Favre. 2009. A scalable global model for summarization. In *Proceedings of the Workshop on Integer Linear Programming for Natural Langauge Processing*, pages 10–18. Association for Computational Linguistics.

Marti A Hearst. 1997. Texttiling: Segmenting text into multi-paragraph subtopic passages. *Computational linguistics*, 23(1):33–64.

Steve Jones, Stephen Lundy, and Gordon W Paynter. 2002. Interactive document summarisation using automatically extracted keyphrases. In *System Sciences, 2002. HICSS. Proceedings of the 35th Annual Hawaii International Conference on*, pages 1160–1169. IEEE.

Anton Leuski, Chin-Yew Lin, and Eduard Hovy. 2003. ineats: interactive multi-document summarization. In *Proceedings of the 41st Annual Meeting on Association for Computational Linguistics-Volume 2*, pages 125–128. Association for Computational Linguistics.

Hui Lin and Jeff Bilmes. 2010. Multi-document summarization via budgeted maximization of submodular functions. In *Human Language Technologies: The 2010 Annual Conference of the North American Chapter of the Association for Computational Linguistics*, pages 912–920. Association for Computational Linguistics.

Peter J Liu, Mohammad Saleh, Etienne Pot, Ben Goodrich, Ryan Sepassi, Lukasz Kaiser, and Noam Shazeer. 2018. Generating wikipedia by summarizing long sequences. *arXiv preprint arXiv:1801.10198*.

Rada Mihalcea and Paul Tarau. 2004. Textrank: Bringing order into text. In *Proceedings of the 2004 conference on empirical methods in natural language processing*.

Ramesh Nallapati, Feifei Zhai, and Bowen Zhou. 2017. Summarunner: A recurrent neural network based sequence model for extractive summarization of documents. In *AAAI*, pages 3075–3081.

Ramesh Nallapati, Bowen Zhou, Caglar Gulcehre, Bing Xiang, et al. 2016. Abstractive text summarization using sequence-to-sequence rnns and beyond. *arXiv preprint arXiv:1602.06023*.

Pengjie Ren, Zhumin Chen, Zhaochun Ren, Furu Wei, Jun Ma, and Maarten de Rijke. 2017. Leveraging contextual sentence relations for extractive summarization using a neural attention model. In *Proceedings of the 40th International ACM SIGIR Conference on Research and Development in Information Retrieval*, pages 95–104. ACM.

Alexander M Rush, Sumit Chopra, and Jason Weston. 2015. A neural attention model for abstractive sentence summarization. *arXiv preprint arXiv:1509.00685.*

Ruben Sipos, Pannaga Shivaswamy, and Thorsten Joachims. 2012. Large-margin learning of submodular summarization models. In *Proceedings of the 13th Conference of the European Chapter of the Association for Computational Linguistics*, pages 224–233. Association for Computational Linguistics.

Jiwei Tan, Xiaojun Wan, and Jianguo Xiao. 2017. Abstractive document summarization with a graph-based attentional neural model. In *Proceedings of the 55th Annual Meeting of the Association for Computational Linguistics (Volume 1: Long Papers)*, volume 1, pages 1171–1181.

Xiaojun Wan and Jianmin Zhang. 2014. Ctsum: extracting more certain summaries for news articles. In *Proceedings of the 37th international ACM SIGIR conference on Research & development in information retrieval*, pages 787–796. ACM.

Kristian Woodsend and Mirella Lapata. 2012. Multiple aspect summarization using integer linear programming. In *Proceedings of the 2012 Joint Conference on Empirical Methods in Natural Language Processing and Computational Natural Language Learning*, pages 233–243. Association for Computational Linguistics.

Conglei Yao, Xu Jia, Sicong Shou, Shicong Feng, Feng Zhou, and Hongyan Liu. 2011. Autopedia: Automatic domain-independent wikipedia article generation. In *Proceedings of the 20th international conference companion on World wide web*, pages 161–162. ACM.

Jianmin Zhang and Xiaojun Wan. 2017. Towards automatic construction of news overview articles by news synthesis. In *Proceedings of the 2017 Conference on Empirical Methods in Natural Language Processing*, pages 2111–2116.

Jianmin Zhang, Tianming Wang, and Xiaojun Wan. 2016. Pkusumsum: a java platform for multilingual document summarization. In *Proceedings of COLING 2016, the 26th International Conference on Computational Linguistics: System Demonstrations*, pages 287–291.

Learning to Respond to Mixed-code Queries using Bilingual Word Embeddings

Chia-Fang Ho[1], Jhih-Jie Chen[2], Ching-Yu Yang[2], Jason S. Chang[2]
[1]Institute of Information Systems and Applications
National Tsing Hua University
[2]Department of Computer Science
National Tsing Hua University
{fun, jjc, chingyu, jason}@nlplab.cc

Abstract

We present a method for learning bilingual word embeddings in order to support second language (L2) learners in finding recurring phrases and example sentences that match mixed-code queries (e.g., *"接受 sentence"*) composed of words in both target language and native language (L1). In our approach, mixed-code queries are transformed into target language queries aimed at maximizing the probability of retrieving relevant target language phrases and sentences. The method involves converting a given parallel corpus into mixed-code data, generating word embeddings from mixed-code data, and expanding queries in target languages based on bilingual word embeddings. We present a prototype search engine, *x.Linggle*, that applies the method to a linguistic search engine for a parallel corpus. Preliminary evaluation on a list of common word-translation shows that the method performs reasonably well.

1 Introduction

Many queries are submitted to search engines on the Web every day to retrieve linguistic information for learning a second language (L2), and an increasing number of search engines specifically target queries for finding translations of phrases and sentences. For example, *Linguee* (www.linguee.com) accepts L1 queries and retrieves bilingual sentences (L1+L2), while *Google Translate* (translate.google.com) is used to translate (mixed-code) texts, and return L2 results.

Due to limited L2 vocabulary knowledge, users often submit mix-coded queries, but search engines such as *Linguee* only retrieve sentences similar to queries without converting them into target language queries.

By transforming L1 keywords in the original query into relevant L2 keywords, we can bias the search engine toward retrieving relevant L2 phrases and sentences for language learning.

We present a system, *x.Linggle*, that automatically processes mixed-code queries into monolingual queries and retrieves relevant phrases and examples to users. See Figure 1 for an example of *x.Linggle* search results of the query "接受 *education*". As shown in Figure 1, *x.Linggle* is accessible at https://x.linggle.com. *x.Linggle* has determined several L2 keywords for the L1 keyword "接受" by calculating cosine similarities between word vectors in the bilingual embedding space and convert the query into L2 queries (e.g., "receive education", "obtain education", "accept education"). Then, *x.Linggle* retrieves and ranks the results of these L2 queries according to occurrence counts, and finally returns relevant phrases with example sentences.

The rest of the article is organized as follows. First, we present our method for deriving bilingual word embeddings to support mixed-code queries. Next, we introduce the search engine in which we integrate our mixed-code query system. Then, we conduct a preliminary evaluation on the most common 7000 vocabulary for ESL learners. Finally, we conclude in Section 6.

2 Related Work

Word representation or word embedding has been an area of active research. It has been shown that predicting instead of counting context words leads to better representation of lexical semantics and relation between words (Mikolov et al., 2013; Pennington et al., 2014). We consider the specific case of learning word representation of two languages simultaneously, instead of a single language.

Previously proposed methods use a rotation matrix to learn the relation between word embeddings of the two languages. Conneau et al. (2017);

Proceedings of NAACL-HLT 2019: Demonstrations, pages 24–28
Minneapolis, Minnesota, June 2 - June 7, 2019. ©2019 Association for Computational Linguistics

Figure 1: The prototype system, *x.Linggle*

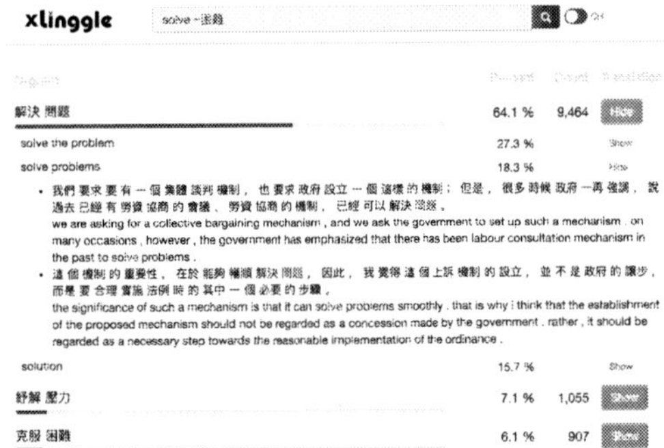

Figure 2: The extended example mechanism of *x.Linggle*

Duong et al. (2017) relate cross-lingual information based on a small set of word-translation pairs. Our approach is different in that we use mixed-code data converted from a parallel corpus, to derive directly an embedding space with word tokens in two languages, instead of learning a matrix transforming between two independent language embedding spaces.

In a study more closely related to our work, Gouws and Søgaard (2015); Vulić and Moens (2015) process a document-aligned comparable corpus as training data while Luong et al. (2015) processes mixed-code sentences for Cross-lingual Document Classification (CLDC) task. We use a similar training methodology for the different purpose of responding to mixed-code queries by converting mixed-code query into L2 queries based on the bilingual embedding.

In area of evaluating embedddings, researchers have typically used Spearman's rank correlation coefficients and Word Similarity to measure the quality of word embeddings (e.g., Mikolov et al. (2013); Pennington et al. (2014)). In contrast, we evaluate bilingual embedding by measuring the coverage of appropriate and relevant translation of the mixed-code queries.

In contrast to the previous research in word representation and bilingual word embeddings, we present a system that automatically converts mixed-code linguistic queries (which may contain L1 keywords or part of speech wildcards) so as to retrieve relevant phrase and sentences to assist language learning.

3   Bilingual Word Embeddings

Combining two separate word embeddings using a limited set of word-translation pairs to form a bilingual word embedding might not work very well. Word embedding vectors typically represent many word senses, while translations may cover only the dominant sense. To develop bilingual word embeddings, a promising approach is to artificially generate a mixed-code dataset based on a parallel corpus.

Problem Statement: We focus on the preprocessing step of mixed-code answering process: training bilingual word embedding model. We are given a mixed-code query Q_{mc}, a parallel corpus, and an L2 linguistic search engine. Our goal is to respond to the query, and retrieve relevant recurring L2 phrases and sentences. For this, we derive a bilingual word embedding V, such that $V(W)$ for an L1 keyword W (e,g,, "接受") in Q_{mc} is close to $V(T)$ for most L2 word T (e.g., "receive") relevant to W. Therefore the system can use V to retrieve "receive education" for the query of "接受 education".

The method involves (i) training a bilingual word embedding beforehand, (ii) searching for similar L2 words for L1 keyword in the embedding space, (iii) convert and expanding the mixed-code query for retrieving relevant phrases and sentences in the target language. To train word embeddings, we adopt the approach proposed by Mikolov et al. (2013), to derive a continuous, *semantic* representation of words based on context. Consider the flexibility, our method provides a framework of methodology and elements can be change according to different target. For example, bilingual word embedding model in different languages can be trained simply replace training data with other language corpus. Moreover, any word embedding training method (e.g., Mikolov et al. (2013); Pennington et al. (2014)) can be applied to train bilingual word embeddings.

However, if we only train with monolingual sentences, we can not find cross-lingual relation for our purpose. Therefore, we transplant the translation of a word into the sentence to generate artificially mixed-code sentences, and then train a word embedding model to encode cross-lingual information.

3.1 Transplanting Translations

In order to train word embeddings that with cross-lingual information, we generate mixed-code sentences from parallel sentences by transplanting word translation into the source sentences. For this, we used *Hong Kong Parallel Text* (HKPT), which consists of pairs of Chinese and English sentence with word-level alignments. The HKPT corpus consists of nearly 3M parallel sentences with 59M English and 98M tokens.

However, the alignment of Chinese and English does not correspond exactly word by word, and some even involve non one-to-one (1-1) alignment, leading to difficulties in transplanting. To cope with this problem, we perform the following training data preprocessing procedure.

Preprocessing Parallel Sentence

First, we merge possible multi-words as inseparable units whenever a word aligns to consecutive multiple words. Due to the differences between Chinese and English segmentation, for example, the alignment of English token "power plant", "發電廠"(which could be segmented into "發電" and "廠"). If that is the case, then the model can learn fine-grained information (e.g., "power" → "發電", "plant" → "廠") during training. For this reason, we change the word segmentation and realign, in order to derive more 1-1 correspondances. A transformation table is built to convert alignment of two English words and one Chinese word (e.g., "power plant" → "發電廠") into two pairs of 1-1 word alignment (e.g., "power" → "發電", "plant" → "廠") based on lexical translation probability derived from the dataset itself. With the transformation table, parallel corpus sentences are re-aligned and our model can perform better because of more information is available for individual words, which was previously not possible due to non 1-1 alignments.

Transplanting Translations

After preprocessing, we generate mixed-code sentence by replacing words with their alignment counterpart. It is important to note that we only replace one token at a time for simplicity. As it turns out, this approach worked just fine.

First, for each of the two languages, we generate mixed-code sentences by replacing one token in the source sentence with its corresponding foreign token. This process repeats for each content word in the L2 sentence to generate mixed-code sentences (e.g., 'I 有 a dream .', 'I have 一個 dream .' ...)

3.2 Word Embedding Training

We apply Skip-Gram models with negative sampling technique which reduces the noise distribution by logistic regression while using parallel corpus data as our training data. With parallel dataset, we generate training sentences by replacing source language tokens with target ones to obtain the neighbors of a token not only in the source language but also in the target language. Skip-gram model tries to predict current word's neighbors (its context) by giving a set of sentences (also called corpus), and the model loops on the words of each sentence and learn relation between words in a vector space. We train word embeddings model with the mixed-code sentences by putting them into pairs of a target word and its context words. (e.g., target word: **have**, context word: [我, 有, 一個, 夢]) Finaly, words in both languages can be represented in the same embeddings space.

When user submits an mixed-code query, L1 tokens in query are converted into candidate tokens in L2 by calculating distances of token vectors in a bilingual word embeddings model.

We convert and expand L1 keywords into L2 queries and re-rank the results to these queries by frequency.

4 x.Linggle: a mixed-code Linguistic Search Engine

We build our system based on an underlying linguistic search engine, *Linggle*, by (Boisson et al., 2013), supporting a set of wildcard query symbols. Figure 1 shows an example search performed by the system. Figure 3 describes the query symbols with examples. In addition to mixed-code query, we also offer on-demand display of example sentences to assist learners in writing or translation. We introduce the query symbol in the next section.

Operators	Description	Example
_	match any single word	drive _ car
*	match zero or more words	ready * change
?	search for TERM optionally	discuss ?about the issue
~	search for similar words	play an/a ~important role
/	either TERM1 or TERM2	in/at/on the afternoon
{}	order of TERM1, TERM2, TERM3, ...	{know where is she}
PoS.	search for words with specific PoS. (v, n, adj, adv, prep, det, conj, pron)	v. death penalty

Figure 3: Query operator instruction

4.1 Query Symbols

An underline (_) match any single word (e.g., "drive _ car"), while wildcards (*) match zero or more words (less than 4) (e.g., "ready * change"). Additionally, the question mark (?) before a word or part of speech symbol match nothing or the word/pos that follows.(e.g., "discuss ?about the issue") Use tilde (~) before a word to search for synonyms(e.g., "play an/a ~important role"). To match any of a list of words, use the symbols (/) (e.g., "in/at/on the afternoon"). Use curly brackets ({}) to match a list of words in any order (e.g., "{know where is she}"). Finally, a set of part of speech symbols can be used to match any single word with the designated POS (e.g., "v. death penalty")

4.2 Example and Translation

The original *Linggle* provides example sentences containing retrieved phrases to help learners learn the usage. We take a step further and extend the example mechanism. In our system, possible translations are shown first, and then parallel examples are provided. In so doing, learners not only learn the actual usage but also understand the nuance between phrases through the examples in their native language. The extended version of example is shown in Figure 2.

5 Preliminary Evaluation

The goal of this work is to enable a cross-language search engine to answer mixed-code queries, the model should be evaluated according to how well it covers relevant translations. We conduct a preliminary evaluation on a list of the most common 7000 words for intermediate high school ESL learners[1], with translations from an official Website of Ministry of Education in Taiwan. With

the dataset, we compare our model with *Cambridge Dictionary* in terms of covering the words and translation. The evaluation results show the proposed model model perform on par with the *Cambridge English-Chinese Dictionary* covering around 51% of the word-translation list.

6 Conclusion

Many avenues exist for future research and improvement of our system. For example, existing methods for ranking relevant phrases from queries could be implemented. Ranking phrases according to TF-IDF score instead of frequency could be used to improve relevance between queries and phrases. Additionally, an interesting direction to explore is disambiguating word sense by constructing a graph linking context words to sense translations based on bilingual word embeddings. Yet another direction of research would be to derive word embedding for units large than a single word, including collocations and compounds in more one language.

In summary, we have introduced a method for learning bilingual word embeddings that supports second language (L2) learners in finding recurring phrases and example sentences. The method involves converting a given parallel corpus into mixed-code data, generating word embeddings from mixed-code data, and expanding queries in the target language based on bilingual word embeddings. We have implemented the method on an underlying linguistic search engine, *Linggle*. Through the evaluation, we have shown that the method performs reasonably well and is useful for L2 learners.

References

Joanne Boisson, Ting-Hui Kao, Jian-Cheng Wu, Tzu-Hsi Yen, and Jason S Chang. 2013. Linggle: a web-

---

[1]https://zh.wikibooks.org/zh-tw/英語/高中7000辭彙

scale linguistic search engine for words in context. In *Proceedings of the 51st Annual Meeting of the Association for Computational Linguistics: System Demonstrations*, pages 139–144.

Alexis Conneau, Guillaume Lample, Marc'Aurelio Ranzato, Ludovic Denoyer, and Hervé Jégou. 2017. Word translation without parallel data. *arXiv preprint arXiv:1710.04087*.

Long Duong, Hiroshi Kanayama, Tengfei Ma, Steven Bird, and Trevor Cohn. 2017. Multilingual training of crosslingual word embeddings. In *Proceedings of the 15th Conference of the European Chapter of the Association for Computational Linguistics: Volume 1, Long Papers*, volume 1, pages 894–904.

Stephan Gouws and Anders Søgaard. 2015. Simple task-specific bilingual word embeddings. In *Proceedings of the 2015 Conference of the North American Chapter of the Association for Computational Linguistics: Human Language Technologies*, pages 1386–1390.

Thang Luong, Hieu Pham, and Christopher D Manning. 2015. Bilingual word representations with monolingual quality in mind. In *Proceedings of the 1st Workshop on Vector Space Modeling for Natural Language Processing*, pages 151–159.

Tomas Mikolov, Kai Chen, Greg Corrado, and Jeffrey Dean. 2013. Efficient estimation of word representations in vector space. *arXiv preprint arXiv:1301.3781*.

Jeffrey Pennington, Richard Socher, and Christopher Manning. 2014. Glove: Global vectors for word representation. In *Proceedings of the 2014 conference on empirical methods in natural language processing (EMNLP)*, pages 1532–1543.

Ivan Vulić and Marie-Francine Moens. 2015. Monolingual and cross-lingual information retrieval models based on (bilingual) word embeddings. In *Proceedings of the 38th international ACM SIGIR conference on research and development in information retrieval*, pages 363–372. ACM.

Train, Sort, Explain: Learning to Diagnose Translation Models

Robert Schwarzenberg[1], David Harbecke[1], Vivien Macketanz[1],
Eleftherios Avramidis[1], Sebastian Möller[1,2]
[1]German Research Center for Artificial Intelligence (DFKI), Berlin, Germany
[2]Technische Universität Berlin, Berlin, Germany
{firstname.lastname}@dfki.de

Abstract

Evaluating translation models is a trade-off between effort and detail. On the one end of the spectrum there are automatic count-based methods such as BLEU, on the other end linguistic evaluations by humans, which arguably are more informative but also require a disproportionately high effort. To narrow the spectrum, we propose a general approach on how to automatically expose systematic differences between human and machine translations to human experts. Inspired by adversarial settings, we train a neural text classifier to distinguish human from machine translations. A classifier that performs and generalizes well after training should recognize systematic differences between the two classes, which we uncover with neural explainability methods. Our proof-of-concept implementation, DiaMaT, is open source. Applied to a dataset translated by a state-of-the-art neural Transformer model, DiaMaT achieves a classification accuracy of 75% and exposes meaningful differences between humans and the Transformer, amidst the current discussion about human parity.

1 Introduction

A multi-dimensional diagnostic evaluation of performance or quality often turns out to be more helpful for system improvement than just considering a one-dimensional utilitarian metric, such as BLEU (Papineni et al., 2002). This is exemplified by, for instance, the pioneering work of Bahdanau et al. (2014). The authors introduced the attention mechanism responding to the findings of Cho et al. (2014) who reported that neural translation quality degraded with sentence length. The attention mechanism was later picked up by Vaswani et al. (2017) for their attention-only Transformer model, which still is state of the art in machine translation (MT) (Bojar et al., 2018). Furthermore, while MT

output approaches human translation quality and the claims for "human parity" (Wu et al., 2016; Hassan et al., 2018) increase, multi-dimensional diagnostic evaluations can be useful to spot the thin line between the machine and the human.

Diagnostic (linguistic) evaluations require human-expert feedback, which, however, is very time-consuming to collect. For this reason, there is a need for tools that mitigate the effort, such as the ones developed by Madnani (2011); Popović (2011); Berka et al. (2012); Klejch et al. (2015).

In this paper we propose a novel approach for developing evaluation tools. Contrary to the above tools that employ string comparison methods such as BLEU, implementations of the new approach derive annotations based on a neural model of explainability. This allows both capturing of semantics as well as focusing on the particular tendencies of MT errors. Using neural methods for the evaluation and juxtaposition of translations has already been done by Rikters et al. (2017). Their method, however, can only be applied to attention-based models and their translations. In contrast, our approach generalizes to arbitrary machine and even human translations. After first discussing the abstract approach in the next section, we present a concrete open-source implementation, "DiaMaT" (from *Dia*gnose *Ma*chine *T*ranslations).

2 Approach

The proposed approach consists of the three steps (1) *train*, (2) *sort*, and (3) *explain*.

2.1 Step 1: Train

In a first step, inspired by generative adversarial networks (Goodfellow et al., 2014; Wu et al., 2017; Yang et al., 2017) we propose to train a model to distinguish machine from human translations. The premise is that if the classifier generalizes well after training, it has learned to recognize

Proceedings of NAACL-HLT 2019: Demonstrations, pages 29–34
Minneapolis, Minnesota, June 2 - June 7, 2019. ©2019 Association for Computational Linguistics

systematic or frequent differences between the two classes (herinafter also referred to as "class evidence"). Class evidence may be, for instance, style differences, overused n-grams but also errors. The text classifier can be implemented through various architectures, ranging from deep CNNs (Conneau et al., 2017) to recurrent classifiers built on top of pre-trained language models (Howard and Ruder, 2018).

2.2 Step 2: Sort

In a second step, we suggest letting the trained classifier predict the labels of a test set which contains human and machine translations and then sort them by classification confidence. This is based on the assumption that if the classifier is very certain that a given translation was produced by a machine (translation moved to the top of the list in this step), then the translation should contain strong evidence for a class, i.e. errors typical for only the machine. Furthermore, even if we are dealing with a very human-like MT output, which means that our classifier may only slightly perform above chance, sorting by classification confidence should still move the few systematic differences that the classifier identified to the top.

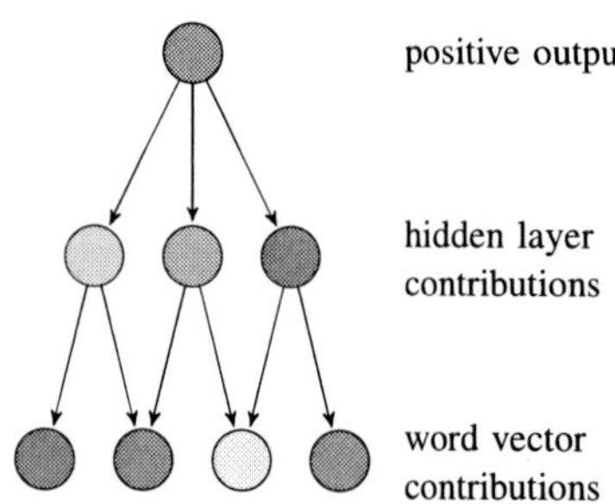

Figure 1: Contributions propagated from output to input space. Colors represent positive (red) and negative (blue) contributions. The Figure is adapted from Kindermans et al. (2018).

2.3 Step 3: Explain

Arras et al. (2016, 2017a,b) demonstrated the data exploratory power of explainability methods in Natural Language Processing (NLP). This is why in a third step, we propose to apply an explainability method to uncover and visualize the class evidence on which the classifier based its decisions. Our definition of an explanation follows Montavon et al. (2018), who define it as "the collection of features of the interpretable domain, that

have contributed for a given example to produce a decision (e.g. classification or regression)."[1] In our case the interpretable domain is the plain text space. There exist several candidate explainability methods, one of which we present in the following as an example.

Figure 2: A heatmap of contribution scores in word vector space over a sequence of tokens. Red means positive contribution (score > 0), blue means negative contribution (score < 0).

2.3.1 Explainability and Interpretability Methods for Data Exploration

In their tutorial paper, Montavon et al. (2018) discuss several groups of explainability methods. One group, for instance, identifies how sensitively a model reacts to a change in the input, others extract patterns typical for a certain class. Here, we discuss methods that propagate back contributions.

The contribution flow is illustrated in Fig. 1. At the top, the depicted binary classifier produced a positive output (input classified as class one). The classification decision is based on the fact that in the previous layer, the evidence for class one exceeded the evidence for class zero: The left and the right neuron contributed positively to the decision (reddish), whereas the middle neuron contributed negatively (blueish). Several explainability methods, such as Layerwise Relevance Propagation (Bach et al., 2015) or PatternAttribution (Kindermans et al., 2018), backtrack contributions layer-wise. The methods have to preserve coherence over highly non-linear activation functions. Eventually, contributions are projected into the input space where they reveal what the model considers emblematic for a class. This is what we exploit in step 3.

---

[1] Montavon et al. (2018) distinguish between explainability and interpretability. Interpretability methods also hold potential for the approach. For brevity, we limit ourselves to explainability methods here.

Source: " das trifft uns schwer , Rama ist ein herber Verlust " .

Machine (2.304, 0.993): " this strikes us hard , Rama is a severe loss . "

Human (-2.625, 0.007): " it 's hit us hard . Rama is a bitter loss . "

Source: Jazz wurde , auch wenn er nicht direkt verboten war , nicht gespielt .

Machine (2.97, 0.998): jazz was not played , even if it was not directly banned

Human (-3.032, 0.002): jazz , too , without exactly being proscribed , wasn ' t played .

Source: Jumbo - Hersteller streiten im Angesicht großer Bestellungen über Sitzbreite

Machine (3.013, 0.999): Jumbo manufacturers argue over seat width in the face of large orders

Human (-3.618, 0.001): jet makers feud over seat width with big orders at stake

Figure 3: Screenshot of demonstrative results in DiaMaT. Filters that allow the user to analyse the corpus are not shown. The bold label is the true label. The activations of the machine neuron are shown in brackets; on the left the unnormalized logit activation, on the right the softmax activation. Positive logits and softmax probabilities greater 0.5 indicate machine evidence, as do tokens highlighted in red. Consequently, blue indicates evidence for the human. The more intense the colour, the stronger the evidence.

Explainability methods in NLP (Arras et al., 2016, 2017a,b; Harbecke et al., 2018) are typically used to first project scores into word-vector space resulting in heat maps as shown in Fig. 2. To interpret them in plain text space, the scores are summed over the word vector dimensions to compute RGB values for each token, resulting in plain text heatmaps as shown in Fig. 3.

3 Implementation

For step 1 (training phase), DiaMaT[2] deploys a CNN text classifier, the architecture of which is depicted in Fig. 4. The classifier consumes three embeddings: the embedding of a source and two translations of the source, one by a machine and one by a human. It then separately convolves over the embeddings and subsequently applies max pooling to the filter activations. The concatenated max features are then passed to the last layer, a fully connected layer with two output neurons. The left neuron fires if the machine translation was passed to the left input layer, the right neuron fires if the machine translation was passed to the right input layer. Note that this layer allows the model to combine features from all three inputs for its classification decision.

For step 2 (sorting phase), DiaMaT offers to sort by unnormalized logit activations or by softmax activations. Furthermore, one can choose to use the machine neuron activation or the human neuron activation as the sorting key.

For step 3 (explaining phase), DiaMaT employs the iNNvestigate toolbox (Alber et al., 2018) in the back-end that offers more than ten explainability methods: Replacing one method with another only requires to change one configuration value in DiaMaT, before repeating step 3 again. In step 3, DiaMaT produces explanations in the form of $(token, score)$ tuple lists that are consumed by a front-end server which visualizes the scores as class evidence (see Fig. 3).[3]

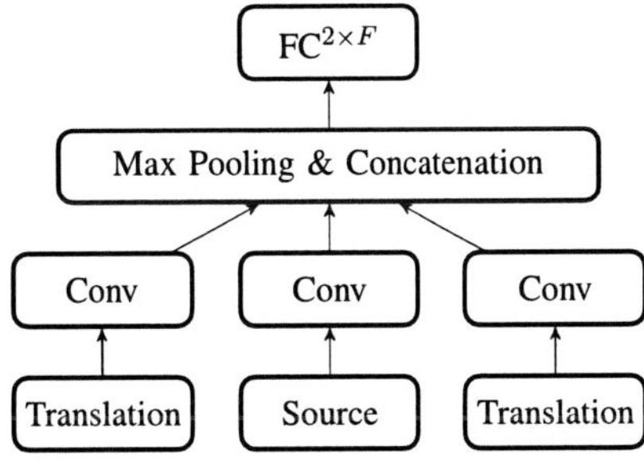

Figure 4: Architecture of the text classifier.

4 Datasets and Experiments

We tested DiaMaT on a corpus translated by an NMT Transformer engine (Vaswani et al., 2017)

---

[2]Source code, data and experiments are available at `https://github.com/dfki-nlp/diamat`.

[3]The front-end was inspired by the demo LRP server of the Fraunhofer HHI insitute `https://lrpserver.hhi.fraunhofer.de/text-classification`, last accessed 2019-01-31.

conforming to the WMT14 data setup (Bojar et al., 2014). The NMT model was optimized on the test-set of WMT13 and an ensemble of 5 best models was used. It was trained using OpenNMT (Klein et al., 2017), including Byte Pair Encoding (Sennrich et al., 2015) but no back-translation, achieving 32.68 BLEU on the test-set of WMT14.

Next, we trained the CNN text classifier sketched in Fig. 4 for which we randomly drew 1M training samples (human references and machine translations alongside their sources) from the WMT18 training data (Bojar et al., 2018), excluding the WMT14 training data. The validation set consisted of 100k randomly drawn samples from the same set and we drew another 100k samples randomly for training the explainability method of choice, PatternAttribution, which learns explanations from data. All texts were embedded using pre-trained fastText word vectors (Grave et al., 2018).

We evaluated the classifier on around 20k samples drawn from the official test sets, excluding WMT13. On this test set, the classifier achieved an accuracy of 75%, which is remarkable, considering the ongoing discussion about human parity (Wu et al., 2016; Hassan et al., 2018). We also used this test set for steps 2 and 3. Thus, neither the translation model, nor the text classifier, nor the explainability method encountered this split during training. For step 2, the machine translation was always passed to the right input layer and contributions to the right output neuron were retrieved with PatternAttribution.[4] We then sorted the inputs by the softmax activation of the machine neuron, which moved inputs for which the classifier is certain that it has identified the machine correctly to the top.

5   Demonstration and Observations

We observed that the top inputs frequently contained sentences in which DiaMaT considered the token after a sentence-ending full stop strong evidence for the human (Fig. 3, top segment). We take this as evidence that DiaMaT correctly recognized that the human generated multiple sentences instead of a single one more often than the machine did. At this point, we cannot, however, offer an explanation for why the token preceding the punctuation mark is frequently considered evidence for the machine.

Furthermore, DiaMaT also regarded reduced negations ("n't") as evidence for the human (see Fig. 3, middle segment) which again is reflected in the statistics. The machine tends to use the unreduced negation more frequently.

The last segment in Fig. 3 shows how DiaMaT points to the fact that the machine more often produced sentence end markers than the human in cases where the source contained no end marker. The claims above are all statistically significant in the test set, according to a χ^2 test with $\alpha = 0.001$.

6   Future Work

The inputs in Fig. 3 contain easily readable evidence. There is, however, also much evidence that is hard to read. In general, we can assume that with increasing architectural complexity, more complex class evidence can be uncovered, which may come at the cost of harder readability.

In the future, it is worth exploring how different architectures and model choices affect the quality, complexity and readability of the uncovered evidence. For instance, one direction would be to to train the classifier on top of a pretrained language model (Howard and Ruder, 2018; Devlin et al., 2019) which could improve the classification performance. Furthermore, other explainability methods should also be tested.

7   Conclusion

We presented a new approach to analyse and juxtapose translations. Furthermore, we also presented an implementation of the approach, DiaMaT. DiaMaT exploits the generalization power of neural networks to learn systematic differences between human and machine translations and then takes advantage of neural explainability methods to uncover these. It learns from corpora containing millions of translations but offers explanations on sentence level. In a stress test, DiaMaT was capable of exposing systematic differences between a state-of-the-art translation model output and human translations.

Acknowledgements

This research was partially supported by the German Federal Ministry of Education and Research through the project DEEPLEE (01IW17001). We would also like to thank the anonymous reviewers and Leonhard Hennig for their helpful feedback.

---

[4]In order to visualize evidence for the human (blue), positive contributions in the left input needed to be inverted.

References

Maximilian Alber, Sebastian Lapuschkin, Philipp Seegerer, Miriam Hägele, Kristof T Schütt, Grégoire Montavon, Wojciech Samek, Klaus-Robert Müller, Sven Dähne, and Pieter-Jan Kindermans. 2018. iNNvestigate neural networks! *arXiv preprint arXiv:1808.04260*.

Leila Arras, Franziska Horn, Grégoire Montavon, Klaus-Robert Müller, and Wojciech Samek. 2016. Explaining Predictions of Non-Linear Classifiers in NLP. In *Proceedings of the 1st Workshop on Representation Learning for NLP*, pages 1–7.

Leila Arras, Franziska Horn, Grégoire Montavon, Klaus-Robert Müller, and Wojciech Samek. 2017a. "What is relevant in a text document?": An interpretable machine learning approach. *PLOS ONE*, 12(8).

Leila Arras, Grégoire Montavon, Klaus-Robert Müller, and Wojciech Samek. 2017b. Explaining recurrent neural network predictions in sentiment analysis. In *Proceedings of the EMNLP'17 Workshop on Computational Approaches to Subjectivity, Sentiment & Social Media Analysis (WASSA)*, pages 159–168. Association for Computational Linguistics.

Sebastian Bach, Alexander Binder, Grégoire Montavon, Frederick Klauschen, Klaus-Robert Müller, and Wojciech Samek. 2015. On pixel-wise explanations for non-linear classifier decisions by layer-wise relevance propagation. *PLoS ONE*, 10(7):e0130140.

Dzmitry Bahdanau, Kyunghyun Cho, and Yoshua Bengio. 2014. Neural machine translation by jointly learning to align and translate. *arXiv preprint arXiv:1409.0473*.

Jan Berka, Ondřej Bojar, Mark Fishel, Maja Popović, and Daniel Zeman. 2012. Automatic MT Error Analysis: Hjerson Helping Addicter. In *Proceedings of the Eight International Conference on Language Resources and Evaluation*, pages 2158–2163, Istanbul, Turkey. European Language Resources Association.

Ondřej Bojar, Christian Buck, Christian Federmann, Barry Haddow, Philipp Koehn, Johannes Leveling, Christof Monz, Pavel Pecina, Matt Post, Herve Saint-Amand, Radu Soricut, Lucia Specia, and Aleš Tamchyna. 2014. Findings of the 2014 Workshop on Statistical Machine Translation. In *Proceedings of the Ninth Workshop on Statistical Machine Translation*, pages 12–58, Baltimore, Maryland, USA. Association for Computational Linguistics.

Ondřej Bojar, Christian Federmann, Mark Fishel, Yvette Graham, Barry Haddow, Matthias Huck, Philipp Koehn, and Christof Monz. 2018. Findings of the 2018 conference on machine translation (wmt18). In *Proceedings of the Third Conference on Machine Translation, Volume 2: Shared Task Papers*, pages 272–307, Belgium, Brussels. Association for Computational Linguistics.

Kyunghyun Cho, Bart van Merriënboer, Dzmitry Bahdanau, and Yoshua Bengio. 2014. On the properties of neural machine translation: Encoder–decoder approaches. *Syntax, Semantics and Structure in Statistical Translation*, page 103.

Alexis Conneau, Holger Schwenk, Loïc Barrault, and Yann Lecun. 2017. Very deep convolutional networks for text classification. In *Proceedings of the European Chapter of the Association for Computational Linguistic (EACL)*.

Jacob Devlin, Ming-Wei Chang, Kenton Lee, and Kristina Toutanova. 2019. BERT: Pre-training of Deep Bidirectional Transformers for Language Understanding. *Proceedings of the 2019 Conference of the North American Chapter of the Association for Computational Linguistics: Human Language Technologies*.

Ian Goodfellow, Jean Pouget-Abadie, Mehdi Mirza, Bing Xu, David Warde-Farley, Sherjil Ozair, Aaron Courville, and Yoshua Bengio. 2014. Generative adversarial nets. In *Advances in neural information processing systems*, pages 2672–2680.

Edouard Grave, Piotr Bojanowski, Prakhar Gupta, Armand Joulin, and Tomas Mikolov. 2018. Learning word vectors for 157 languages. In *Proceedings of the International Conference on Language Resources and Evaluation (LREC 2018)*.

David Harbecke, Robert Schwarzenberg, and Christoph Alt. 2018. Learning explanations from language data. In *Proceedings of the 2018 EMNLP Workshop BlackboxNLP: Analyzing and Interpreting Neural Networks for NLP*, pages 316–318.

Hany Hassan, Anthony Aue, Chang Chen, Vishal Chowdhary, Jonathan Clark, Christian Federmann, Xuedong Huang, Marcin Junczys-Dowmunt, William Lewis, Mu Li, Shujie Liu, Tie-Yan Liu, Renqian Luo, Arul Menezes, Tao Qin, Frank Seide, Xu Tan, Fei Tian, Lijun Wu, Shuangzhi Wu, Yingce Xia, Dongdong Zhang, Zhirui Zhang, and Ming Zhou. 2018. Achieving Human Parity on Automatic Chinese to English News Translation. *CoRR*, abs/1803.05567.

Jeremy Howard and Sebastian Ruder. 2018. Universal language model fine-tuning for text classification. In *Proceedings of the 56th Annual Meeting of the Association for Computational Linguistics (Volume 1: Long Papers)*, volume 1, pages 328–339.

Pieter-Jan Kindermans, Kristof T. Schütt, Maximilian Alber, Klaus-Robert Müller, Dumitru Erhan, Been Kim, and Sven Dähne. 2018. Learning how to explain neural networks: PatternNet and PatternAttribution. In *International Conference on Learning Representations (ICLR)*.

Guillaume Klein, Yoon Kim, Yuntian Deng, Jean Senellart, and Alexander M Rush. 2017. OpenNMT:

Open-source toolkit for neural machine translation. *arXiv preprint arXiv:1701.02810*.

Ondrej Klejch, Eleftherios Avramidis, Aljoscha Burchardt, and Martin Popel. 2015. MT-ComparEval: Graphical evaluation interface for Machine Translation development. *The Prague Bulletin of Mathematical Linguistics*, 104(1):63–74.

Nitin Madnani. 2011. iBLEU: interactively debugging and scoring statistical machine translation systems. In *2011 IEEE Fifth International Conference on Semantic Computing*, pages 213–214.

Grégoire Montavon, Wojciech Samek, and Klaus-Robert Müller. 2018. Methods for interpreting and understanding deep neural networks. *Digital Signal Processing*, 73:1–15.

Kishore Papineni, Salim Roukos, Todd Ward, and Wei-Jing Zhu. 2002. BLEU: a method for automatic evaluation of machine translation. In *Proceedings of the 40th annual meeting on association for computational linguistics*, pages 311–318. Association for Computational Linguistics.

Maja Popović. 2011. Hjerson: An Open Source Tool for Automatic Error Classification of Machine Translation Output. *The Prague Bulletin of Mathematical Linguistics*, 96(-1):59–68.

Matīss Rikters, Mark Fishel, and Ondřej Bojar. 2017. Visualizing Neural Machine Translation Attention and Confidence. *The Prague Bulletin of Mathematical Linguistics*, 109(1):39–50.

Rico Sennrich, Barry Haddow, and Alexandra Birch. 2015. Neural Machine Translation of Rare Words with Subword Units. *CoRR*, abs/1508.0.

Ashish Vaswani, Noam Shazeer, Niki Parmar, Jakob Uszkoreit, Llion Jones, Aidan N Gomez, Łukasz Kaiser, and Illia Polosukhin. 2017. Attention is all you need. In *Advances in Neural Information Processing Systems*, pages 5998–6008.

Lijun Wu, Yingce Xia, Li Zhao, Fei Tian, Tao Qin, Jianhuang Lai, and Tie-Yan Liu. 2017. Adversarial Neural Machine Translation. *CoRR*, abs/1704.06933.

Yonghui Wu, Mike Schuster, Zhifeng Chen, Quoc V. Le, Mohammad Norouzi, Wolfgang Macherey, Maxim Krikun, Yuan Cao, Qin Gao, Klaus Macherey, Jeff Klingner, Apurva Shah, Melvin Johnson, Xiaobing Liu, Łukasz Kaiser, Stephan Gouws, Yoshikiyo Kato, Taku Kudo, Hideto Kazawa, Keith Stevens, George Kurian, Nishant Patil, Wei Wang, Cliff Young, Jason Smith, Jason Riesa, Alex Rudnick, Oriol Vinyals, Greg Corrado, Macduff Hughes, and Jeffrey Dean. 2016. Google's Neural Machine Translation System: Bridging the Gap between Human and Machine Translation. *Computer Research Repository*, abs/1609.0.

Zhen Yang, Wei Chen, Feng Wang, and Bo Xu. 2017. Improving Neural Machine Translation with Conditional Sequence Generative Adversarial Nets. *CoRR*, abs/1703.04887.

`compare-mt:`
A Tool for Holistic Comparison of Language Generation Systems

Graham Neubig, Zi-Yi Dou, Junjie Hu, Paul Michel, Danish Pruthi, Xinyi Wang

Language Technologies Institute, Carnegie Mellon University

`gneubig@cs.cmu.edu`

Abstract

In this paper, we describe `compare-mt`, a tool for *holistic* analysis and comparison of the results of systems for language generation tasks such as machine translation. The main goal of the tool is to give the user a high-level and coherent view of the salient differences between systems that can then be used to guide further analysis or system improvement. It implements a number of tools to do so, such as analysis of accuracy of generation of particular types of words, bucketed histograms of sentence accuracies or counts based on salient characteristics, and extraction of characteristic n-grams for each system. It also has a number of advanced features such as use of linguistic labels, source side data, or comparison of log likelihoods for probabilistic models, and also aims to be easily extensible by users to new types of analysis. `compare-mt` is a pure-Python open source package,[1] that has already proven useful to generate analyses that have been used in our published papers.

1 Introduction

Tasks involving the generation of natural language are ubiquitous in NLP, including machine translation (MT; Koehn (2010)), language generation from structured data (Reiter and Dale, 2000), summarization (Mani, 1999), dialog response generation (Oh and Rudnicky, 2000), image captioning (Mitchell et al., 2012). Unlike tasks that involve prediction of a single label such as text classification, natural language texts are nuanced, and there are not clear yes/no distinctions about whether outputs are correct or not. Evaluation measures such as BLEU (Papineni et al., 2002), ROUGE (Lin, 2004), METEOR (Denkowski and Lavie, 2011), and many others attempt to give an

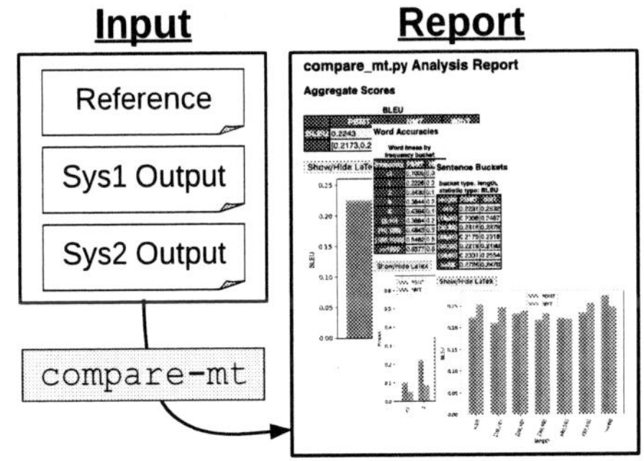

Figure 1: Workflow of using `compare-mt` for analysis of two systems

overall idea of system performance, and technical research often attempts to improve accuracy according to these metrics.

However, as useful as these metrics are, they are often opaque: if we see, for example, that an MT model has achieved a gain in one BLEU point, this does not tell us what characteristics of the output have changed. Without fine-grained analysis, readers of research papers, or even the writers themselves can be left scratching their heads asking *"what exactly is the source of the gains in accuracy that we're seeing?"*

Unfortunately, this analysis can be time-consuming and difficult. Manual inspection of individual examples can be informative, but finding salient patterns for unusual phenomena requires perusing a large number of examples. There is also a risk that confirmation bias will simply affirm pre-existing assumptions. If a developer has some hypothesis about specifically what phenomena their method should be helping with, they can develop scripts to automatically test these assumptions. However, this requires deep intuitions with respect to what changes to expect in advance, which cannot be taken for granted in beginning researchers

---

[1] Code http://github.com/neulab/compare-mt and video demo https://youtu.be/K-MNPOGKnDQ are available.

35

Proceedings of NAACL-HLT 2019: Demonstrations, pages 35–41

Minneapolis, Minnesota, June 2 - June 7, 2019. ©2019 Association for Computational Linguistics

or others not intimately familiar with the task at hand. In addition, creation of special-purpose one-off analysis scripts is time-consuming.

In this paper, we present `compare-mt`, a tool for *holistic comparison and analysis* of the results of language generation systems. The main use case of `compare-mt`, illustrated in 1, is that once a developer obtains multiple system outputs (e.g. from a baseline system and improved system), they feed these outputs along with a reference output into `compare-mt`, which extracts aggregate statistics comparing various aspects of these outputs. The developer can then quickly browse through this holistic report and note salient differences between the systems, which will then guide fine-grained analysis of specific examples that elucidate exactly what is changing between the two systems.

Examples of the aggregate statistics generated by `compare-mt` are shown in §2, along with description of how these lead to discovery of salient differences between systems. These statistics include word-level accuracies for words of different types, sentence-level accuracies or counts for sentences of different types, and salient n-grams or sentences where one system does better than the other. §4 demonstrates `compare-mt`'s practical applicability by showing some case studies where has *already* been used for analysis in our previously published work. Appendix A further details more advanced functionality of `compare-mt` that can make use of specific labels, perform analysis over source side text through alignments, and allow simple extension to new types of analysis. The methodology in `compare-mt` is inspired by several previous works on *automatic error analysis* (Popović and Ney, 2011), and we perform an extensive survey of the literature, note how many of the methods proposed in previous work can be easily realized by using functionality in `compare-mt`, and detail the differences with other existing toolkits in Appendix B.

2   Basic Analysis using `compare-mt`

Using `compare-mt` with the default settings is as simple as typing

```
compare-mt ref sys1 sys2
```

where `ref` is a manually curated reference file, and `sys1` and `sys2` are the outputs of two systems that we would like to compare. These analy-

	PBMT	NMT	Win?
BLEU	22.43	**24.03**	s2>s1
	[21.76,23.19]	[23.33,24.65]	p<0.001
RIBES	80.00	80.00	-
	[79.39,80.64]	[79.44,80.92]	p=0.44
Length	**94.79**	93.82	s1>s2
	[94.10,95.49]	[92.90,94.85]	p<0.001

Table 1: Aggregate score analysis with scores, confidence intervals, and pairwise significance tests.

sis results can be written to the terminal in text format, but can also be written to a formatted HTML file with charts and LaTeX tables that can be directly used in papers or reports.[2]

In this section, we demonstrate the types of analysis that are provided by this standard usage of `compare-mt`. Specifically, we use the example of comparing phrase-based (Koehn et al., 2003) and neural (Bahdanau et al., 2015) Slovak-English machine translation systems from Neubig and Hu (2018).

Aggregate Score Analysis   The first variety of analysis is not unique to `compare-mt`, answering the standard question posed by most research papers: *"given two systems, which one has better accuracy overall?"* It can calculate scores according to standard BLEU (Papineni et al., 2002), as well as other measures such as output-to-reference length ratio (which can discover systematic biases towards generating too-long or too-short sentences) or alternative evaluation metrics such as chrF (Popović, 2015) and RIBES (Isozaki et al., 2010). `compare-mt` also has an extensible `Scorer` class, which will be used to expand the metrics supported by `compare-mt` in the future, and can be used by users to implement their own metrics as well. Confidence intervals and significance of differences in these scores can be measured using bootstrap resampling (Koehn, 2004).

Fig. 1 shows the concrete results of this analysis on our PBMT and NMT systems. From the results we can see that the NMT achieves higher BLEU but shorter sentence length, while there is no significant difference in RIBES.

Bucketed Analysis   A second, and more nuanced, variety of analysis supported by

---

[2]In fact, all of the figures and tables in this paper (with the exception of Fig. 1) were generated by `compare-mt`, and only slightly modified for formatting. An example of the command used to do so is shown in the Appendix.

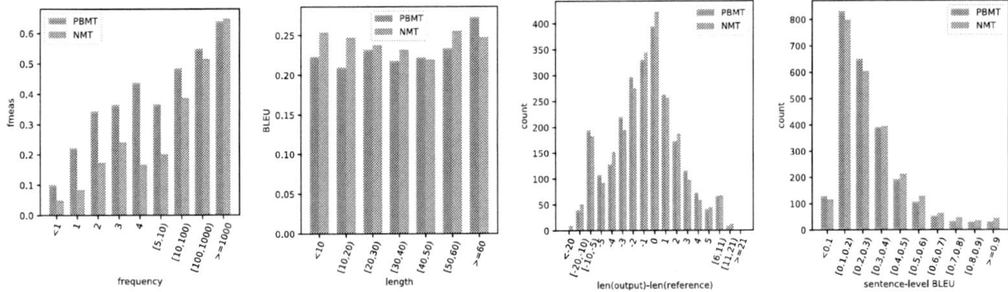

(a) Word F-measure bucketed by frequency.
(b) BLEU bucketed by sentence length.
(c) Counts of sentences by length difference.
(d) Counts of sentences by sentence-level BLEU.

Figure 2: Examples of bucketed analysis

`compare-mt` is *bucketed* analysis, which assigns words or sentences to buckets, and calculates salient statistics over these buckets.

Specifically, bucketed word accuracy analysis attempts to answer the question *"which types of words can each system generate better than the other?"* by calculating word accuracy by bucket. One example of this, shown in Fig. 2a, is measurement of word accuracy bucketed by frequency in the training corpus. By default this "accuracy" is defined as f-measure of system outputs with respect to the reference, which gives a good overall picture of how well the system is doing, but it is also possible to separately measure precision or recall, which can demonstrate how much a system over- or under-produces words of a specific type as well. From the results in the example, we can see that both PBMT and NMT systems do more poorly on rare words, but the PBMT system tends to be more robust to low-frequency words while the NMT system does a bit better on very high-frequency words.

A similar analysis can be done on the sentence level, attempting to answer questions of *"on what types of sentences can one system perform better than the other?"* In this analysis we define the "bucket type", which determines how we split sentences into bucket, and the "statistic" that we calculate for each of these buckets. For example, `compare-mt` calculates three types of analysis by default:

- **bucket=length, statistic=score:** This calculates the BLEU score by reference sentence length, indicating whether a system does better or worse at shorter or longer sentences. From the Fig. 2b, we can see that the PBMT system does better at very long sentences, while the NMT system does better at very short sentences.

- **bucket=lengthdiff, statistic=count:** This outputs a histogram of the number of sentences that have a particular length difference from the reference output. A distribution peaked around 0 indicates that a system generally matches the output length, while a flatter distribution indicates a system has trouble generating sentences of the correct length Fig. 2c indicates that while PBMT rarely generates extremely short sentences, NMT has a tendency to do so in some cases.

- **bucket=score, statistic=count:** This outputs a histogram of the number of sentences receiving a particular score (e.g. sentence-level BLEU score). This shows how many sentences of a particular accuracy each system outputs. Fig. 2d, we can see that the PBMT system has slightly more sentences with low scores.

These are just three examples of the many different types of sentence-level analysis that are possible with difference settings of the bucket and statistic types.

N-gram Difference Analysis The holistic analysis above is quite useful when word or sentence buckets can uncover salient accuracy differences between the systems. However, it is also common that we may not be able to predict *a-priori* what kinds of differences we might expect between two systems. As a method for more fine-grained analysis, `compare-mt` implements a method that looks at differences in the n-grams produced by

n-gram	m_1	m_2	s
phantom	34	1	0.945
Amy	9	0	0.909
, who	8	0	0.900
my mother	7	0	0.889
else happened	5	0	0.857
going to show you	0	6	0.125
going to show	0	6	0.125
hemisphere	0	5	0.143
Is	0	5	0.143
'm going to show	0	5	0.143

Table 2: Examples discovered by n-gram analysis

Ref/Sys	BLEU	Text
Ref	-	Beth Israel 's in Boston .
PBMT	1.00	Beth Israel 's in Boston .
NMT	0.41	Beat Isaill is in Boston .
Ref	-	And what I 'm talking about is this .
PBMT	0.35	And that 's what I 'm saying is this .
NMT	1.00	And what I 'm talking about is this .

Table 3: Sentence-by-sentence examples

each system, and tries to find n-grams that each system is better at producing than the other (Akabe et al., 2014). Specifically, it counts the number of times each system matches each ngram x, defined as $m_1(x)$ and $m_2(x)$ respectively, and calculates a smoothed probability of an n-gram match coming from one system or another:

$$p(x) = \frac{m_1(x) + \alpha}{m_1(x) + m_2(x) + 2\alpha}. \tag{1}$$

Intuitively, n-grams where the first system excels will have a high value (close to 1), and when the second excels the value will be low (close to 0). If smoothing coefficient α is set high, the system will prefer frequent n-grams with robust statistcs, and when α is low, the system will prefer highly characteristic n-grams with a high ratio of matches in one system compared to the other.

An example of n-grams discovered with this analysis is shown in Tab. 2. From this, we can then explore the references and outputs of each system, and figure out what phenomena resulted in these differences in n-gram accuracy. For example, further analysis showed that the relatively high accuracy of "hemisphere" for the NMT system was due to the propensity of the PBMT system to output the mis-spelling "hemispher," which it picked up from a mistaken alignment. This may indicate the necessity to improve alignments for word stems, a problem that could not have easily been discovered from the bucketed analysis in the previous section.

Sentence Example Analysis Finally, compare-mt makes it possible to analyze and compare individual sentence examples based on statistics, or differences of statistics. Specifically, we can calculate a measure of accuracy of each sentence (e.g. sentence-level BLEU score), sort the sentences in the test set according to the difference in this measure, then display the

examples where the difference in evaluation is largest in either direction.

Tab. 3 shows two examples (cherry-picked from the top 10 sentence examples due to space limitations). We can see that in the first example, the PBMT-based system performs better on accurately translating a low-frequency named entity, while in the second example the NMT system accurately generates a multi-word expression with many frequent words. These concrete examples can both help reinforce our understanding of the patterns found in the holistic analysis above, or uncover new examples that may lead to new methods for holistic analysis.

3 Advanced Features

Here we discuss advanced features that allow for more sophisticated types of analysis using other sources of information than the references and system outputs themselves.

Label-wise Abstraction One feature that greatly improves the flexibility of analysis is compare-mt's ability to do analysis over arbitrary word labels. For example, we can perform word accuracy analysis where we bucket the words by POS tags, as shown in 4. In the case of the PBMT vs. NMT analysis above, this uncovers the interesting fact that PBMT was better at generating base-form verbs, whereas NMT was better at generating conjugated verbs. This can also be applied to the n-gram analysis, finding which POS n-grams are generated well by one system or another, a type of analysis that was performed by Chiang et al. (2005) to understand differences in reordering between different systems.

Labels are provided by external files, where there is one label per word in the reference and system outputs, which means that generating these labels can be an arbitrary pre-processing step performed by the user without any direct modifications to the compare-mt code itself. These labels do not have to be POS tags, of course, and can

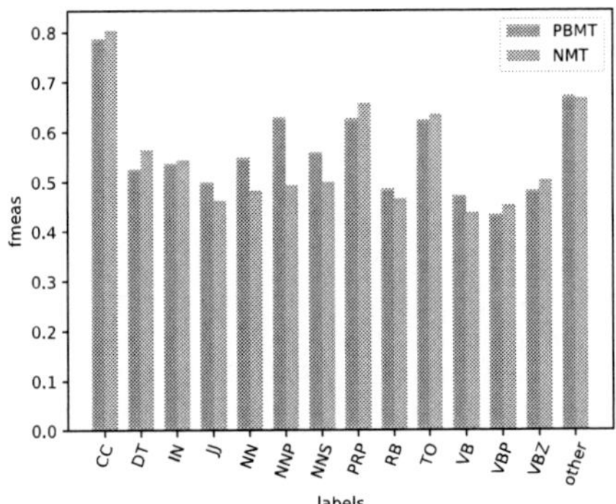

Figure 3: Word F-measure bucketed by POS tag.

also be used for other kinds of analysis. For example, one may perform analysis to find accuracy of generation of words with particular morphological tags (Popović et al., 2006), or words that appear in a sentiment lexicon (Mohammad et al., 2016).

Source-side Analysis While most analysis up until this point focused on whether a particular word on the *target* side is accurate or not, it is also of interest what source-side words are or are not accurately translated. compare-mt also supports word accuracy analysis for source-language words given the source language input file, and alignments between the input, and both the reference and the system outputs. Using alignments, compare-mt finds what words on the source side were generated correctly or incorrectly on the target side, and can do aggregate word accuracy analysis, either using word frequency or labels such as POS tags.

Word Likelihood Analysis Finally, as many recent methods can directly calculate a log likelihood for each word, we also provide another tool compare-ll that makes it possible to perform holistic analysis of these log likelihoods. First, the user creates a file where there is one log likelihood for each word in the reference file, and then, like the word accuracy analysis above, compare-ll can calculate aggregate statistics for this log likelihood based on word buckets.

Extending compare-mt One other useful feature is compare-mt's ability to be easily extended to new types of analysis. For example,

- If a user is interested in using a different evaluation metric, they could implement a new instance of the Scorer class and use it for both aggregate score analysis (with significance tests), sentence bucket analysis, or sentence example analysis.

- If a user wanted to bucket words according to a different type of statistic or feature, they could implement their own instance of a Bucketer class, and use this in the word accuracy analysis.

4 Example Use-cases

To emphasize compare-mt's practical utility, we also provide examples of how it has *already* been used in analyses in published research papers: Figs. 4 and 5 of Wang et al. (2018) use sentence-level bucketed analysis. Tab. 7 of Qi et al. (2018) and Tab. 8 of Michel and Neubig (2018) show the results of n-gram analysis. Fig. 2 of Qi et al. (2018), Fig. 4 of Sachan and Neubig (2018), Tab. 5 of Kumar and Tsvetkov (2019) show the results of word accuracy analysis.

5 Conclusion

In this paper, we presented an open-source tool for holistic analysis of the results of machine translation or other language generation systems. It makes it possible to discover salient patterns that may help guide further analysis.

compare-mt is evolving, and we plan to add more functionality as it becomes necessary to further understand cutting-edge techniques for MT. One concrete future plan includes better integration with example-by-example analysis (after doing holistic analysis, clicking through to individual examples that highlight each trait), but many more improvements will be made as the need arises.

Acknowledgements: The authors thank the early users of compare-mt and anonymous reviewers for their feedback and suggestions (especially Reviewer 1, who found a mistake in a figure!). This work is sponsored in part by Defense Advanced Research Projects Agency Information Innovation Office (I2O) Program: Low Resource Languages for Emergent Incidents (LORELEI) under Contract No. HR0011-15-C0114. The views and conclusions contained in this document are those of the authors and should not be interpreted as representing the official policies, either expressed or implied, of the U.S. Government. The U.S. Government is authorized to reproduce and distribute reprints for Government purposes notwithstanding any copyright notation here on.

References

Koichi Akabe, Graham Neubig, Sakriani Sakti, Tomoki Toda, and Satoshi Nakamura. 2014. Discriminative language models as a tool for machine translation error analysis. In *Proc. COLING*, pages 1124–1132.

Wilker Aziz, Sheila Castilho, and Lucia Specia. 2012. Pet: a tool for post-editing and assessing machine translation. In *Proc. LREC*, pages 3982–3987.

Dzmitry Bahdanau, Kyunghyun Cho, and Yoshua Bengio. 2015. Neural machine translation by jointly learning to align and translate. In *Proc. ICLR*.

Rachel Bawden, Rico Sennrich, Alexandra Birch, and Barry Haddow. 2018. Evaluating Discourse Phenomena in Neural Machine Translation. In *Proc. NAACL*, pages 1304–1313, New Orleans, Louisiana. Association for Computational Linguistics.

Luisa Bentivogli, Arianna Bisazza, Mauro Cettolo, and Marcello Federico. 2016. Neural versus phrase-based machine translation quality: a case study. In *Proc. EMNLP*, pages 257–267, Austin, Texas. Association for Computational Linguistics.

Alexandra Birch, Miles Osborne, and Phil Blunsom. 2010. Metrics for mt evaluation: evaluating reordering. *Machine Translation*, 24(1):15–26.

Konstantinos Chatzitheodorou and Stamatis Chatzistamatis. 2013. COSTA MT evaluation tool: An open toolkit for human machine translation evaluation. *The Prague Bulletin of Mathematical Linguistics*, 100(1):83–89.

David Chiang, Adam Lopez, Nitin Madnani, Christof Monz, Philip Resnik, and Michael Subotin. 2005. The hiero machine translation system: Extensions, evaluation, and analysis. In *Proc. EMNLP*, pages 779–786.

Steve DeNeefe, Kevin Knight, and Hayward H. Chan. 2005. Interactively exploring a machine translation model. In *Proc. ACL*, pages 97–100. Association for Computational Linguistics.

Michael Denkowski and Alon Lavie. 2011. Meteor 1.3: Automatic Metric for Reliable Optimization and Evaluation of Machine Translation Systems. In *Proc. WMT*, pages 85–91.

Yanzhuo Ding, Yang Liu, Huanbo Luan, and Maosong Sun. 2017. Visualizing and understanding neural machine translation. In *Proceedings of the 55th Annual Meeting of the Association for Computational Linguistics (Volume 1: Long Papers)*, volume 1, pages 1150–1159.

Ahmed El Kholy and Nizar Habash. 2011. Automatic error analysis for morphologically rich languages. In *Proc. MT Summit*, pages 225–232.

Christian Federmann. 2012. Appraise: an open-source toolkit for manual evaluation of mt output. *The Prague Bulletin of Mathematical Linguistics*, 98(1):25–35.

Mark Fishel, Rico Sennrich, Maja Popović, and Ondřej Bojar. 2012. Terrorcat: a translation error categorization-based mt quality metric. In *Proc. WMT*, pages 64–70.

Mary Flanagan. 1994. Error classification for mt evaluation. In *Proc. AMTA*, pages 65–72.

Meritxell Gonzàlez, Jesús Giménez, and Lluís Màrquez. 2012. A graphical interface for mt evaluation and error analysis. In *Proceedings of the ACL 2012 System Demonstrations*, pages 139–144.

Pierre Isabelle, Colin Cherry, and George Foster. 2017. A challenge set approach to evaluating machine translation. In *Proc. EMNLP*, pages 2476–2486.

Hideki Isozaki, Tsutomu Hirao, Kevin Duh, Katsuhito Sudoh, and Hajime Tsukada. 2010. Automatic evaluation of translation quality for distant language pairs. In *Proc. EMNLP*, pages 944–952.

Ondřej Klejch, Eleftherios Avramidis, Aljoscha Burchardt, and Martin Popel. 2015. Mt-compareval: Graphical evaluation interface for machine translation development. *The Prague Bulletin of Mathematical Linguistics*, 104(1):63–74.

Philipp Koehn. 2004. Statistical significance tests for machine translation evaluation. In *Proc. EMNLP*, pages 388–395.

Philipp Koehn. 2010. *Statistical Machine Translation*. Cambridge Press.

Phillip Koehn, Franz Josef Och, and Daniel Marcu. 2003. Statistical phrase-based translation. In *Proc. HLT*, pages 48–54.

Sachin Kumar and Yulia Tsvetkov. 2019. Von mises-fisher loss for training sequence to sequence models with continuous outputs. In *Proc. of ICLR*.

Jaesong Lee, Joong-Hwi Shin, and Jun-Seok Kim. 2017. Interactive visualization and manipulation of attention-based neural machine translation. In *Proceedings of the 2017 Conference on Empirical Methods in Natural Language Processing: System Demonstrations*, pages 121–126, Copenhagen, Denmark. Association for Computational Linguistics.

Chin-Yew Lin. 2004. Rouge: A package for automatic evaluation of summaries. In *Text Summarization Branches Out: Proceedings of the ACL-04 Workshop*, pages 74–81.

Adam Lopez and Philip Resnik. 2005. Pattern visualization for machine translation output. In *Proceedings of HLT/EMNLP 2005 Interactive Demonstrations*, pages 12–13.

Nitin Madnani. 2011. ibleu: Interactively debugging and scoring statistical machine translation systems. In *2011 IEEE Fifth International Conference on Semantic Computing*, pages 213–214. IEEE.

Inderjeet Mani. 1999. *Advances in automatic text summarization*. MIT press.

Paul Michel and Graham Neubig. 2018. MTNT: A testbed for machine translation of noisy text. In *Conference on Empirical Methods in Natural Language Processing (EMNLP)*, Brussels, Belgium.

Margaret Mitchell, Jesse Dodge, Amit Goyal, Kota Yamaguchi, Karl Stratos, Xufeng Han, Alyssa Mensch, Alex Berg, Tamara Berg, and Hal Daume III. 2012. Midge: Generating image descriptions from computer vision detections. In *Proc. EACL*, pages 747–756.

Saif M Mohammad, Mohammad Salameh, and Svetlana Kiritchenko. 2016. How translation alters sentiment. *Journal of Artificial Intelligence Research*, 55:95–130.

Mathias Müller, Annette Rios, Elena Voita, and Rico Sennrich. 2018. A large-scale test set for the evaluation of context-aware pronoun translation in neural machine translation. In *Proc. WMT*, pages 61–72, Belgium, Brussels. Association for Computational Linguistics.

Masaki Murata, Kiyotaka Uchimoto, Qing Ma, Toshiyuki Kanamaru, and Hitoshi Isahara. 2005. Analysis of machine translation systems' errors in tense, aspect, and modality. In *Proc. PACLIC*.

Sudip Kumar Naskar, Antonio Toral, Federico Gaspari, and Andy Way. 2011. A framework for diagnostic evaluation of mt based on linguistic checkpoints. *Proc. MT Summit*, pages 529–536.

Graham Neubig and Junjie Hu. 2018. Rapid adaptation of neural machine translation to new languages. In *Proc. EMNLP*, Brussels, Belgium.

Alice H Oh and Alexander I Rudnicky. 2000. Stochastic language generation for spoken dialogue systems. In *Proceedings of the 2000 ANLP/NAACL Workshop on Conversational systems-Volume 3*, pages 27–32. Association for Computational Linguistics.

Kishore Papineni, Salim Roukos, Todd Ward, and Wei-Jing Zhu. 2002. BLEU: a method for automatic evaluation of machine translation. In *Proc. ACL*, pages 311–318.

Maja Popović. 2015. chrf: character n-gram f-score for automatic mt evaluation. In *Proceedings of the Tenth Workshop on Statistical Machine Translation*, pages 392–395, Lisbon, Portugal. Association for Computational Linguistics.

Maja Popović, Adrià de Gispert, Deepa Gupta, Patrik Lambert, Hermann Ney, José B. Mariño, Marcello Federico, and Rafael Banchs. 2006. Morphosyntactic information for automatic error analysis of statistical machine translation output. In *Proc. WMT*, pages 1–6.

Maja Popović and Hermann Ney. 2007. Word error rates: Decomposition over POS classes and applications for error analysis. In *Proceedings of the Second Workshop on Statistical Machine Translation*, pages 48–55.

Maja Popović and Hermann Ney. 2011. Towards automatic error analysis of machine translation output. *Computational Linguistics*, 37(4):657–688.

Ye Qi, Devendra Sachan, Matthieu Felix, Sarguna Padmanabhan, and Graham Neubig. 2018. When and why are pre-trained word embeddings useful for neural machine translation? In *Proc. NAACL*, New Orleans, USA.

Ehud Reiter and Robert Dale. 2000. *Building natural language generation systems*. Cambridge university press.

Devendra Sachan and Graham Neubig. 2018. Parameter sharing methods for multilingual self-attentional translation models. In *Proc. WMT*, Brussels, Belgium.

Rico Sennrich. 2017. How Grammatical is Character-level Neural Machine Translation? Assessing MT Quality with Contrastive Translation Pairs. In *Proc. EACL*, pages 376–382, Valencia, Spain.

Sara Stymne. 2011. BLAST: A tool for error analysis of machine translation output. In *Proceedings of the ACL-HLT 2011 System Demonstrations*, pages 56–61.

David Vilar, Jia Xu, Luis Fernando d'Haro, and Hermann Ney. 2006. Error analysis of statistical machine translation output. In *Proc. LREC*, pages 697–702.

Xinyi Wang, Hieu Pham, Pengcheng Yin, and Graham Neubig. 2018. A tree-based decoder for neural machine translation. In *Conference on Empirical Methods in Natural Language Processing (EMNLP)*, Brussels, Belgium.

Jonathan Weese and Chris Callison-Burch. 2010. Visualizing data structures in parsing-based machine translation. *The Prague Bulletin of Mathematical Linguistics*, 93:127–136.

Daniel Zeman, Mark Fishel, Jan Berka, and Ondřej Bojar. 2011. Addicter: What is wrong with my translations? *The Prague Bulletin of Mathematical Linguistics*, 96(1):79–88.

Ming Zhou, Bo Wang, Shujie Liu, Mu Li, Dongdong Zhang, and Tiejun Zhao. 2008. Diagnostic evaluation of machine translation systems using automatically constructed linguistic check-points. In *Proc. COLING*, pages 1121–1128, Manchester, UK. Coling 2008 Organizing Committee.

Eidos, INDRA, & Delphi: From Free Text to Executable Causal Models

Rebecca Sharp, Adarsh Pyarelal, Benjamin M. Gyori[†], Keith Alcock,
Egoitz Laparra, Marco A. Valenzuela-Escárcega, Ajay Nagesh, Vikas Yadav,
John A. Bachman[†], Zheng Tang, Heather Lent, Fan Luo, Mithun Paul,
Steven Bethard, Kobus Barnard, Clayton T. Morrison, Mihai Surdeanu
University of Arizona, Tucson, Arizona, USA
[†]Harvard Medical School, Boston, Massachusetts, USA
{bsharp,adarsh}@email.arizona.edu

Abstract

Building causal models of complicated phenomena such as food insecurity is currently a slow and labor-intensive manual process. In this paper, we introduce an approach that builds executable probabilistic models from raw, free text. The proposed approach is implemented through three systems: Eidos[1], INDRA[2] and Delphi[3]. Eidos is an open-domain machine reading system designed to extract causal relations from natural language. It is rule-based, allowing for rapid domain transfer, customizability, and interpretability. INDRA aggregates multiple sources of causal information and performs assembly to create a coherent knowledge base and assess its reliability. This assembled knowledge serves as the starting point for modeling. Delphi is a modeling framework that assembles quantified causal fragments and their contexts into executable probabilistic models that respect the semantics of the original text and can be used to support decision making.

1 Introduction

Food insecurity is an extremely complex phenomenon that affects wide swathes of the global population, and is governed by factors ranging from biophysical variables that affect crop yields, to social, economic, and political factors such as migration, trade patterns, and conflict.

For any attempt to combat food insecurity to be effective, it must be informed by a model that comprehensively considers the myriad of factors influencing it. Furthermore, for analysts and decision makers to truly trust such a model, it must be *causal* and *interpretable*, as in, it must provide a mechanistic explanation of the phenomenon, rather than just being a black-box statistical construction.

Currently, however, these models are hand-built for each new situation and require many months to construct, resulting in long delays for much-needed interventions.

Here we propose an end-to-end system that combines open-domain information extraction (IE) with a quantitative model-building framework, transforming free text into executable probabilistic models that capture complex real-world systems. All code and data described here is open-source and publicly available, and we provide a short video demonstration[4].

Contributions:

(1) We introduce Eidos, a rule-based open-domain IE system that extracts causal statements from raw text. To maximize domain independence, Eidos is largely unlexicalized (with the exception of causal cues such as *promotes*), and implements a top-down approach where causal interactions are extracted first, followed by the participating concepts, which are grounded with specific geospatial and temporal contexts for model contextualization. Eidos also extracts quantifiable adjectives (e.g. *significant*) that can be used to form a bridge between qualitative statements and quantitative modeling.

(2) We describe an extension of the Integrated Network and Dynamical Reasoning Assembler (INDRA, Gyori et al., 2017), an automated knowledge and model assembly system which implements interfaces to Eidos and multiple other machine reading systems. Originally developed to assemble models of biochemical mechanisms, we generalized INDRA to represent general causal influences as INDRA Statements, and load a taxonomy of concepts to align related Statements from multiple readers and documents.

(3) We introduce Delphi, a Bayesian modeling

---

[1]https://github.com/clulab/eidos
[2]https://github.com/sorgerlab/indra
[3]https://github.com/ml4ai/delphi

[4]https://youtu.be/FcLEJejluAg

Proceedings of NAACL-HLT 2019: Demonstrations, pages 42–47
Minneapolis, Minnesota, June 2 - June 7, 2019. ©2019 Association for Computational Linguistics

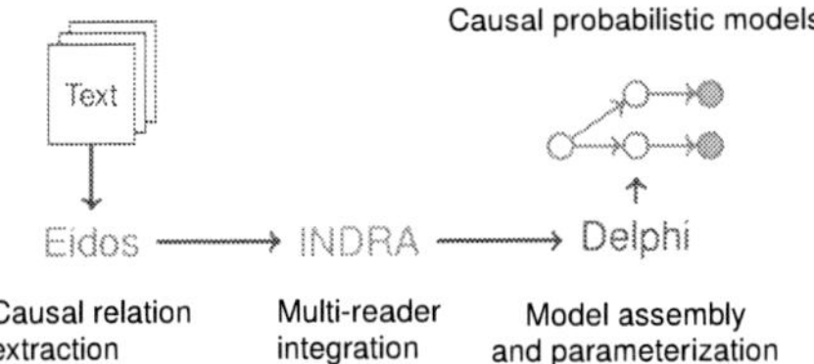

Figure 1: Overall architecture showing the flow of information between the systems.

framework that converts the above statements into executable probabilistic models that respect the semantics of the source text. These models can help decision-makers rapidly build intuition about complicated systems and their dynamics. The proposed framework is interpretable due to its foundation in rule-based IE and Bayesian generative modeling.

Architecture: In Fig. 1, we show a high-level depiction of the information flow pipeline. First, natural language texts serve as inputs to Eidos, which performs causal relation extraction, grounding, and spatiotemporal contextualization. The extracted relations are subsequently aggregated by INDRA into data structures called INDRA Statements for downstream modeling. These serve as an input to Delphi, which assembles a causal probabilistic model from them.

2 Causal Information Extraction

Eidos was designed as an open-domain IE system (Banko et al., 2007) with a top-down approach that allows us to not be limited to a fixed set of concepts, as determining this set across multiple distinct domains (e.g., agronomy and socioeconomics) is close to impossible. First, we find trigger words signaling a relation of interest and then extract and expand the participating concepts (2.1), link these concepts to a taxonomy (2.2), and annotate them with temporal and spatial context (2.3).[5,6]

In addition to an API that can be used for machine reading at scale, Eidos has a webapp that provides users a way to see what rules were responsible for the extracted content, as well as brat visualizations (Stenetorp et al., 2012) of the output,

facilitating rapid development of the interpretable rule-grammars.

2.1 Reading Approach

To understand our top-down approach, let us consider the individual steps involved in processing the following sentence: *The significantly increased conflict seen in South Sudan forced many families to flee in 2017.*

(1) We begin by preprocessing the text with dependency syntax using Stanford CoreNLP (Manning et al., 2014) and the processors library[7].

(2) Then, Eidos finds any occurrences of *quantifiers* (gradable adjectives and adverbs). These are common in the high-level texts relevant to food insecurity, such as reports from UN agencies and nonprofits, but they are difficult to use in quantitative models without additional information. In the example above, the word *significantly* is found as a quantifier of *increased*. Delphi uses these quantifiers to construct probability density functions using the crowdsourced data of Sharp et al. (2018), as detailed in 4.

(3) Next, Eidos uses a set of trigger words to find causal and correlational relations with an Odin grammar (Valenzuela-Escárcega et al., 2016). Odin is an information extraction framework which includes a declarative language supporting both surface and syntactic patterns and a runtime system. Eidos's grammar was based in part on the biomedical grammar developed by Valenzuela-Escárcega et al. (2018) but adapted to the open domain and our representation of concepts. This rule grammar is fully interpretable and easily editable, allowing users to make modifications without needing to retrain a complex model. In the example sentence from earlier, the extraction of a causal relation would be triggered by the word *forced*, with *conflict* and *families* identified as the initial cause and effect, respectively.

(4) The initial cause and effect are then expanded using dependency syntax following the approach of Hahn-Powell et al. (2017). Namely, from each of the initial arguments, we traverse outgoing dependency links to expand the arguments into their dependency subgraph. Here, the resulting arguments are *significantly increased conflict seen in South Sudan* and *many families to flee in 2017.*

---

[5] This has some similarities to FrameNet (Baker et al., 1998), whose Causation frame has targets (triggers) and frame elements (participating concepts) that are associated with a taxonomy (the FrameNet hierarchy). In our case, the concepts come from a domain-specific taxonomy.

[6] We assume here that causal relations are specified within sentences rather than across sentences at the document level, and that the concepts involved in the causal relations can be linked to an appropriate taxonomy.

[7] https://github.com/clulab/processors

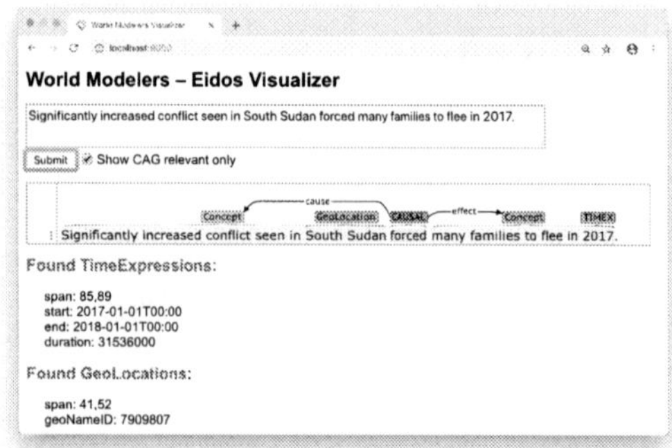

Figure 2: Screenshot of the Eidos output for the running example sentence, visualized in Eidos's webapp.

(5) Relevant state information is then added to the expanded concepts. Representing the polarity of an influence on the causal relation edge (i.e., in terms of *promotes* or *inhibits*) can be lossy, so Eidos instead uses concept states (i.e., concepts can be increased, decreased, and/or quantified). In the example above, Eidos marks the concept pertaining to conflict as being increased and quantified. If desired, the promotion/inhibition representation with edge polarity can be straightforwardly recovered. The final output of the Eidos system for the running example sentence, as displayed in the Eidos webapp, is shown in Fig. 2.

2.2 Concept linking

The Eidos reading system, with its top-down approach, was designed to keep extracted concepts as close to the text as possible, intentionally allowing downstream users to make decisions about event semantics depending on their use cases. As a result, linking concepts to a taxonomy becomes critical for preventing sparsity.

Eidos's concept linking is based on word-embedding similarities. A given concept (with stop words removed), is represented by the average of the word embeddings for each of its words. A vector for each node in the taxonomy is similarly calculated (using the provided "examples" for the node), and the taxonomy node whose vector is closest to the concept vector is considered to be the grounding. In practice, Eidos returns the top k groundings, allowing for downstream disambiguation. The concept linking strategy is modular and allows for grounding to any taxonomy provided in the human-readable YAML format. With this method, Eidos is able to link to an arbitrary number of taxonomies, at both high and low levels of abstraction.

2.3 Temporal and geospatial normalization

Time normalization The context surrounding the extractions is often critical for downstream reasoning. Eidos integrates the temporal parser of Laparra et al. (2018) that uses a character recurrent neural network to identify time expressions in the text which are then linked together with a set of rules into semantic graphs which follow the SCATE schema (Bethard and Parker, 2016) and can be interpreted using temporal logic to obtain the intervals referred to by the time expressions.

After the time expressions are identified and normalized, an Odin grammar attaches them to the causal relations extracted by Eidos. If the document creation time is provided, it is also parsed by our model and used as the default temporal attachment for those causal relations without a temporal expression in their close context.

Geospatial normalization Eidos's geospatial normalization module (Yadav et al., 2019) has two components: a detection component consisting of the word-level LSTM named entity recognition (NER) model of Yadav and Bethard (2018), and a normalization component which implements population heuristics (i.e., selecting the most populous location (Magge et al., 2018)) and filters using a distance-based heuristic (Magge et al., 2018).

3 Assembly of causal relations

The output of Eidos is processed by INDRA into a collection of INDRA Statements, each of which represents a causal influence relation. INDRA is also able to process the output of multiple other reading systems that extract causal relations from text (these systems are not described in detail here). INDRA implements input processor modules to extract standardized Statements from each reading system. A Statement represents a causal influence between two Concepts (a subject and an object), each of which is linked to one or more taxonomies (see Section 2.2). The Statement also captures the polarity and magnitude of change in both subject and object, if available. Finally, one or more Evidences are attached to each Statement capturing provenance (reader, document, sentence) and context (time, location) information. This common representation establishes a link between diverse knowledge sources and several model formalism endpoints.

Given the attributes of each Statement and a taxonomy to which Concepts are linked, INDRA creates a Statement graph whose edges capture (i) redundancy between two Statements (ii) hierarchical refinement between two Statements, and (iii) contradiction between two Statements. Statements that are redundant, or in other words, capture the same causal relation, are merged and their evidences are aggregated. A probability model is then used which captures the empirical precision of each reader to calculate the overall support (a "belief" score) for a Statement given the joint probability of correctness implied by the evidence. As a seed to this probability model, INDRA loads empirical precision values collected via human curation for each Eidos rule. INDRA exposes a collection of methods to filter Statements that can be composed to form a problem-specific assembly pipeline, including (i) filtering by Statement belief and Concept linking accuracy (ii) filtering to more general or specific Statements (with respect to a taxonomy), and (iii) filtering contradictions by belief. INDRA also exposes a REST API and JSON-based serialization of Statements.

INDRA contains multiple modules that can assemble Statements into causal graphs (for visualization or inference) and executable ODE models. In the architecture presented here, Delphi (our Bayesian modeling framework) takes INDRA Statements directly as input, and serves as a probabilistic model assembly system.

4   Causal Probabilistic Models from Text

Statements produced by INDRA are assembled by Delphi into a structure called a *causal analysis graph*, or CAG. In Fig. 3, we show the CAG resulting from our running example sentence (cell [1]). The node labels (*conflict* and *human migration*) in the CAG correspond to entries in the high-level taxonomy that the concepts have been grounded to.

Representation   We represent abstract concepts such as *conflict* and *human migration* as real-valued *latent* variables in a dynamic Bayes network (DBN) (Dagum et al., 1992), and the indicators corresponding to these concepts as *observed* variables. By an indicator, we mean a tangible quantity that serves as a proxy for the abstract concept[8]. For example, the variable *Net migration* (as defined in World Bank (2018)) is one of several indicators for the

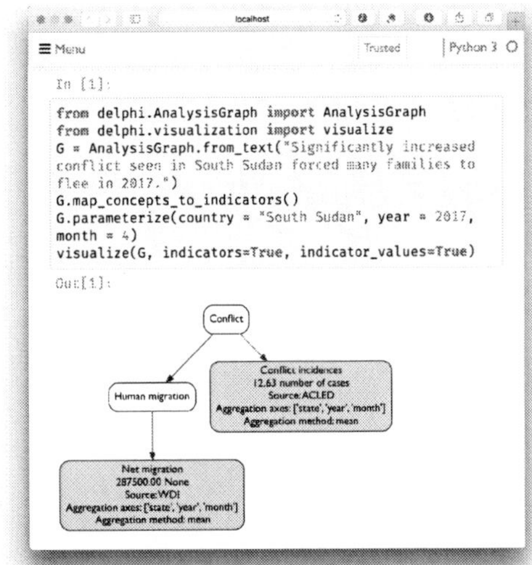

Figure 3: Construction of a causal analysis graph from the running example sentence.

concept of *human migration*. To capture the uncertainty inherent in interpreting natural language, we take the transition model of the DBN itself to be a random variable with an associated probability distribution. We interpret sentences about causal relations as saying something about the functional relationship between the concepts involved. For example, we interpret the running example sentence as giving us a clue about the shape of $\partial(\text{human migration})/\partial(\text{conflict})$.

Assembly   To assemble our model, we do the following[9]:

(1) We construct the aforementioned distribution over the transition model of the DBN using the extracted polarities of the causal relations as well as the gradable adjectives associated with the concepts involved in the relations. The transition model is a matrix whose elements are random variables representing the coefficients of a system of linear differential equations (Guan et al., 2015), with distributions obtained by constructing a Gaussian kernel density estimator over Cartesian products of the crowdsourced responses collected by Sharp et al. (2018) for the adjectives in each relation.

(2) To provide more tangible results, we map the abstract concepts to indicator variables for which we have time series data. This data is gathered from a number of databases, including but not limited to

---

[8]Note that these are not the same as the indicator random variables encountered in probability theory.

[9]The complete mathematical details of the model assembly process are out of the scope of this paper, but can be found at: http://vision.cs.arizona.edu/adarsh/Arizona_Text_to_Model_Procedure.pdf

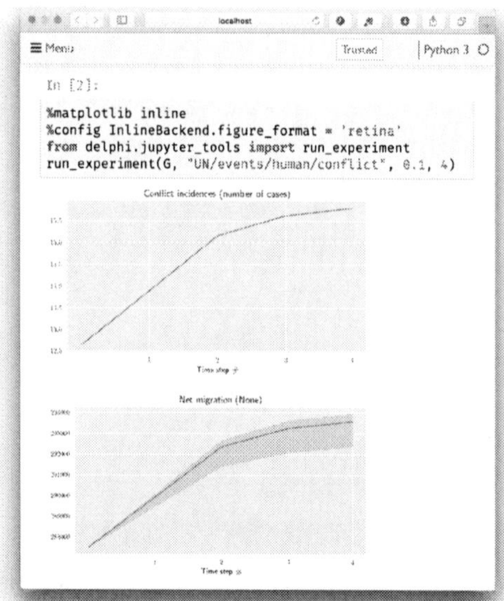

Figure 4: Results of conditional forecasting experiment with CAG built from example sentence.

the FAOSTAT (Food and Agriculture Organization of the United Nations, 2018) and the World Development Indicators (World Bank, 2018) databases. The mapping is done using the OntologyMapper tool in Eidos that uses word embedding similarities to map entries in the high-level taxonomy to the lower-level variables in the time series data.

(3) Then, we associate values with indicators using a parameterization algorithm that takes as input some spatiotemporal context, and retrieves values for the indicators from the time series data, falling back to aggregation over a (configurable) set of aggregation axes in order to prevent null results. In Fig. 3, we show the indicators automatically mapped to the conflict and human migration nodes (*conflict incidences* and *net migration*, respectively) and their values for the spatiotemporal context of South Sudan in April 2017.

Conditional forecasting Once the model is assembled, we can run experiments to obtain quantitative predictions for indicators, which can build intuitions about the complex system in question and support decision making. The outputs take the form of time series data, with associated uncertainty estimates. An example is shown in Fig. 4, in which we investigate the impact of increasing conflict on human migration using our model, with $\partial(\text{conflict})/\partial t = 0.1e^{-t}$. The predictions of the model reflect (i) the semantics of the source text (increased conflict leads to increased migration)

and (ii) the uncertainty in interpreting the source sentence. The confidence bands in the lower plot reflect the distribution of the crowdsourced gradable adjective data.

5 Assessment

We are currently in the process of developing a framework to quantitatively evaluate the models assembled using this pipeline, primarily via backcasting. However, the systems have been qualitatively evaluated by MITRE, an independent performer group in the World Modelers program charged with designing and conducting evaluations of the technologies developed. For the evaluation, a causal analysis graph larger than the toy running example in this paper ($\approx$ 20 nodes) was created and executed. Noted strengths of the system include the ability to *drill down* into the provenance of the causal relations, the integration of multiple machine readers, and the plausible directionality of the produced forecast (given the sentences used to construct the models). Some limitations were also noted, i.e., that the initialization and parameterization of the models were somewhat opaque (which hindered explainability) and some aspects of uncertainty are captured by the readers but not fully propagated to the model. We are actively working on addressing both of these limitations.

6 Conclusion

Complex causal models are required in order to address key issues such as food insecurity that span multiple domains. As an alternative to expensive, hand-built models which can take months to years to construct, we propose an end-to-end framework for creating executable probabilistic causal models from free text. Our entire pipeline is interpretable and intervenable, such that domain experts can use our tools to greatly reduce the time required to develop new causal models for urgent situations.

Acknowledgments: This work was supported by the Defense Advanced Research Projects Agency (DARPA) under the World Modelers program, grant W911NF1810014 and by the Bill and Melinda Gates Foundation HBGDki Initiative. Marco Valenzuela-Escárcega and Mihai Surdeanu declare a financial interest in lum.ai. This interest has been properly disclosed to the University of Arizona Institutional Review Committee and is managed in accordance with its conflict of interest policies.

References

Collin F. Baker, Charles J. Fillmore, and John B. Lowe. 1998. The Berkeley FrameNet project. In *Proceedings of the 17th international conference on Computational Linguistics-Volume 1*, pages 86–90. Association for Computational Linguistics.

Michele Banko, Michael J. Cafarella, Stephen Soderland, Matt Broadhead, and Oren Etzioni. 2007. Open information extraction from the web. In *Proceedings of the 20th International Joint Conference on Artifical Intelligence*, IJCAI'07, pages 2670–2676, San Francisco, CA, USA. Morgan Kaufmann Publishers Inc.

Steven Bethard and Jonathan Parker. 2016. A semantically compositional annotation scheme for time normalization. In *Proceedings of the Tenth International Conference on Language Resources and Evaluation (LREC 2016)*, Paris, France. European Language Resources Association (ELRA). [Acceptance rate 60%].

Paul Dagum, Adam Galper, and Eric Horvitz. 1992. Dynamic network models for forecasting. In Didier Dubois, Michael P. Wellman, Bruce D'Ambrosio, and Phillipe Smets, editors, *Uncertainty in Artificial Intelligence*, pages 41 – 48. Morgan Kaufmann.

Food and Agriculture Organization of the United Nations. 2018. FAOSTAT Database.

Jinyan Guan, Kyle Simek, Ernesto Brau, Clayton T. Morrison, Emily Butler, and Kobus Barnard. 2015. Moderated and drifting linear dynamical systems. In *Proceedings of the 32nd International Conference on Machine Learning*, volume 37 of *Proceedings of Machine Learning Research*, pages 2473–2482, Lille, France. PMLR.

Benjamin M. Gyori, John A. Bachman, Kartik Subramanian, Jeremy L. Muhlich, Lucian Galescu, and Peter K. Sorger. 2017. From word models to executable models of signaling networks using automated assembly. *Molecular Systems Biology*, 13(11).

Gus Hahn-Powell, Marco A. Valenzuela-Escárcega, and Mihai Surdeanu. 2017. Swanson linking revisited: Accelerating literature-based discovery across domains using a conceptual influence graph. *Proceedings of ACL 2017, System Demonstrations*, pages 103–108.

Egoitz Laparra, Dongfang Xu, and Steven Bethard. 2018. From characters to time intervals: New paradigms for evaluation and neural parsing of time normalizations. *Transactions of the Association for Computational Linguistics*, 6:343–356.

Arjun Magge, Davy Weissenbacher, Abeed Sarker, Matthew Scotch, and Graciela Gonzalez-Hernandez. 2018. Deep neural networks and distant supervision for geographic location mention extraction. *Bioinformatics*, 34(13):i565–i573.

Christopher D. Manning, Mihai Surdeanu, John Bauer, Jenny Finkel, Steven J. Bethard, and David McClosky. 2014. The Stanford CoreNLP natural language processing toolkit. In *Association for Computational Linguistics (ACL) System Demonstrations*, pages 55–60.

Rebecca Sharp, Mithun Paul, Ajay Nagesh, Dane Bell, and Mihai Surdeanu. 2018. Grounding gradable adjectives through crowdsourcing. In *Proceedings of the Eleventh International Conference on Language Resources and Evaluation (LREC 2018)*, Paris, France. European Language Resources Association (ELRA).

Pontus Stenetorp, Sampo Pyysalo, Goran Topić, Tomoko Ohta, Sophia Ananiadou, and Jun'ichi Tsujii. 2012. brat: a web-based tool for nlp-assisted text annotation. In *Proceedings of the Demonstrations at the 13th Conference of the European Chapter of the Association for Computational Linguistics*, pages 102–107. Association for Computational Linguistics.

Marco A. Valenzuela-Escárcega, Özgün Babur, Gus Hahn-Powell, Dane Bell, Thomas Hicks, Enrique Noriega-Atala, Xia Wang, Mihai Surdeanu, Emek Demir, and Clayton T. Morrison. 2018. Large-scale automated machine reading discovers new cancer driving mechanisms. *Database: The Journal of Biological Databases and Curation*.

Marco A. Valenzuela-Escárcega, Gustave Hahn-Powell, and Mihai Surdeanu. 2016. Odin's runes: A rule language for information extraction. In *Proceedings of the 10th edition of the Language Resources and Evaluation Conference (LREC)*.

World Bank. 2018. World Development Indicators Database.

Vikas Yadav and Steven Bethard. 2018. A survey on recent advances in named entity recognition from deep learning models. In *Proceedings of the 27th International Conference on Computational Linguistics*, pages 2145–2158.

Vikas Yadav, Egoitz Laparra, Ti-Tai Wang, Mihai Surdeanu, and Steven Bethard. 2019. University of arizona at semeval-2019 task 12: Deep-affix named entity recognition of geolocation entities. In *Proceedings of The 13th International Workshop on Semantic Evaluation*, Minneapolis, USA. Association for Computational Linguistics.

FAIRSEQ: A Fast, Extensible Toolkit for Sequence Modeling

Myle Ott△*   Sergey Edunov△*   Alexei Baevski△   Angela Fan△   Sam Gross△
Nathan Ng△   David Grangier▽†   Michael Auli△
△ Facebook AI Research
▽ Google Brain

Abstract

FAIRSEQ is an open-source sequence modeling toolkit that allows researchers and developers to train custom models for translation,
summarization, language modeling, and other
text generation tasks. The toolkit is based
on PyTorch and supports distributed training
across multiple GPUs and machines. We also
support fast mixed-precision training and inference on modern GPUs. A demo video can
be found here: `https://www.youtube.`
`com/watch?v=OtgDdWtHvto`.

1 Introduction

Neural sequence-to-sequence models have been
successful on a variety of text generation tasks, including machine translation, abstractive document
summarization, and language modeling. Accordingly, both researchers and industry professionals
can benefit from a fast and easily extensible sequence modeling toolkit.

There are several toolkits with similar basic
functionality, but they differ in focus area and intended audiences. For example, OpenNMT (Klein
et al., 2017) is a community-built toolkit written
in multiple languages with an emphasis on extensibility. MarianNMT (Junczys-Dowmunt et al.,
2018) focuses on performance and the backend is
written in C++ for fast automatic differentiation.
OpenSeq2Seq (Kuchaiev et al., 2018) provides
reference implementations for fast distributed and
mixed precision training. Tensor2tensor (Vaswani
et al., 2018) and Sockeye (Hieber et al., 2018) focus on production-readiness.

In this paper, we present FAIRSEQ, a sequence
modeling toolkit written in PyTorch that is fast,
extensible, and useful for both research and production. FAIRSEQ features: (i) a common interface across models and tasks that can be extended

---

*equal contribution
†Work done while at Facebook AI Research.

with user-supplied plug-ins (§2); (ii) efficient distributed and mixed precision training, enabling
training over datasets with hundreds of millions
of sentences on current hardware (§3); (iii) state-
of-the-art implementations and pretrained models
for machine translation, summarization, and language modeling (§4); and (iv) optimized inference
with multiple supported search algorithms, including beam search, diverse beam search (Vijayakumar et al., 2016), and top-k sampling. FAIRSEQ
is distributed with a BSD license and is available on GitHub at `https://github.com/`
`pytorch/fairseq`.

2 Design

Extensibility.   FAIRSEQ can be extended through
five types of user-supplied plug-ins, which enable
experimenting with new ideas while reusing existing components as much as possible.

Models   define the neural network architecture
and encapsulate all learnable parameters. Models
extend the `BaseFairseqModel` class, which
in turn extends `torch.nn.Module`. Thus any
FAIRSEQ model can be used as a stand-alone module in other PyTorch code. Models can additionally predefine named *architectures* with common
network configurations (e.g., embedding dimension, number of layers, etc.). We also abstracted
the methods through which the model interacts
with the generation algorithm, e.g., beam search,
through step-wise prediction. This isolates model
implementation from the generation algorithm.

Criterions   compute the loss given the model
and a batch of data, roughly: `loss =`
`criterion(model, batch)`. This formulation makes criterions very expressive, since they
have complete access to the model. For example, a criterion may perform on-the-fly genera-

Proceedings of NAACL-HLT 2019: Demonstrations, pages 48–53
Minneapolis, Minnesota, June 2 - June 7, 2019. ©2019 Association for Computational Linguistics

tion to support sequence-level training (Edunov et al., 2018b) or online backtranslation (Edunov et al., 2018a; Lample et al., 2018). Alternatively, in a mixture-of-experts model, a criterion may implement EM-style training and backpropagate only through the expert that produces the lowest loss (Shen et al., 2019).

Tasks store dictionaries, provide helpers for loading and batching data and define the training loop. They are intended to be immutable and primarily interface between the various components. We provide tasks for translation, language modeling, and classification.

Optimizers update the model parameters based on the gradients. We provide wrappers around most PyTorch optimizers and an implementation of Adafactor (Shazeer and Stern, 2018), which is a memory-efficient variant of Adam.

Learning Rate Schedulers update the learning rate over the course of training. We provide several popular schedulers, e.g., the inverse square-root scheduler from Vaswani et al. (2017) and cyclical schedulers based on warm restarts (Loshchilov and Hutter, 2016).

Reproducibility and forward compatibility. FAIRSEQ includes features designed to improve reproducibility and forward compatibility. For example, checkpoints contain the full state of the model, optimizer and dataloader, so that results are reproducible if training is interrupted and resumed. FAIRSEQ also provides forward compatibility, i.e., models trained using old versions of the toolkit will continue to run on the latest version through automatic checkpoint upgrading.

3 Implementation

FAIRSEQ is implemented in PyTorch and it provides efficient batching, mixed precision training, multi-GPU as well as multi-machine training.

Batching. There are multiple strategies to batch input and output sequence pairs (Morishita et al., 2017). FAIRSEQ minimizes padding within a mini-batch by grouping source and target sequences of similar length. The content of each mini-batch stays the same throughout training, however mini-batches themselves are shuffled randomly every epoch. When training on more than one GPU or machine, then the mini-batches for each worker

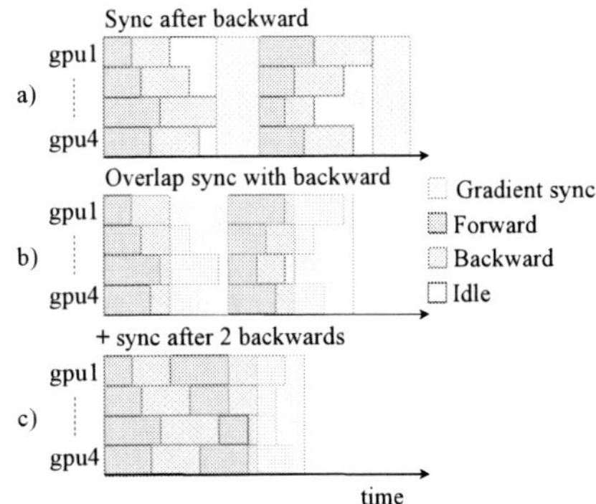

Figure 1: Illustration of (a) gradient synchronization and idle time during training, (b) overlapping back-propagation (backward) with gradient synchronization to improve training speed, (c) how accumulating gradient updates can reduce variance in processing time and reduce communication time.

are likely to differ in the average sentence length which results in more representative updates.

Multi-GPU training. FAIRSEQ uses the NCCL2 library and `torch.distributed` for inter-GPU communication. Models are trained in a synchronous optimization setup where each GPU has a copy of the model to process a sub-batch of data after which gradients are synchronized between GPUs; all sub-batches constitute a mini-batch. Even though sub-batches contain a similar number of tokens, we still observe a high variance in processing times. In multi-GPU or multi-machine setups, this results in idle time for most GPUs while slower workers are finishing their work (Figure 1 (a)). FAIRSEQ mitigates the effect of stragglers by overlapping gradient synchronization between workers with the backward pass and by accumulating gradients over multiple mini-batches for each GPU (Ott et al., 2018b).

Overlapping gradient synchronization starts to synchronize gradients of parts of the network when they are computed. In particular, when the gradient computation for a layer finishes, FAIRSEQ adds the result to a buffer. When the size of the buffer reaches a predefined threshold, the gradients are synchronized in a background thread while back-propagation continues as usual (Figure 1 (b)). Next, we accumulate gradients for multiple sub-batches on each GPU which reduces the variance in processing time between workers since there is no need to wait for stragglers after each sub-batch (Figure 1 (c)). This also increases the

	Sentences/sec
FAIRSEQ FP32	88.1
FAIRSEQ FP16	**136.0**

Table 1: Translation speed measured on a V100 GPU on the test set of the standard WMT'14 English-German benchmark using a big Transformer model.

effective batch size but we found that models can still be trained effectively (Ott et al., 2018b).

Mixed precision. Recent GPUs enable efficient half precision floating point (FP16) computation. FAIRSEQ provides support for both full precision (FP32) and FP16 at training and inference. We perform all forward-backward computations as well as the all-reduce for gradient synchronization between workers in FP16. However, the parameter updates remain in FP32 to preserve accuracy. FAIRSEQ implements dynamic loss scaling (Micikevicius et al., 2018) in order to avoid underflows for activations and gradients because of the limited precision offered by FP16. This scales the loss right after the forward pass to fit into the FP16 range while the backward pass is left unchanged. After the FP16 gradients are synchronized between workers, we convert them to FP32, restore the original scale, and update the weights.

Inference. FAIRSEQ provides fast inference for non-recurrent models (Gehring et al., 2017; Vaswani et al., 2017; Fan et al., 2018b; Wu et al., 2019) through incremental decoding, where the model states of previously generated tokens are cached in each active beam and re-used. This can speed up a naïve implementation without caching by up to an order of magnitude, since only new states are computed for each token. For some models, this requires a component-specific caching implementation, e.g., multi-head attention in the Transformer architecture.

During inference we build batches with a variable number of examples up to a user-specified number of tokens, similar to training. FAIRSEQ also supports inference in FP16 which increases decoding speed by 54% compared to FP32 with no loss in accuracy (Table 1).

4 Applications

FAIRSEQ has been used in many applications, such as machine translation (Gehring et al., 2017; Edunov et al., 2018b,a; Chen et al., 2018; Ott et al., 2018a; Song et al., 2018; Wu et al., 2019), language modeling (Dauphin et al., 2017; Baevski and Auli, 2019), abstractive document summarization (Fan et al., 2018a; Liu et al., 2018; Narayan et al., 2018), story generation (Fan et al., 2018b, 2019), error correction (Chollampatt and Ng, 2018), multilingual sentence embeddings (Artetxe and Schwenk, 2018), and dialogue (Miller et al., 2017; Dinan et al., 2019).

4.1 Machine translation

We provide reference implementations of several popular sequence-to-sequence models which can be used for machine translation, including LSTM (Luong et al., 2015), convolutional models (Gehring et al., 2017; Wu et al., 2019) and Transformer (Vaswani et al., 2017).

We evaluate a "big" Transformer encoder-decoder model on two language pairs, WMT English to German (En–De) and WMT English to French (En–Fr). For En–De we replicate the setup of Vaswani et al. (2017) which relies on WMT'16 for training with 4.5M sentence pairs, we validate on newstest13 and test on newstest14. The 32K vocabulary is based on a joint source and target byte pair encoding (BPE; Sennrich et al. 2016). For En–Fr, we train on WMT'14 and borrow the setup of Gehring et al. (2017) with 36M training sentence pairs. We use newstest12+13 for validation and newstest14 for test. The 40K vocabulary is based on a joint source and target BPE.

We measure case-sensitive tokenized BLEU with multi-bleu (Hoang et al., 2006) and detokenized BLEU with SacreBLEU[1] (Post, 2018). All results use beam search with a beam width of 4 and length penalty of 0.6, following Vaswani et al. 2017. FAIRSEQ results are summarized in Table 2. We reported improved BLEU scores over Vaswani et al. (2017) by training with a bigger batch size and an increased learning rate (Ott et al., 2018b).

4.2 Language modeling

FAIRSEQ supports language modeling with gated convolutional models (Dauphin et al., 2017) and Transformer models (Vaswani et al., 2017). Models can be trained using a variety of input and output representations, such as standard token embeddings, convolutional character embeddings (Kim

---

[1] SacreBLEU hash: `BLEU+case.mixed+lang.en-{de,fr}+ numrefs.1+smooth.exp+test.wmt14/full+tok.13a+version.1.2.9`

	En–De	En–Fr
a. Gehring et al. (2017)	25.2	40.5
b. Vaswani et al. (2017)	28.4	41.0
c. Ahmed et al. (2017)	28.9	41.4
d. Shaw et al. (2018)	29.2	41.5
FAIRSEQ Transformer base	28.1	41.1
FAIRSEQ Transformer big	**29.3**	**43.2**
detok. SacreBLEU	*28.6*	*41.4*
8 GPU training time	*~12 h*	*~73 h*
128 GPU training time	*~1.3 h*	*~7.2 h*

Table 2: BLEU on news2014 for WMT English-German (En–De) and English-French (En–Fr). All results are based on WMT'14 training data, except for En–De (b), (c), (d) and our models which were trained on WMT'16. Train times based on V100 GPUs.

	Perplexity
Grave et al. (2016)	40.8
Dauphin et al. (2017)	37.2
Merity et al. (2018)	33.0
Rae et al. (2018)	29.2
FAIRSEQ Adaptive inputs	**18.7**

Table 3: Test perplexity on WikiText-103 (cf. Table 4).

et al., 2016), adaptive softmax (Grave et al., 2017), and adaptive inputs (Baevski and Auli, 2019). We also provide tutorials and pre-trained models that replicate the results of Dauphin et al. (2017) and Baevski and Auli (2019) on WikiText-103 and the One Billion Word datasets.

We evaluate two Transformer language models, which use only a decoder network and adaptive input embeddings, following Baevski and Auli (2019). The first model has 16 blocks, inner dimension 4K and embedding dimension 1K; results on WikiText-103 are in Table 3. The second model has 24 blocks, inner dimension 8K and embedding dimension 1.5K; results on the One Billion Word benchmark are in Table 4.

4.3 Abstractive document summarization

Next, we experiment with abstractive document summarization where we use a base Transformer to encode the input document and then generate a summary with a decoder network. We use the CNN-Dailymail dataset (Hermann et al., 2015; Nallapati et al., 2016) of news articles paired with multi-sentence summaries. We evaluate on

	Perplexity
Dauphin et al. (2017)	31.9
Józefowicz et al. (2016)	30.0
Shazeer et al. (2017)	28.0
FAIRSEQ Adaptive inputs	**23.0**

Table 4: Test perplexity on the One Billion Word benchmark. Adaptive inputs share parameters with an adaptive softmax.

	ROUGE		
	1	2	L
See et al. (2017)	39.5	17.3	36.4
Gehrmann et al. (2018)	41.2	18.7	38.3
FAIRSEQ	40.1	17.6	36.8
+ pre-trained LM	**41.6**	**18.9**	**38.5**

Table 5: Abstractive summarization results on the full-text version of CNN-DailyMail dataset.

the full-text version with no entity anonymization (See et al., 2017); we truncate articles to 400 tokens (See et al., 2017). We use BPE with 30K operations to form our vocabulary following Fan et al. (2018a). To evaluate, we use the standard ROUGE metric (Lin, 2004) and report ROUGE-1, ROUGE-2, and ROUGE-L. To generate summaries, we follow standard practice in tuning the minimum output length and disallow repeating the same trigram (Paulus et al., 2017). Table 5 shows results of FAIRSEQ. We also consider a configuration where we input pre-trained language model representations to the encoder network and this language model was trained on newscrawl and CNN-Dailymail, totalling 193M sentences.

5 Conclusion

We presented FAIRSEQ, a fast, extensible toolkit for sequence modeling that is scalable and suitable for many applications. In the future, we will continue the development of the toolkit to enable further research advances.

Acknowledgements

We thank Jonas Gehring for writing the original Lua/Torch version of fairseq.

References

Karim Ahmed, Nitish Shirish Keskar, and Richard Socher. 2017. Weighted transformer network for machine translation. *arxiv*, 1711.02132.

Mikel Artetxe and Holger Schwenk. 2018. Massively multilingual sentence embeddings for zero-shot cross-lingual transfer and beyond. *arXiv*, abs/1812.10464.

Alexei Baevski and Michael Auli. 2019. Adaptive input representations for neural language modeling. In *Proc. of ICLR*.

Yun Chen, Victor OK Li, Kyunghyun Cho, and Samuel R Bowman. 2018. A stable and effective learning strategy for trainable greedy decoding. *arXiv*, abs/1804.07915.

Shamil Chollampatt and Hwee Tou Ng. 2018. A multilayer convolutional encoder-decoder neural network for grammatical error correction. *arXiv*, abs/1801.08831.

Yann N. Dauphin, Angela Fan, Michael Auli, and David Grangier. 2017. Language modeling with gated convolutional networks. In *Proc. of ICML*.

Emily Dinan, Stephen Roller, Kurt Shuster, Angela Fan, Michael Auli, and Jason Weston. 2019. Wizard of Wikipedia: Knowledge-powered conversational agents. In *Proc. of ICLR*.

Sergey Edunov, Myle Ott, Michael Auli, and David Grangier. 2018a. Understanding back-translation at scale. In *Conference of the Association for Computational Linguistics (ACL)*.

Sergey Edunov, Myle Ott, Michael Auli, David Grangier, et al. 2018b. Classical structured prediction losses for sequence to sequence learning. In *Proc. of NAACL*.

Angela Fan, David Grangier, and Michael Auli. 2018a. Controllable abstractive summarization. In *ACL Workshop on Neural Machine Translation and Generation*.

Angela Fan, Mike Lewis, and Yann Dauphin. 2018b. Hierarchical neural story generation. In *Proc. of ACL*.

Angela Fan, Mike Lewis, and Yann Dauphin. 2019. Strategies for structuring story generation. *arXiv*, abs/1902.01109.

Jonas Gehring, Michael Auli, David Grangier, Denis Yarats, and Yann N Dauphin. 2017. Convolutional Sequence to Sequence Learning. In *Proc. of ICML*.

Sebastian Gehrmann, Yuntian Deng, and Alexander M Rush. 2018. Bottom-up abstractive summarization. *arXiv*, abs/1808.10792.

Edouard Grave, Armand Joulin, Moustapha Cissé, David Grangier, and Hervé Jégou. 2017. Efficient softmax approximation for gpus. In *Proc. of ICML*.

Edouard Grave, Armand Joulin, and Nicolas Usunier. 2016. Improving neural language models with a continuous cache. *arXiv*, abs/1612.04426.

Karl Moritz Hermann, Tomas Kocisky, Edward Grefenstette, Lasse Espeholt, Will Kay, Mustafa Suleyman, and Phil Blunsom. 2015. Teaching machines to read and comprehend. In *NIPS*.

Felix Hieber, Tobias Domhan, Michael Denkowski, David Vilar, Artem Sokolov, Ann Clifton, and Matt Post. 2018. Sockeye: A Toolkit for Neural Machine Translation. *arXiv*, abs/1712.05690.

Hieu Hoang, Philipp Koehn, Ulrich Germann, Kenneth Heafield, and Barry Haddow. 2006. multi-bleu.perl. `https://github.com/moses-smt/ mosesdecoder/blob/master/scripts/ generic/multi-bleu.perl`.

Rafal Józefowicz, Oriol Vinyals, Mike Schuster, Noam Shazeer, and Yonghui Wu. 2016. Exploring the limits of language modeling. *arXiv*, abs/1602.02410.

Marcin Junczys-Dowmunt, Roman Grundkiewicz, Tomasz Dwojak, Hieu Hoang, Kenneth Heafield, Tom Neckermann, Frank Seide, Ulrich Germann, Alham Fikri Aji, Nikolay Bogoychev, André F. T. Martins, and Alexandra Birch. 2018. Marian: Fast neural machine translation in C++. In *Proc. of ACL 2018, System Demonstrations*.

Yoon Kim, Yacine Jernite, David Sontag, and Alexander M Rush. 2016. Character-aware neural language models. In *Proc. of AAAI*.

Guillaume Klein, Yoon Kim, Yuntian Deng, Jean Senellart, and Alexander M. Rush. 2017. OpenNMT: Open-source toolkit for neural machine translation. In *Proc. ACL*.

Oleksii Kuchaiev, Boris Ginsburg, Igor Gitman, Vitaly Lavrukhin, Carl Case, and Paulius Micikevicius. 2018. OpenSeq2Seq: Extensible Toolkit for Distributed and Mixed Precision Training of Sequence-to-Sequence Models. In *Proc. of Workshop for NLP Open Source Software*.

Guillaume Lample, Myle Ott, Alexis Conneau, Ludovic Denoyer, and Marc'Aurelio Ranzato. 2018. Phrase-based & neural unsupervised machine translation. In *Proc. of EMNLP*.

Chin-Yew Lin. 2004. Rouge: a package for automatic evaluation of summaries. In *ACL Workshop on Text Summarization Branches Out*.

Yizhu Liu, Zhiyi Luo, and Kenny Zhu. 2018. Controlling length in abstractive summarization using a convolutional neural network. In *Proc. of EMNLP*.

Ilya Loshchilov and Frank Hutter. 2016. Sgdr: Stochastic gradient descent with warm restarts. In *Proc. of ICLR*.

Minh-Thang Luong, Hieu Pham, and Christopher D Manning. 2015. Effective approaches to attention-based neural machine translation. In *Proc. of EMNLP*.

Stephen Merity, Nitish Shirish Keskar, and Richard Socher. 2018. An analysis of neural language modeling at multiple scales. *arXiv*, abs/1803.08240.

Paulius Micikevicius, Sharan Narang, Jonah Alben, Gregory F. Diamos, Erich Elsen, David Garcia, Boris Ginsburg, Michael Houston, Oleksii Kuchaiev, Ganesh Venkatesh, and Hao Wu. 2018. Mixed Precision Training. In *Proc. of ICLR*.

A. H. Miller, W. Feng, A. Fisch, J. Lu, D. Batra, A. Bordes, D. Parikh, and J. Weston. 2017. Parlai: A dialog research software platform. *arXiv*, abs/1705.06476.

Makoto Morishita, Yusuke Oda, Graham Neubig, Koichiro Yoshino, Katsuhito Sudoh, and Satoshi Nakamura. 2017. An empirical study of mini-batch creation strategies for neural machine translation. In *Proc. of WMT*.

Ramesh Nallapati, Bowen Zhou, Cicero dos Santos, Caglar Gulcehre, and Bing Xiang. 2016. Abstractive text summarization using sequence-to-sequence rnns and beyond. In *SIGNLL Conference on Computational Natural Language Learning*.

Shashi Narayan, Shay B Cohen, and Mirella Lapata. 2018. Don't give me the details, just the summary! topic-aware convolutional neural networks for extreme summarization. *arXiv*, abs/1808.08745.

Myle Ott, Michael Auli, David Grangier, and MarcAurelio Ranzato. 2018a. Analyzing uncertainty in neural machine translation. In *Proc. of ICML*.

Myle Ott, Sergey Edunov, David Grangier, and Michael Auli. 2018b. Scaling neural machine translation. In *Proc. of WMT*.

Romain Paulus, Caiming Xiong, and Richard Socher. 2017. A deep reinforced model for abstractive summarization. *arXiv preprint arXiv:1705.04304*.

Matt Post. 2018. A call for clarity in reporting bleu scores. *arXiv*, abs/1804.08771.

Jack W. Rae, Chris Dyer, Peter Dayan, and Timothy P. Lillicrap. 2018. Fast parametric learning with activation memorization. *arXiv*, abs/1803.10049.

Abigail See, Peter J. Liu, and Christopher D. Manning. 2017. Get to the point: Summarization with pointer-generator networks. In *ACL*.

Rico Sennrich, Barry Haddow, and Alexandra Birch. 2016. Neural machine translation of rare words with subword units. In *Proc. of ACL*.

Peter Shaw, Jakob Uszkoreit, and Ashish Vaswani. 2018. Self-attention with relative position representations. In *Proc. of NAACL*.

Noam Shazeer, Azalia Mirhoseini, Krzysztof Maziarz, Andy Davis, Quoc V. Le, Geoffrey E. Hinton, and Jeff Dean. 2017. Outrageously large neural networks: The sparsely-gated mixture-of-experts layer. *arXiv*, abs/1701.06538.

Noam Shazeer and Mitchell Stern. 2018. Adafactor: Adaptive learning rates with sublinear memory cost. *arXiv preprint arXiv:1804.04235*.

Tianxiao Shen, Myle Ott, Michael Auli, and Marc'Aurelio Ranzato. 2019. Mixture models for diverse machine translation: Tricks of the trade. *arXiv*, abs/1902.07816.

Kaitao Song, Xu Tan, Di He, Jianfeng Lu, Tao Qin, and Tie-Yan Liu. 2018. Double path networks for sequence to sequence learning. *arXiv*, abs/1806.04856.

A. Vaswani, S. Bengio, E. Brevdo, F. Chollet, A. N. Gomez, S. Gouws, L. Jones, Ł. Kaiser, N. Kalchbrenner, N. Parmar, R. Sepassi, N. Shazeer, and J. Uszkoreit. 2018. Tensor2Tensor for Neural Machine Translation. *arXiv*, abs/1803.07416.

Ashish Vaswani, Noam Shazeer, Niki Parmar, Jakob Uszkoreit, Llion Jones, Aidan N. Gomez, Lukasz Kaiser, and Illia Polosukhin. 2017. Attention Is All You Need. In *Proc. of NIPS*.

Ashwin K Vijayakumar, Michael Cogswell, Ramprasath R Selvaraju, Qing Sun, Stefan Lee, David Crandall, and Dhruv Batra. 2016. Diverse beam search: Decoding diverse solutions from neural sequence models. *arXiv preprint arXiv:1610.02424*.

Felix Wu, Angela Fan, Alexei Baevski, Yann N. Dauphin, and Michael Auli. 2019. Pay less attention with lightweight and dynamic convlutions. In *Proc. of ICLR*.

FLAIR: An Easy-to-Use Framework for State-of-the-Art NLP

Alan Akbik[†]   Tanja Bergmann[†*]   Duncan Blythe[†*]

Kashif Rasul[†]   Stefan Schweter[‡]   Roland Vollgraf[†]

[†]Zalando Research, Mühlenstraße 25, 10243 Berlin
[‡]Bayerische Staatsbibliothek München, Digital Library/Munich Digitization Center, 80539 Munich
[*]Aleph-One GmbH, Rigaer Straße 8, 12047 Berlin [*]RASA AI, Berlin

Abstract

We present FLAIR, an NLP framework designed to facilitate training and distribution of state-of-the-art sequence labeling, text classification and language models. The core idea of the framework is to present a simple, unified interface for conceptually very different types of word and document embeddings. This effectively hides all embedding-specific engineering complexity and allows researchers to "mix and match" various embeddings with little effort. The framework also implements standard model training and hyperparameter selection routines, as well as a data fetching module that can download publicly available NLP datasets and convert them into data structures for quick set up of experiments. Finally, FLAIR also ships with a "model zoo" of pre-trained models to allow researchers to use state-of-the-art NLP models in their applications. This paper gives an overview of the framework and its functionality.

The framework is available on GitHub at
`https://github.com/zalandoresearch/flair`.

1 Introduction

Classic pre-trained word embeddings have been shown to be of great use for downstream NLP tasks, both due to their ability to assist learning and generalization with information learned from unlabeled data, as well as the relative ease of including them into any learning approach (Mikolov et al., 2013; Pennington et al., 2014). Many recently proposed approaches go beyond the initial "one word, one embedding" paradigm to better model additional features such as subword structures (Ma and Hovy, 2016; Bojanowski et al., 2017) and meaning ambiguity (Peters et al., 2018a). Though shown to be extremely powerful, such embeddings have the drawback that they cannot be used to simply initialize the embedding layer of a neural network and thus require specific reworkings of the overall model architecture.

Hierarchical architectures. A common example is that many current approaches combine classic word embeddings with character-level features trained on task data (Ma and Hovy, 2016; Lample et al., 2016). To accomplish this, they use a hierarchical learning architecture in which the output states of a character-level CNN or RNN are concatenated with the output of the embedding layer. While modern deep learning frameworks such as PYTORCH (Paszke et al., 2017) make the construction of such architectures relatively straightforward, architectural changes are nevertheless required for something that is fundamentally just another method for embedding words.

Contextualized embeddings. Similarly, recent works—including our own—have proposed methods that produce different embeddings for the same word depending on its contextual usage (Peters et al., 2018a; Akbik et al., 2018; Devlin et al., 2018). The string "Washington" for instance would be embedded differently depending on whether the context indicates this string to be a last name or a location. While shown to be highly powerful, especially in combination with classic word embeddings, such methods require an architecture in which the output states of a trained language model (LM) are concatenated with the output of the embedding layer, thus adding architectural complexity.

These examples illustrate that word embeddings typically cannot simply be mixed and matched with minimal effort, but rather require specific reworkings of the model architecture.

Proposed solution: FLAIR framework. With this paper, we present a new framework designed to address this problem. The principal design goal is to abstract away from specific engineering challenges that different types of word embeddings

Proceedings of NAACL-HLT 2019: Demonstrations, pages 54–59
Minneapolis, Minnesota, June 2 - June 7, 2019. ©2019 Association for Computational Linguistics

raise. We created a simple, unified interface for all word embeddings as well as arbitrary combinations of embeddings. This interface, we argue, allows researchers to build a single model architecture that can then make use of any type of word embedding with no additional engineering effort.

To further simplify the process of setting up and executing experiments, FLAIR includes convenience methods for downloading standard NLP research datasets and reading them into data structures for the framework. It also includes model training and hyperparameter selection routines to facilitate typical training and testing workflows. In addition, FLAIR also ships with a growing list of pre-trained models allowing users to apply already trained models to their text. This paper gives an overview of the framework.

2 Framework Overview

2.1 Setup

FLAIR only requires a current version of Python (at least version 3.6) to be available on a system or a virtual environment. Then, the simplest way to install the library is via `pip`, by issuing the command: `pip install flair`. This downloads the latest release of FLAIR and sets up all required libraries, such as PyTorch.

Alternatively, users can clone or fork the current master branch of FLAIR from the GitHub repository. This allows users to work on the latest version of the code and create pull requests. The GitHub page[1] has extensive documentation on training and applying models and embedding.

2.2 Base Classes

With code readability and ease-of-use in mind, we represent NLP concepts such as tokens, sentences and corpora with simple base (non-tensor) classes that we use throughout the library. For instance, the following code instantiates an example Sentence object:

```
# init sentence
sentence = Sentence('I love Berlin')
```

Each Sentence is instantiated as a list of Token objects, each of which represents a word and has fields for tags (such as part-of-speech or named entity tags) and embeddings (embeddings of this word in different embedding spaces).

---

[1]https://github.com/zalandoresearch/flair

2.3 Embeddings

Embeddings are the core concept of FLAIR. Each embedding class implements either the TokenEmbedding or the DocumentEmbedding interface for word and document embeddings respectively. Both interfaces define the .embed() method to embed a Sentence or a list of Sentence objects into a specific embedding space.

2.3.1 Classic Word Embeddings

The simplest examples are classic word embeddings, such as GLOVE or FASTTEXT. Simply instantiate one of the supported word embeddings and call .embed() to embed a sentence:

```
# init GloVe embeddings
glove = WordEmbeddings('glove')

# embed sentence
glove.embed(sentence)
```

Here, the framework checks if the requested GLOVE embeddings are already available on local disk. If not, the embeddings are first downloaded. Then, GLOVE embeddings are added to each Token in the Sentence.

Note that all logic is handled by the embedding class, i.e. it is not necessary to run common preprocessing steps such as constructing a vocabulary of words in the dataset or encoding words as one-hot vectors. Rather, each embedding is immediately applicable to any text wrapped in a Sentence object.

2.3.2 Other Word Embeddings

As noted in the introduction, FLAIR supports a growing list of embeddings such as hierarchical character features (Lample et al., 2016), ELMo embeddings (Peters et al., 2018a), ELMo transformer embeddings (Peters et al., 2018b), BERT embeddings (Devlin et al., 2018), byte pair embeddings (Heinzerling and Strube, 2018), Flair embeddings (Akbik et al., 2018) and *Pooled Flair* embeddings. See Table 1 for an overview.

Importantly, all embeddings implement the same interface and may be called and applied just like in the WordEmbedding example above. For instance, to use BERT embeddings to embed a sentence, simply call:

```
# init BERT embeddings
bert = BertEmbeddings()

# embed sentence
bert.embed(sentence)
```

Class	Type	Pretrained?
WordEmbeddings	classic word embeddings (Pennington et al., 2014)	yes
CharacterEmbeddings	character features (Lample et al., 2016)	no
BytePairEmbeddings	byte-pair embeddings (Heinzerling and Strube, 2018)	yes
FlairEmbeddings	character-level LM embeddings (Akbik et al., 2018)	yes
PooledFlairEmbeddings	pooled version of FLAIR embeddings (Akbik et al., 2019b)	yes
ELMoEmbeddings	word-level LM embeddings (Peters et al., 2018a)	yes
ELMoTransformerEmbeddings	word-level transformer LM embeddings (Peters et al., 2018b)	yes
BertEmbeddings	byte-pair masked LM embeddings (Devlin et al., 2018)	yes
DocumentPoolEmbeddings	document embeddings from pooled word embeddings (Joulin et al., 2017)	yes
DocumentLSTMEmbeddings	document embeddings from LSTM over word embeddings	no

Table 1: Summary of word and document embeddings currently supported by FLAIR. Note that some embedding types are not pre-trained; these embeddings are automatically trained or fine-tuned when training a model for a downstream task.

2.3.3 Stacked Embeddings

In many cases, we wish to mix and match several different types of embeddings. For instance, Lample et al. (2016) combine classic word embeddings with character features. To achieve this in FLAIR, we need to combine the embedding classes WordEmbeddings and CharacterEmbeddings. To enable such combinations, e.g. the "stacking" of embeddings, we include the StackedEmbeddings class. It is instantiated by passing a list of embeddings to stack, but then behaves like any other embedding class. This means that by calling the .embed() method, a StackedEmbeddings class instance embeds a sentence like any other embedding class instance.

Our recommended setup is to stack WordEmbeddings with FlairEmbeddings, which gives state-of-the-art accuracies across many sequence labeling tasks. See Akbik et al. (2018) for a comparative evaluation.

2.3.4 Document Embeddings

FLAIR also supports methods for producing vector representations not of words, but of entire documents. There are two main embedding classes for this, namely DocumentPoolEmbeddings and DocumentLSTMEmbeddings. The former applies a pooling operation, such as *mean pooling*, to all word embeddings in a document to derive a document representation. The latter applies an LSTM over the word embeddings in a document to output a document representation.

2.4 NLP Dataset Downloader

To facilitate setting up experiments, we include convenience methods to download publicly available benchmark datasets for a variety of NLP tasks and read them into data structures for training. For instance, to download the universal dependency

Dataset	Task	Language(s)
CoNLL 2000	NP Chunking	en
CoNLL 2003	NER	dt, es
EIEC	NER	basque
IMDB	Classification	en
TREC-6	Classification	en
TREC-50	Classification	en
Universal Dependencies	PoS, Parsing	30 languages
WikiNER	NER	9 languages
WNUT-17	NER	en

Table 2: Summary of NLP datasets in the downloader. References: CoNLL 2000 (Sang and Buchholz, 2000), CoNLL 2003 (Sang and De Meulder, 2003), EIEC (Alegria et al.), IMDB (Maas et al., 2011), TREC-6 (Voorhees and Harman, 2000), TREC-50 (Li and Roth, 2002), Universal Dependencies (Zeman et al., 2018), WikiNER (Nothman et al., 2012) and WNUT-17 (Derczynski et al., 2017).

treebank for English, simply execute these lines:

```
# define dataset
task = NLPTask.UD_English

# load dataset
corpus = NLPTaskDataFetcher.load_corpus(
    task)
```

Internally, the data fetcher checks if the requested dataset is already present on local disk and if not, downloads it. The dataset is then read into an object of type TaggedCorpus which defines training, testing and development splits.

Table 2 gives an overview of all datasets that are currently downloadable. Other datasets, such as the CoNLL-03 datasets for English and German, require licences and thus cannot be automatically downloaded.

2.5 Model Training

To train a downstream task model, FLAIR includes the ModelTrainer class which implements a host of mechanisms that are typically applied during training. This includes features such as mini-batching, model checkpointing, learning rate annealing schedulers, evaluation methods and logging. This unified training interface is designed to

Task	Dataset	Language(s)	Variant(s)
4-class NER	CoNLL 2003 (Sang and De Meulder, 2003)	en, de, nl, es	default, fast, multilingual
4-class NER	WikiNER (Nothman et al., 2012)	fr	default
12-class NER	Ontonotes (Hovy et al., 2006)	en	default, fast
NP Chunking	CoNLL 2000 (Sang and Buchholz, 2000)	en	default, fast
Offensive Language Detection	GermEval 2018 (Wiegand et al., 2018)	de	default
PoS tagging	Ontonotes (Hovy et al., 2006)	en	default, fast
Semantic Frame Detection	PropBank (Bonial et al., 2014)	en	default, fast
Sentiment Analysis	IMDB (Maas et al., 2011)	en	default
Universal PoS	Universal Dependencies (Zeman et al., 2018)	12 languages	multilingual

Table 3: Summary of pre-trained sequence labeling and text classification models currently available. The "default" variant are single-language models optimized for GPU-systems. The "fast" variant are smaller models optimized for CPU-systems. The "multilingual" variants are single models that can label text in different languages.

facilitate experimentation with standard learning parameters.

The `ModelTrainer` can be applied to any FLAIR model that implements the `flair.nn.Model` interface, such as our sequence tagging and text classification classes. Refer to the online tutorials for examples on how to train different types of downstream task models.

2.6 Hyperparameter Selection

To further facilitate training models, FLAIR includes native support for the HYPEROPT library which implements a Tree of Parzen Estimators (TPE) approach to hyperparameter optimization (Bergstra et al., 2013). Hyperparameter selection is performed against the development data split by default. This allows users to first run hyperparameter selection using the training and development data splits, and then evaluate the final parameters with the held-out testing data.

3 Model Zoo

In addition to providing a framework for embedding text and training models, FLAIR also includes a model zoo of pre-trained sequence labeling, text classification and language models. They allow users to apply pre-trained models to their own text, or to fine-tune them for their use cases. A list of currently shipped models is provided in Table 3.

For example, to load and apply the default named entity recognizer for English, simply execute the following lines of code:

```
# make a sentence
sentence = Sentence('I love Berlin .')

# load the NER tagger
tagger = SequenceTagger.load('ner')

# run NER over sentence
tagger.predict(sentence)
```

This first checks if the corresponding model is already available on local disk and if not, downloads it. Entity tags are then added to the Token objects in the Sentence. In this specific example, this will mark up "Berlin" as an entity of type *location*.

3.1 Model Variants

We distribute different variants of models with FLAIR (see Table 3). The *default* variant are single-language models intended to be run on GPU, typically using embeddings from language models with 2048 hidden states. The *fast* variant models use computationally less demanding embeddings, typically from LMs with 1024 hidden states, and are suited to be run on CPU setups.

We also include multilingual models for some tasks. These are "one model, many languages" models that can predict tags for text in multiple languages. For instance, Flair includes multilingual part-of-speech tagging models that predict universal PoS tags for text in 12 languages. See Akbik et al. (2019a) for an overview of multilingual models and preliminary evaluation numbers.

4 Conclusion and Outlook

We presented FLAIR as a framework designed to facilitate experimentation with different embedding types, as well as training and distributing sequence labeling and text classification models.

Together with the open source community, we are working to extend the framework along multiple directions. This includes supporting *more embedding approaches* such as transformer embeddings (Radford et al., 2018; Dai et al., 2019), InferSent representations (Conneau et al., 2017) and LASER embeddings (Artetxe and Schwenk, 2018), and expanding our coverage of *NLP datasets* and formats for automatic data fetching.

Current research also focuses on developing new embedding types, investigating further downstream tasks and extending the framework to facilitate multi-task learning approaches.

Acknowledgements

We would like to thank the anonymous reviewers for their helpful comments. This project has received funding from the European Union's Horizon 2020 research and innovation programme under grant agreement no 732328 ("FashionBrain").

The development of FLAIR has benefited enormously from the open source community. We wish to thank the many individuals who contributed (see `https://github.com/zalandoresearch/flair/graphs/contributors`) since without a doubt the usability and features of FLAIR have only gotten better due to their work or feedback. Thank you also to Zalando's Open Source team (see `https://opensource.zalando.com`).

References

Alan Akbik, Tanja Bergmann, and Roland Vollgraf. 2019a. Multilingual sequence labeling with one model. In *NLDL 2019, Northern Lights Deep Learning Workshop*.

Alan Akbik, Tanja Bergmann, and Roland Vollgraf. 2019b. Pooled contextualized embeddings for named entity recognition. In *NAACL, 2019 Annual Conference of the North American Chapter of the Association for Computational Linguistics*, page to appear.

Alan Akbik, Duncan Blythe, and Roland Vollgraf. 2018. Contextual string embeddings for sequence labeling. In *COLING 2018, 27th International Conference on Computational Linguistics*, pages 1638–1649.

Inaki Alegria, Olatz Arregi, Irene Balza, Nerea Ezeiza, Izaskun Fernandez, and Ruben Urizar. Design and development of a named entity recognizer for an agglutinative language.

Mikel Artetxe and Holger Schwenk. 2018. Massively multilingual sentence embeddings for zero-shot cross-lingual transfer and beyond. *arXiv preprint arXiv:1812.10464*.

James Bergstra, Daniel Yamins, and David Daniel Cox. 2013. Making a science of model search: Hyperparameter optimization in hundreds of dimensions for vision architectures.

Piotr Bojanowski, Edouard Grave, Armand Joulin, and Tomas Mikolov. 2017. Enriching word vectors with subword information. *Transactions of the Association for Computational Linguistics*, 5:135–146.

Claire Bonial, Julia Bonn, Kathryn Conger, Jena D. Hwang, and Martha Palmer. 2014. Propbank: Semantics of new predicate types. In *Proceedings of the Ninth International Conference on Language Resources and Evaluation (LREC-2014)*. European Language Resources Association (ELRA).

Alexis Conneau, Douwe Kiela, Holger Schwenk, Loïc Barrault, and Antoine Bordes. 2017. Supervised learning of universal sentence representations from natural language inference data. In *Proceedings of the 2017 Conference on Empirical Methods in Natural Language Processing*, pages 670–680, Copenhagen, Denmark. Association for Computational Linguistics.

Zihang Dai, Zhilin Yang, Yiming Yang, Jaime G. Carbonell, Quoc V. Le, and Ruslan Salakhutdinov. 2019. Transformer-xl: Attentive language models beyond a fixed-length context. *CoRR*, abs/1901.02860.

Leon Derczynski, Eric Nichols, Marieke van Erp, and Nut Limsopatham. 2017. Results of the wnut2017 shared task on novel and emerging entity recognition. In *Proceedings of the 3rd Workshop on Noisy User-generated Text*, pages 140–147.

Jacob Devlin, Ming-Wei Chang, Kenton Lee, and Kristina Toutanova. 2018. Bert: Pre-training of deep bidirectional transformers for language understanding. *arXiv preprint arXiv:1810.04805*.

Benjamin Heinzerling and Michael Strube. 2018. BPEmb: Tokenization-free Pre-trained Subword Embeddings in 275 Languages. In *Proceedings of the Eleventh International Conference on Language Resources and Evaluation (LREC 2018)*, Miyazaki, Japan. European Language Resources Association (ELRA).

Eduard Hovy, Mitchell Marcus, Martha Palmer, Lance Ramshaw, and Ralph Weischedel. 2006. Ontonotes: the 90% solution. In *Proceedings of the human language technology conference of the NAACL, Companion Volume: Short Papers*, pages 57–60. Association for Computational Linguistics.

Armand Joulin, Edouard Grave, Piotr Bojanowski, and Tomas Mikolov. 2017. Bag of tricks for efficient text classification. In *Proceedings of the 15th Conference of the European Chapter of the Association for Computational Linguistics: Volume 2, Short Papers*, volume 2, pages 427–431.

Guillaume Lample, Miguel Ballesteros, Sandeep Subramanian, Kazuya Kawakami, and Chris Dyer. 2016. Neural architectures for named entity recognition. *arXiv preprint arXiv:1603.01360*.

Xin Li and Dan Roth. 2002. Learning question classifiers. In *Proceedings of the 19th international conference on Computational linguistics-Volume 1*, pages 1–7. Association for Computational Linguistics.

Xuezhe Ma and Eduard Hovy. 2016. End-to-end sequence labeling via bi-directional LSTMs-CNNs-CRF. *arXiv preprint arXiv:1603.01354.*

Andrew L. Maas, Raymond E. Daly, Peter T. Pham, Dan Huang, Andrew Y. Ng, and Christopher Potts. 2011. Learning word vectors for sentiment analysis. In *Proceedings of the 49th Annual Meeting of the Association for Computational Linguistics: Human Language Technologies*, pages 142–150, Portland, Oregon, USA. Association for Computational Linguistics.

Tomas Mikolov, Ilya Sutskever, Kai Chen, Greg S Corrado, and Jeff Dean. 2013. Distributed representations of words and phrases and their compositionality. In *Advances in neural information processing systems*, pages 3111–3119.

Joel Nothman, Nicky Ringland, Will Radford, Tara Murphy, and James R. Curran. 2012. Learning multilingual named entity recognition from Wikipedia. *Artificial Intelligence*, 194:151–175.

Adam Paszke, Sam Gross, Soumith Chintala, Gregory Chanan, Edward Yang, Zachary DeVito, Zeming Lin, Alban Desmaison, Luca Antiga, and Adam Lerer. 2017. Automatic differentiation in pytorch.

Jeffrey Pennington, Richard Socher, and Christopher Manning. 2014. Glove: Global vectors for word representation. In *Proceedings of the 2014 conference on empirical methods in natural language processing (EMNLP)*, pages 1532–1543.

Matthew Peters, Mark Neumann, and Christopher Clark Kenton Lee Luke Zettlemoyer Mohit Iyyer, Matt Gardner. 2018a. Deep contextualized word representations. *6th International Conference on Learning Representations.*

Matthew Peters, Mark Neumann, Luke Zettlemoyer, and Wen-tau Yih. 2018b. Dissecting contextual word embeddings: Architecture and representation. In *Proceedings of the 2018 Conference on Empirical Methods in Natural Language Processing*, pages 1499–1509.

Alec Radford, Karthik Narasimhan, Time Salimans, and Ilya Sutskever. 2018. Improving language understanding with unsupervised learning. Technical report, Technical report, OpenAI.

Erik F Tjong Kim Sang and Sabine Buchholz. 2000. Introduction to the CoNLL-2000 shared task: Chunking. In *Proceedings of the 2nd workshop on Learning language in logic and the 4th conference on Computational natural language learning-Volume 7*, pages 127–132. Association for Computational Linguistics.

Erik F Tjong Kim Sang and Fien De Meulder. 2003. Introduction to the CoNLL-2003 shared task: Language-independent named entity recognition. In *Proceedings of the seventh conference on Natural language learning at HLT-NAACL 2003-Volume 4,*

pages 142–147. Association for Computational Linguistics.

Ellen M Voorhees and Donna Harman. 2000. Overview of the sixth text retrieval conference (trec-6). *Information Processing & Management*, 36(1):3–35.

Michael Wiegand, Melanie Siegel, and Josef Ruppenhofer. 2018. Overview of the germeval 2018 shared task on the identification of offensive language. *Austrian Academy of Sciences, Vienna September 21, 2018.*

Daniel Zeman, Jan Haji, Martin Popel, Martin Potthast, Milan Straka, Filip Ginter, Joakim Nivre, and Slav Petrov. 2018. Conll 2018 shared task: Multilingual parsing from raw text to universal dependencies. *Proceedings of the CoNLL 2018 Shared Task: Multilingual Parsing from Raw Text to Universal Dependencies*, pages 1–21.

ChatEval: A Tool for Chatbot Evaluation

João Sedoc⋆   Daphne Ippolito⋆   Arun Kirubarajan   Jai Thirani   Lyle Ungar   Chris Callison-Burch

⋆Authors contributed equally

University of Pennsylvania

`{joao,daphnei,kiruba,jthirani,ungar,ccb}@seas.upenn.edu`

Abstract

Open-domain dialog systems (i.e., chatbots) are difficult to evaluate. The current best practice for analyzing and comparing these dialog systems is the use of human judgments. However, the lack of standardization in evaluation procedures, and the fact that model parameters and code are rarely published hinder systematic human evaluation experiments. We introduce a unified framework for human evaluation of chatbots that augments existing tools and provides a web-based hub for researchers to share and compare their dialog systems. Researchers can submit their trained models to the ChatEval web interface and obtain comparisons with baselines and prior work. The evaluation code is open-source to ensure standardization and transparency. In addition, we introduce open-source baseline models and evaluation datasets. ChatEval can be found at `https://chateval.org`.

Introduction

Reproducibility and model assessment for open-domain dialog systems is challenging, as many small variations in the training setup or evaluation technique can result in significant differences in perceived model performance (Fokkens et al., 2013). While reproducibility is problematic for NLP in general, this is especially true for dialog systems due to the lack of automatic metrics. In addition, as the field has grown, it has become increasingly fragmented in human evaluation methodologies.

Papers often focus on novel methods, but insufficient attention is paid to ensuring that datasets and evaluation remain consistent and reproducible. For example, while human evaluation of chatbot quality is extremely common, few papers publish the set of prompts used for this evaluation, and almost no papers release their

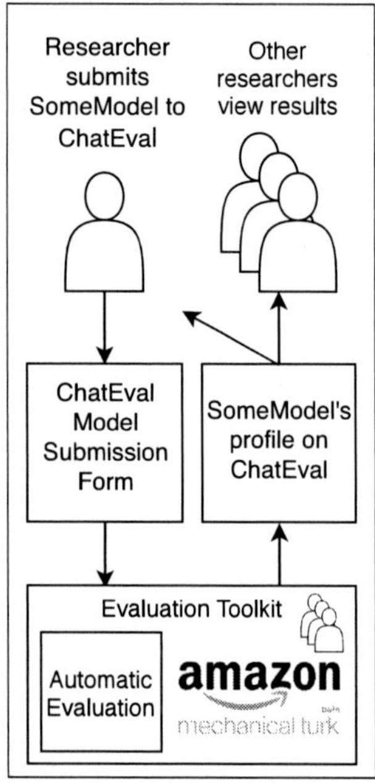

Figure 1: Flow of information in ChatEval. A researcher submits information about her model, including its responses to prompts in a standard evaluation set. Automatic evaluation as well as human evaluation are conducted, then the results are posted publicly on the ChatEval website.

learned model parameters. Because of this, papers tend to evaluate their methodological improvement against a sequence-to-sequence (Seq2Seq) baseline (Sutskever et al., 2014) rather than against each other.

Seq2Seq was first proposed for dialog generation by Vinyals and Le (2015) in a system they called the Neural Conversational Model (NCM). Due to the NCM being closed-source, nearly all papers compare against their own reimplementations of the model, which can vary widely in performance. Indeed, we found no model, neither

60

Proceedings of NAACL-HLT 2019: Demonstrations, pages 60–65

Minneapolis, Minnesota, June 2 - June 7, 2019. ©2019 Association for Computational Linguistics

among those we trained nor those available online, that matched the performance of the original NCM, as evaluated by humans.

Another issue is that human evaluation experiments, which are currently the gold standard for model evaluation, are equally fragmented, with almost no two papers by different authors adopting the same evaluation dataset or experimental procedure.

To address these concerns, we have built ChatEval, a scientific framework for evaluating chatbots. ChatEval consists of two main components: (1) an open-source codebase for conducting automatic and human evaluation of chatbots in a standardized way, and (2) a web portal for accessing model code, trained parameters, and evaluation results, which grows with participation. In addition, ChatEval includes newly created and curated evaluation datasets with both human annotated and automated baselines.

Related Work

Competitions such as the Alexa Prize,[1] ConvAI[2] and WOCHAT,[3] rank submitted chatbots by having humans converse with them and then rate the quality of the conversation. However, asking for absolute assessments of quality yields less discriminative results than soliciting direct comparisons of quality. In the dataset introduced for the ConvAI2 competition, nearly all the proposed algorithms were evaluated to be within one standard deviation of each other (Zhang et al., 2018). Therefore, for our human evaluation task, we ask humans to directly compare the responses of two models given the previous utterances in the conversation.

Both Facebook and Amazon have developed evaluation systems that allow humans to converse with (and then rate) a chatbot (Venkatesh et al., 2018; Miller et al., 2017). Facebook's ParlAI [4] is the most comparable system for a unified framework for sharing, training, and evaluating chatbots; however, ChatEval is different in that it entirely focuses on the evaluation and warehousing of models. Our infrastructure takes as input text files containing model responses and does not require any code base integration.

RankME[5] (Novikova et al., 2018) is an evaluation system for natural language generation. While RankME could be adapted for chatbot evaluation, this would require significant modification of the source code. Furthermore, RankME is only a crowdsourcing framework, which is more narrow than ChatEval. DialCrowd[6] (Lee et al., 2018) is a tool for the easy creation of human evaluation tasks for conversational agents. Finally, Kaggle[7] is another important venue for competitions, which allows for multiple test beds. However, none of these tools and websites offer a unified solution to public baselines, evaluation sets, and an integrated A/B model testing framework.

In many ways, the goal of ChatEval is similar to Appraise: an Open-Source Toolkit for Manual Evaluation of MT Output (Federmann, 2012). Just as Appraise is integrated with WMT, ChatEval should also be used in shared tasks in dialog competitions.

The ChatEval Web Interface

The ChatEval web interface consists of four primary pages. Aside from the overview page, there is a model submission form, a page for viewing the profile of any submitted model, and a page for comparing the responses of multiple models.

Model Submission When researchers submit their model for evaluation, they are asked to upload the model's responses on at least one of our evaluation datasets. They also submit a description of the model which could include a link to paper or project page. Researchers may also optionally include a URL to a public code repository and a URL to download trained model parameters.

After the submission is manually checked, we use the ChatEval evaluation toolkit to launch evaluation on the submitted responses. Two-choice human evaluation experiments compare the researchers' model against baselines of their choice. Automatic evaluation metrics are also computed. If researchers opt to make their model results publicly accessible, the newly submitted model becomes available for future researchers to compare against.

Model Profile Each submitted model, as well as each of our baseline models, have a profile page on

---

[1] https://developer.amazon.com/alexaprize
[2] http://convai.io/
[3] http://workshop.colips.org/wochat/
[4] https://parl.ai

[5] https://github.com/jeknov/RankME
[6] https://dialrc.org/dialcrowd.html
[7] https://www.kaggle.com

the ChatEval website. The profile consists of the URLs and description provided by the researcher, the responses of the model to each prompt in the evaluation set, and a visualization of the results of human and automatic evaluation.

Response Comparison   To facilitate the qualitative comparison of models, we offer a response comparison interface where users can see all the prompts in a particular evaluation set and the responses generated by each model.

Evaluation Datasets

We propose using the dataset collected by the dialogue breakdown detection (DBDC) task (Higashinaka et al., 2017) as a standard benchmark. The DBDC dataset was created by presenting participants with a short paragraph of context and then asking them to converse with three possible chatbots: TickTock (Yu et al., 2015), Iris[8], and Conversational Intelligence Challenge[9]. Participants knew that they were speaking with a chatbot, and the conversations reflect this. We randomly selected 200 human utterances from this dataset, after manually filtering out utterances which were too ambiguous or short to be easily answerable. As the DBDC dataset does not contain any human-human dialog, we collected reference human responses to each utterance.

For compatibility with prior work, we publish random subsets of 200 query-response pairs from the test sets of Twitter and OpenSubtitles. We also make available the list of 200 prompts used as the evaluation set by Vinyals and Le (2015) in their analysis of the NCM's performance.

We believe that the DBDC dataset best represents the kind of conversations we would expect a user to have with a text-based conversational agent. The datasets used for chatbot evaluation ought to reflect the goal of the chatbot. For example, it only makes sense to evaluate a model trained on Twitter using a test set derived from Twitter if the chatbot's aim is to be skilled at responding to Tweets. With the DBDC dataset, we emphasize the goal of engaging in text-based interactions with users who know they are speaking with a chatbot.

Overfitting   One important feature of ChatEval is the ease of adding new evaluation datasets. In order to assure that researchers are not overfitting to any evaluation set, the ChatEval team will take top performing models and also apply them to other datasets. New evaluation datasets can be added upon request from the ChatEval team. We plan to add both the prompts as well as the model responses from Baheti et al. (2018) as well as Li et al. (2019). Finally, we have added the ability to interact with baseline models using FlowAI (Wubben, 2018).[10]

Evaluation Toolkit

The ChatEval evaluation toolkit is used to evaluate submitted models. It consists of an automatic evaluation and a human evaluation component.

Automatic Evaluation   Automatic evaluation metrics include:

- Lexical diversity (*distinct-n*), the number of unique n-grams in the model's responses divided by the total number of generated tokens (Li et al., 2016).
- Average cosine-similarity between the mean of the word embeddings of a generated response and ground-truth response (Liu et al., 2016).
- Sentence average BLEU-2 score (Liu et al., 2016).
- Response perplexity, measured using the likelihood that the model predicts the correct response (Zhang et al., 2018).[11]

Our system is easily extensible to support other evaluation metrics.

Human Evaluation   A/B comparison tests consist of showing the evaluator a prompt and two possible responses from models which are being compared. The prompt can consist of a single utterance or a series of utterances. The user picks the better response or specifies a tie. When both model responses are exactly the same, a tie is automatically recorded. The instructions seen by AMT workers are shown in Figure 2.

The evaluation prompts are split into blocks (currently defaulted to 10). Crowd workers are paid \$0.01 per single evaluation. We used three evaluators per prompt, so, if there are 200

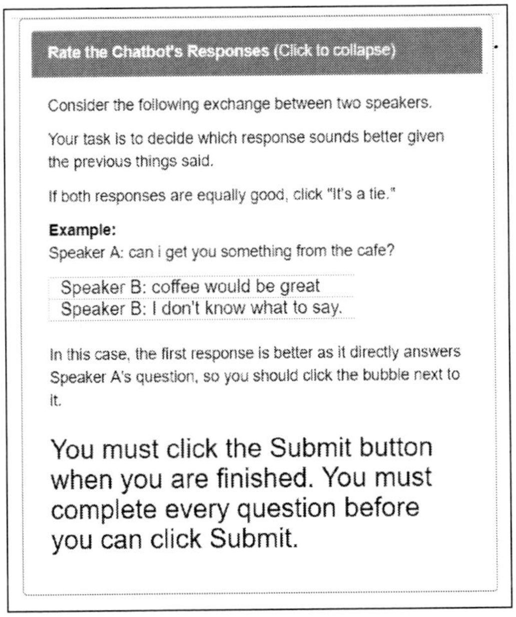

Rate the Chatbot's Responses (Click to collapse)

Consider the following exchange between two speakers.

Your task is to decide which response sounds better given the previous things said.

If both responses are equally good, click "It's a tie."

Example:
Speaker A: can i get you something from the cafe?

Speaker B: coffee would be great
Speaker B: I don't know what to say.

In this case, the first response is better as it directly answers Speaker A's question, so you should click the bubble next to it.

You must click the Submit button when you are finished. You must complete every question before you can click Submit.

Figure 2: The instructions seen by AMT workers.

prompt/response pairs, we have 600 ratings, and the net cost of the experiment is \$7.20 after fees. On the submission form, we ask researchers to pay for the cost of the AMT experiment.

The overall inter-annotator agreement (IAA) varies depending on the vagueness of the prompt as well as the similarity of the models. Out of 18 different experiments run, we found that IAA, as measured by Cohen's weighted kappa (Cohen, 1968), varies between .2 to .54 if we include tie choices. The low IAA is similar to the findings of Yuwono et al. (2018) who also found low inter-annotator agreement. Unfortunately, there are occasionally bad workers, which we automatically remove from our results. In order to identify such workers, we examine the worker against the other annotators.

For analysis of relative performance between models in ChatEval, we use item response theory (IRT) to select prompts as well as test statistical significance. IRT is the basis for almost all psychometric studies (Embretson and Reise, 2013). We follow the work of Otani et al. (2016), who used head-to-head pairwise testing to compare machine translation systems. However, we further this work by also examining the discriminative power of prompts. For instance *"my name is david . what is my name ?"* from the NCM evaluation dataset has been shown to have low discriminative power,

whereas, *"tell me something about your parents ?"* is useful to distinguish between the relative performance of models.

Availability of Toolkit

We expect it will be common for researchers to want to test out several of their models privately before submitting to the public ChatEval website. The ChatEval evaluation toolkit is available on Github for anyone to run.[12] We provide clear instructions for researchers to perform the human and automatic evaluation on their own with the toolkit as an alternative to using our web interface.

Availability of the Raw Data

All raw data including AMT evaluations are publicly available at `https://s3.amazonaws.com/chatbot-eval-data/index.html`. For ease of analysis, the data is also available in a MySQL database hosted on Google Cloud Engine as well as in JSON file format. A template analysis script Python Notebook is available in our repository and also on Google Colab. The ChatEval dataset is potentially useful for the creation and evaluation of automatic metrics.

Selection of Baselines

We seek to establish reasonable public baselines for Seq2Seq-based chatbots. All models trained by us use the OpenNMT-py (Klein et al., 2017) Seq2Seq implementation with its default parameters: two layers of LSTMs with 512 hidden neurons for the bidirectional encoder and the unidirectional decoder. We trained models on three standard datasets: OpenSubtitles, SubTle, and Twitter, and plan to introduce baselines trained on other datasets.

The number of baseline methods will continue to grow. We plan to add an information retrieval baseline, the hierarchical encoder-decoder model (Serban et al., 2017), and several other baselines from ParlAI.

Conclusion and Future Work

ChatEval is a framework for systematic evaluation of chatbots. The ChatEval website provides a repository of model code and parameters, evaluation sets, model comparisons, and a standard

---

[12] `https://github.com/chateval/chateval`

human evaluation setup. ChatEval seamlessly allows researchers to make systematic and consistent comparisons of conversational agents. We hope that future researchers–and the entire field–will benefit from ChatEval.

Future work includes optional larger evaluation sets for automatic descriptive metrics, such as lexical diversity (*distinct-n*), as these methods are often better suited for larger datasets.

We also plan to extend the ChatEval framework to further tasks by creating multiple new websites (IREval for information retreval, TaskEval for task-based chatbot evaluation, and NLGEval for natural language generation). Each of these will be specialized with small changes to the common framework for the different tasks.

Acknowledgements

We would like to thank Marianna Apidianaki for her helpful feedback on ChatEval and Claire Daniele for proofreading. We thank Sander Wubben and Flow.ai for the helpful API and hosting our interactive baseline session. Finally, we thank the anonymous reviewers for their feedback.

This work was partially supported by João Sedoc's Microsoft Research Dissertation Grant. Thank you to all of the workers on Amazon Mechanical Turk who contribute to our system.

References

Ashutosh Baheti, Alan Ritter, Jiwei Li, and Bill Dolan. 2018. Generating more interesting responses in neural conversation models with distributional constraints. In *Proceedings of the 2018 Conference on Empirical Methods in Natural Language Processing*, pages 3970–3980. Association for Computational Linguistics.

Jacob Cohen. 1968. Weighted kappa: Nominal scale agreement provision for scaled disagreement or partial credit. *Psychological bulletin*, 70(4):213–220.

Susan E. Embretson and Steven P. Reise. 2013. *Item response theory*. Psychology Press.

Christian Federmann. 2012. Appraise: An open-source toolkit for manual evaluation of machine translation output. *The Prague Bulletin of Mathematical Linguistics*, 98:25–35.

Antske Fokkens, Marieke Erp, Marten Postma, Ted Pedersen, Piek Vossen, and Nuno Freire. 2013. Offspring from reproduction problems: What replication failure teaches us. In *Proceedings of the 51st Annual Meeting of the Association for Computational Linguistics (Volume 1: Long Papers)*, volume 1, pages 1691–1701.

Ryuichiro Higashinaka, Kotaro Funakoshi, Michimasa Inaba, Yuiko Tsunomori, Tetsuro Takahashi, and Nobuhiro Kaji. 2017. Overview of dialogue breakdown detection challenge 3. *Proceedings of Dialog System Technology Challenge*, 6.

Guillaume Klein, Yoon Kim, Yuntian Deng, Jean Senellart, and Alexander Rush. 2017. Opennmt: Open-source toolkit for neural machine translation. In *ACL, System Demonstrations*, pages 67–72. Association for Computational Linguistics.

Kyusong Lee, Tiancheng Zhao, Alan W Black, and Maxine Eskenazi. 2018. Dialcrowd: A toolkit for easy dialog system assessment. In *Proceedings of the 19th Annual SIGdial Meeting on Discourse and Dialogue*, pages 245–248. Association for Computational Linguistics.

Jiwei Li, Michel Galley, Chris Brockett, Jianfeng Gao, and Bill Dolan. 2016. A diversity-promoting objective function for neural conversation models. In *Proceedings of the 2016 Conference of the North American Chapter of the Association for Computational Linguistics: Human Language Technologies*, pages 110–119, San Diego, California. Association for Computational Linguistics.

Ziming Li, Julia Kiseleva, and Maarten de Rijke. 2019. Dialogue generation: From imitation learning to inverse reinforcement learning. In *Thirty-Third AAAI Conference on Artificial Intelligence*.

Chia-Wei Liu, Ryan Lowe, Iulian Serban, Mike Noseworthy, Laurent Charlin, and Joelle Pineau. 2016. How not to evaluate your dialogue system: An empirical study of unsupervised evaluation metrics for dialogue response generation. In *Proceedings of the 2016 Conference on Empirical Methods in Natural Language Processing*, pages 2122–2132, Austin, Texas. Association for Computational Linguistics.

Alexander Miller, Will Feng, Dhruv Batra, Antoine Bordes, Adam Fisch, Jiasen Lu, Devi Parikh, and Jason Weston. 2017. Parlai: A dialog research software platform. In *Proceedings of the 2017 Conference on Empirical Methods in Natural Language Processing: System Demonstrations*, pages 79–84, Copenhagen, Denmark. Association for Computational Linguistics.

Jekaterina Novikova, Ondřej Dušek, and Verena Rieser. 2018. Rankme: Reliable human ratings for natural language generation. In *Proceedings of the 2018 Conference of the North American Chapter of the Association for Computational Linguistics: Human Language Technologies, Volume 2 (Short Papers)*, pages 72–78, New Orleans, Louisiana. Association for Computational Linguistics.

Naoki Otani, Toshiaki Nakazawa, Daisuke Kawahara, and Sadao Kurohashi. 2016. Irt-based aggregation model of crowdsourced pairwise comparison for evaluating machine translations. In *Proceedings of the 2016 Conference on Empirical Methods in Natural Language Processing*, pages 511–520. Association for Computational Linguistics.

Iulian V. Serban, Alessandro Sordoni, Ryan Lowe, Laurent Charlin, Joelle Pineau, Aaron Courville, and Yoshua Bengio. 2017. A hierarchical latent variable encoder-decoder model for generating dialogues. In *Thirty-First AAAI Conference on Artificial Intelligence*.

Ilya Sutskever, Oriol Vinyals, and Quoc V. Le. 2014. Sequence to sequence learning with neural networks. In *Advances in neural information processing systems*, pages 3104–3112.

Anu Venkatesh, Chandra Khatri, Ashwin Ram, Fenfei Guo, Raefer Gabriel, Ashish Nagar, Rohit Prasad, Ming Cheng, Behnam Hedayatnia, Angeliki Metallinou, Rahul Goel, Shaohua Yang, and Anirudh Raju. 2018. On evaluating and comparing conversational agents. In *NIPS 2017 Conversational AI workshop*.

Oriol Vinyals and Quoc V. Le. 2015. A neural conversational model. In *ICML Deep Learning Workshop*.

Sander Wubben. 2018. Flowai-nlg-api. `https://github.com/flow-ai/flowai-nlg-api`.

Zhou Yu, Alexandros Papangelis, and Alexander Rudnicky. 2015. Ticktock: A non-goal-oriented multimodal dialog system with engagement awareness. In *2015 AAAI Spring symposium series*.

Steven Kester Yuwono, Wu Biao, and Luis Fernando DHaro. 2018. Automated scoring of chatbot responses in conversational dialogue. In *Third Workshop on Chatbots and Conversational Agent Technologies*.

Saizheng Zhang, Emily Dinan, Jack Urbanek, Arthur Szlam, Douwe Kiela, and Jason Weston. 2018. Personalizing dialogue agents: I have a dog, do you have pets too? In *Proceedings of the 56th Annual Meeting of the Association for Computational Linguistics (Volume 1: Long Papers)*, pages 2204–2213, Melbourne, Australia. Association for Computational Linguistics.

LeafNATS: An Open-Source Toolkit and Live Demo System for Neural Abstractive Text Summarization

Tian Shi
Virginia Tech
tshi@vt.edu

Ping Wang
Virginia Tech
ping@vt.edu

Chandan K. Reddy
Virginia Tech
reddy@cs.vt.edu

Abstract

Neural abstractive text summarization (NATS) has received a lot of attention in the past few years from both industry and academia. In this paper, we introduce an open-source toolkit, namely LeafNATS, for training and evaluation of different sequence-to-sequence based models for the NATS task, and for deploying the pre-trained models to real-world applications. The toolkit is modularized and extensible in addition to maintaining competitive performance in the NATS task. A live news blogging system has also been implemented to demonstrate how these models can aid blog/news editors by providing them suggestions of headlines and summaries of their articles.

1 Introduction

Being one of the prominent natural language generation tasks, neural abstractive text summarization (NATS) has gained a lot of popularity (Rush et al., 2015; See et al., 2017; Paulus et al., 2017). Different from extractive text summarization (Gambhir and Gupta, 2017; Nallapati et al., 2017; Verma and Lee, 2017), NATS relies on modern deep learning models, particularly sequence-to-sequence (Seq2Seq) models, to generate words from a vocabulary based on the representations/features of source documents (Rush et al., 2015; Nallapati et al., 2016), so that it has the ability to generate high-quality summaries that are verbally innovative and can also easily incorporate external knowledge (See et al., 2017). Many NATS models have achieved better performance in terms of the commonly used evaluation measures (such as *ROUGE* (Lin, 2004) score) compared to extractive text summarization approaches (Paulus et al., 2017; Celikyilmaz et al., 2018; Gehrmann et al., 2018).

We recently provided a comprehensive survey of the Seq2Seq models (Shi et al., 2018), including their network structures, parameter inference methods, and decoding/generation approaches, for the task of abstractive text summarization. A variety of NATS models share many common properties and some of the key techniques are widely used to produce well-formed and human-readable summaries that are inferred from source articles, such as encoder-decoder framework (Sutskever et al., 2014), word embeddings (Mikolov et al., 2013), attention mechanism (Bahdanau et al., 2014), pointing mechanism (Vinyals et al., 2015) and beam-search algorithm (Rush et al., 2015). Many of these features have also found applications in other language generation tasks, such as machine translation (Bahdanau et al., 2014) and dialog systems (Serban et al., 2016). In addition, other techniques that can also be shared across different tasks include training strategies (Goodfellow et al., 2014; Keneshloo et al., 2018; Ranzato et al., 2015), data pre-processing, results post-processing and model evaluation. Therefore, having an open-source toolbox that modularizes different network components and unifies the learning framework for each training strategy can benefit researchers in language generation from various aspects, including efficiently implementing new models and generalizing existing models to different tasks.

In the past few years, different toolkits have been developed to achieve this goal. Some of them were designed specifically for a single task, such as ParlAI (Miller et al., 2017) for dialog research, and some have been further extended to other tasks. For example, OpenNMT (Klein et al., 2017) and XNMT (Neubig et al., 2018) are primarily for neural machine translation (NMT), but have been applied to other areas. The bottom-up attention model (Gehrmann et al., 2018), which

Proceedings of NAACL-HLT 2019: Demonstrations, pages 66–71
Minneapolis, Minnesota, June 2 - June 7, 2019. ©2019 Association for Computational Linguistics

has achieved state-of-the-art performance for abstractive text summarization, is implemented in OpenNMT. There are also several other general purpose language generation packages, such as Texar (Hu et al., 2018). Compared with these toolkits, LeafNATS is specifically designed for NATS research, but can also be adapted to other tasks. In this toolkit, we implement an end-to-end training framework that can minimize the effort in writing codes for training/evaluation procedures, so that users can focus on building models and pipelines. This framework also makes it easier for the users to transfer pre-trained parameters of user-specified modules to newly built models.

In addition to the learning framework, we have also developed a web application, which is driven by databases, web services and NATS models, to show a demo of deploying a new NATS idea to a real-life application using LeafNATS. Such an application can help front-end users (e.g., blog/news authors and editors) by providing suggestions of headlines and summaries for their articles.

The rest of this paper is organized as follows: Section 2 introduces the structure and design of LeafNATS learning framework. In Section 3, we describe the architecture of the live system demo. Based on the request of the system, we propose and implement a new model using LeafNATS for headline and summary generation. We conclude this paper in Section 4.

2   LeafNATS Toolkit[1]

In this section, we introduce the structure and design of LeafNATS toolkit, which is built upon the lower level deep learning platform – Pytorch (Paszke et al., 2017). As shown in Fig. 1, it consists of four main components, i.e., engines, modules, data and tools and playground.

Engines: In LeafNATS, an engine represents a training algorithm. For example, end-to-end training (See et al., 2017) and adversarial training (Goodfellow et al., 2014) are two different training frameworks. Therefore, we need to develop two different engines for them.

Specifically for LeafNATS, we implement a task-independent end-to-end training engine for NATS, but it can also be adapted to other NLP tasks, such as NMT, question-answering, sentiment classification, etc. The engine uses abstract data, models, pipelines, and loss functions

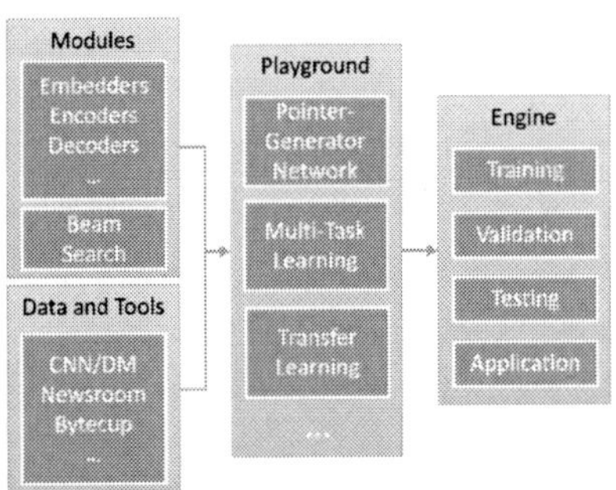

Figure 1: The framework of LeafNATS toolkit.

to build procedures of training, validation, testing/evaluation and application, respectively, so that they can be completely reused when implementing a new model. For example, these procedures include saving/loading check-point files during training, selecting N-best models during validation, and using the best model for generation during testing, etc. Another feature of this engine is that it allows users to specify part of a neural network to train and reuse parameters from other models, which is convenient for transfer learning.

Modules: Modules are the basic building blocks of different models. In LeafNATS, we provide ready-to-use modules for constructing recurrent neural network (RNN)-based sequence-to-sequence (Seq2Seq) models for NATS, e.g., pointer-generator network (See et al., 2017). These modules include embedder, RNN encoder, attention (Luong et al., 2015), temporal attention (Nallapati et al., 2016), attention on decoder (Paulus et al., 2017) and others. We also use these basic modules to assemble a pointer-generator decoder module and the corresponding beam search algorithms. The embedder can also be used to realize the embedding-weights sharing mechanism (Paulus et al., 2017).

Data and Tools: Different models in LeafNATS are tested on three datasets (see Table 1), namely, CNN/Daily Mail (CNN/DM) (Hermann et al., 2015), Newsroom (Grusky et al., 2018) and Bytecup[2]. The pre-processed CNN/DM data is available online[3]. Here, we provide tools to pre-process the last two datasets. Data modules are used to prepare the input data for mini-batch optimization.

Playground: With the engine and modules, we can develop different models by just assembling

---

[1] https://github.com/tshi04/LeafNATS

[2] https://biendata.com/competition/bytecup2018/

[3] https://github.com/JafferWilson/Process-Data-of-CNN-DailyMail

Dataset	Train	Validation	Test
CNN/DM	287,227	13,368	11,490
Newsroom	992,985	108,612	108,655
Bytecup	892,734	111,592	111,592

Table 1: Basic statistics of the datasets used.

these modules and building pipelines in playground. We re-implement different models in the NATS toolkit (Shi et al., 2018) to this framework. The performance (ROUGE scores (Lin, 2004)) of the pointer-generator model on different datasets has been reported in Table 2, where we find that most of the results are better than our previous implementations (Shi et al., 2018) due to some minor changes to the neural network.

Dataset	Model	R-1	R-2	R-L
Newsroom-S	Pointer-Generator	39.91	28.38	36.87
Newsroom-H	Pointer-Generator	27.11	12.48	25.47
CNN/DM	Pointer-Generator	37.02	15.97	34.18
	+coverage	39.26	17.21	36.16
Bytecup	Pointer-Generator	40.50	24.57	37.63

Table 2: Performance of our implemented pointer-generator network on different datasets. Newsroom-S and -H represent Newsroom summary and headline datasets, respectively.

3 A Live System Demonstration[4]

In this section, we present a real-world web application of the abstractive text summarization models, which can help front-end users to write headlines and summaries for their articles/posts. We will first discuss the architecture of the system, and then, provide more details of the front-end design and a new model built by LeafNATS that makes automatic summarization and headline generation possible.

3.1 Architecture

This is a news/blog website, which allows people to read, duplicate, edit, post, delete and comment articles. It is driven by web-services, databases and our NATS models. This web application is developed with PHP, HTML/CSS, and jQuery following the concept of Model-View-Controller (see Fig. 2).

In this framework, when people interact with the front-end views, they send HTML requests to controllers that can manipulate models. Then, the views will be changed with the updated information. For example, in NATS, we first write an article in a text-area. Then, this article along with

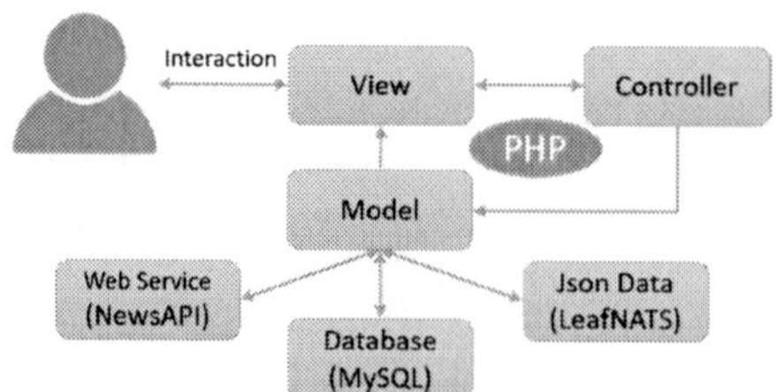

Figure 2: The architecture of the live system.

the summarization request will be sent to the controller via jQuery Ajax call. The controller communicates with our NATS models asynchronously via JSON format data. Finally, generated headlines and summaries are shown in the view.

3.2 Design of Frontend

Fig. 4 presents the front-end design of our web application for creating a new post, where labels represent the sequence of actions. In this website, an author can first click on "New Post" (step 1) to bring a new post view. Then, he/she can write content of an article in the corresponding text-area (step 2) without specifying it's headline and highlights, i.e., summary. By clicking "NATS" button (step 3) and waiting for a few seconds, he/she will see the generated headlines and highlights for the article in a new tab on the right hand side of the screen. Here, each of the buttons in gray color denotes the resource of the training data. For example, "Bytecup" means the model is trained with Bytecup headline generation dataset. The tokenized article content is shown in the bottom. Apart from plain-text headlines and highlights, our system also enables users to get a visual understanding of how each word is generated via attention weights (Luong et al., 2015). When placing the mouse tracker (step 4) on any token in the headlines or highlights, related content in the article will be labeled with red color. If the author would like to use one of the suggestions, he/she can click on the gray button (step 5) to add it to the text-area on the left hand side and edit it. Finally, he/she can click "Post" (step 6) to post the article.

3.3 The Proposed Model

As shown in the Fig. 3, our system can suggest to the users two headlines (based on Newsroom headline and Bytecup datasets) and summaries (based on Newsroom summary and CNN/DM datasets). They are treated as four tasks in this section. To achieve this goal, we use the mod-

[4] http://dmkdt3.cs.vt.edu/leafNATS

Figure 3: Front-end design of the live demonstration of our system.

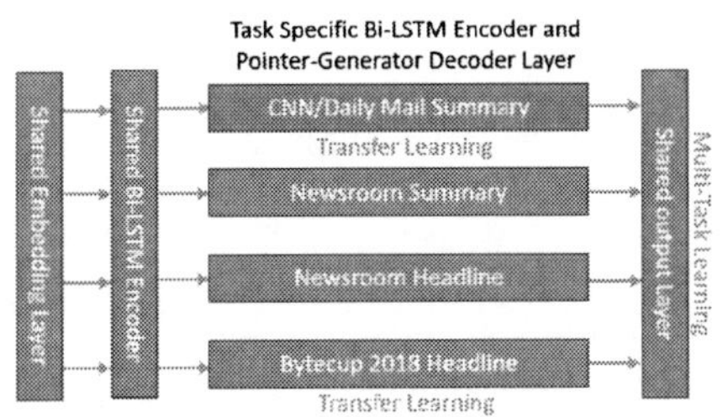

Figure 4: Overview of the model used to generate headlines and summaries.

Dataset	Model	R-1	R-2	R-L
Newsroom-S	multi-task	39.85	28.37	36.91
Newsroom-H	multi-task	28.31	13.40	26.64
CNN/DM	transfer	35.55	15.19	33.00
	+coverage	38.49	16.78	35.68
Bytecup	transfer	40.92	24.51	38.01

Table 3: Performance of our model.

ules provided in LeafNATS toolkit to assemble a new model (see Fig. 4), which has a shared embedding layer, a shared encoder layer, a task specific encoder-decoder (Bi-LSTM encoder and pointer-generator decoder) layer and a shared output layer.

To train this model, we first build a multi-task learning pipeline for Newsroom dataset to learn parameters for the modules that are colored in orange in Fig. 4, because (1) articles in this dataset have both headlines and highlights, (2) the size of the dataset is large, and (3) the articles come from a variety of news agents. Then, we build a transfer learning pipeline for CNN/Daily and Bytecup dataset, and learn the parameters for modules labeled with blue and green color, respectively. With LeafNATS, we can accomplish this work efficiently.

The performance of the proposed model on the corresponding testing sets are shown in Table 3. From the table, we observe that our model performs better in headline generation tasks. However, the ROUGE scores in summarization tasks are lower than the models without sharing embedding, encoder and output layers. It should be noted that by sharing the parameters, this model requires less than 20 million parameters to achieve such performance.

4 Conclusion

In this paper, we have introduced a LeafNATS toolkit for building, training, testing/evaluating, and deploying NATS models, as well as a live news blogging system to demonstrate how the NATS models can make the work of writing headlines and summaries for news articles more efficient. An extensive set of experiments on different benchmark datasets has demonstrated the effectiveness of our implementations. The newly proposed model for this system has achieved competitive results with fewer number of parameters.

Acknowledgments

This work was supported in part by the US National Science Foundation grants IIS-1619028, IIS-1707498 and IIS-1838730.

References

Dzmitry Bahdanau, Kyunghyun Cho, and Yoshua Bengio. 2014. Neural machine translation by jointly learning to align and translate. *arXiv preprint arXiv:1409.0473*.

Asli Celikyilmaz, Antoine Bosselut, Xiaodong He, and Yejin Choi. 2018. Deep communicating agents for abstractive summarization. In *Proceedings of the 2018 Conference of the North American Chapter of the Association for Computational Linguistics: Human Language Technologies, Volume 1 (Long Papers)*, volume 1, pages 1662–1675.

Mahak Gambhir and Vishal Gupta. 2017. Recent automatic text summarization techniques: a survey. *Artificial Intelligence Review*, 47(1):1–66.

Sebastian Gehrmann, Yuntian Deng, and Alexander Rush. 2018. Bottom-up abstractive summarization. In *Proceedings of the 2018 Conference on Empirical Methods in Natural Language Processing*, pages 4098–4109.

Ian Goodfellow, Jean Pouget-Abadie, Mehdi Mirza, Bing Xu, David Warde-Farley, Sherjil Ozair, Aaron Courville, and Yoshua Bengio. 2014. Generative adversarial nets. In *Advances in neural information processing systems*, pages 2672–2680.

Max Grusky, Mor Naaman, and Yoav Artzi. 2018. Newsroom: A dataset of 1.3 million summaries with diverse extractive strategies. In *Proceedings of the 2018 Conference of the North American Chapter of the Association for Computational Linguistics: Human Language Technologies, Volume 1 (Long Papers)*, volume 1, pages 708–719.

Karl Moritz Hermann, Tomas Kocisky, Edward Grefenstette, Lasse Espeholt, Will Kay, Mustafa Suleyman, and Phil Blunsom. 2015. Teaching machines to read and comprehend. In *Advances in Neural Information Processing Systems*, pages 1693–1701.

Zhiting Hu, Haoran Shi, Zichao Yang, Bowen Tan, Tiancheng Zhao, Junxian He, Wentao Wang, Xingjiang Yu, Lianhui Qin, Di Wang, et al. 2018. Texar: A modularized, versatile, and extensible toolkit for text generation. *arXiv preprint arXiv:1809.00794*.

Yaser Keneshloo, Tian Shi, Chandan K Reddy, and Naren Ramakrishnan. 2018. Deep reinforcement learning for sequence to sequence models. *arXiv preprint arXiv:1805.09461*.

Guillaume Klein, Yoon Kim, Yuntian Deng, Jean Senellart, and Alexander Rush. 2017. Opennmt: Open-source toolkit for neural machine translation. *Proceedings of ACL 2017, System Demonstrations*, pages 67–72.

Chin-Yew Lin. 2004. ROUGE: A package for automatic evaluation of summaries. *Text Summarization Branches Out*.

Thang Luong, Hieu Pham, and Christopher D Manning. 2015. Effective approaches to attention-based neural machine translation. In *Proceedings of the 2015 Conference on Empirical Methods in Natural Language Processing*, pages 1412–1421.

Tomas Mikolov, Ilya Sutskever, Kai Chen, Greg S Corrado, and Jeff Dean. 2013. Distributed representations of words and phrases and their compositionality. In *Advances in neural information processing systems*, pages 3111–3119.

Alexander Miller, Will Feng, Dhruv Batra, Antoine Bordes, Adam Fisch, Jiasen Lu, Devi Parikh, and Jason Weston. 2017. Parlai: A dialog research software platform. In *Proceedings of the 2017 Conference on Empirical Methods in Natural Language Processing: System Demonstrations*, pages 79–84.

Ramesh Nallapati, Feifei Zhai, and Bowen Zhou. 2017. Summarunner: A recurrent neural network based sequence model for extractive summarization of documents. In *Thirty-First AAAI Conference on Artificial Intelligence*.

Ramesh Nallapati, Bowen Zhou, Cicero dos Santos, Ça glar Gulçehre, and Bing Xiang. 2016. Abstractive text summarization using sequence-to-sequence RNNs and beyond. *CoNLL 2016*, page 280.

Graham Neubig, Matthias Sperber, Xinyi Wang, Matthieu Felix, Austin Matthews, Sarguna Padmanabhan, Ye Qi, Devendra Singh Sachan, Philip Arthur, Pierre Godard, et al. 2018. Xnmt: The extensible neural machine translation toolkit. *Vol. 1: MT Researchers Track*, page 185.

Adam Paszke, Sam Gross, Soumith Chintala, Gregory Chanan, Edward Yang, Zachary DeVito, Zeming Lin, Alban Desmaison, Luca Antiga, and Adam Lerer. 2017. Automatic differentiation in pytorch.

Romain Paulus, Caiming Xiong, and Richard Socher. 2017. A deep reinforced model for abstractive summarization. *arXiv preprint arXiv:1705.04304*.

Marc'Aurelio Ranzato, Sumit Chopra, Michael Auli, and Wojciech Zaremba. 2015. Sequence level training with recurrent neural networks. *arXiv preprint arXiv:1511.06732*.

Alexander M Rush, Sumit Chopra, and Jason Weston. 2015. A neural attention model for abstractive sentence summarization. In *Proceedings of the 2015 Conference on Empirical Methods in Natural Language Processing*, pages 379–389.

Abigail See, Peter J. Liu, and Christopher D. Manning. 2017. Get to the point: Summarization with pointer-generator networks. In *Proceedings of the 55th Annual Meeting of the Association for Computational Linguistics (Volume 1: Long Papers)*, pages 1073–1083. Association for Computational Linguistics.

Iulian Vlad Serban, Alessandro Sordoni, Yoshua Bengio, Aaron C Courville, and Joelle Pineau. 2016. Building end-to-end dialogue systems using generative hierarchical neural network models.

Tian Shi, Yaser Keneshloo, Naren Ramakrishnan, and Chandan K Reddy. 2018. Neural abstractive text summarization with sequence-to-sequence models. *arXiv preprint arXiv:1812.02303*.

Ilya Sutskever, Oriol Vinyals, and Quoc V Le. 2014. Sequence to sequence learning with neural networks. In *Advances in neural information processing systems*, pages 3104–3112.

Rakesh M. Verma and Daniel Lee. 2017. Extractive summarization: Limits, compression, generalized model and heuristics. *Computación y Sistemas*, 21.

Oriol Vinyals, Meire Fortunato, and Navdeep Jaitly. 2015. Pointer networks. In *Advances in Neural Information Processing Systems*, pages 2692–2700.

End-to-End Open-Domain Question Answering with BERTserini

Wei Yang,[1,2]* Yuqing Xie,[1,2]* Aileen Lin,[2] Xingyu Li,[2]
Luchen Tan,[2] Kun Xiong,[2] Ming Li,[1,2] and Jimmy Lin[1,2]

[1] David R. Cheriton School of Computer Science, University of Waterloo
[2] RSVP.ai

Abstract

We demonstrate an end-to-end question answering system that integrates BERT with the open-source Anserini information retrieval toolkit. In contrast to most question answering and reading comprehension models today, which operate over small amounts of input text, our system integrates best practices from IR with a BERT-based reader to identify answers from a large corpus of Wikipedia articles in an end-to-end fashion. We report large improvements over previous results on a standard benchmark test collection, showing that fine-tuning pretrained BERT with SQuAD is sufficient to achieve high accuracy in identifying answer spans.

1 Introduction

BERT (Devlin et al., 2018), the latest refinement of a series of neural models that make heavy use of pretraining (Peters et al., 2018; Radford et al., 2018), has led to impressive gains in many natural language processing tasks, ranging from sentence classification to question answering to sequence labeling. Most relevant to our task, Nogueira and Cho (2019) showed impressive gains in using BERT for query-based passage reranking. In this demonstration, we integrate BERT with the open-source Anserini IR toolkit to create BERTserini, an end-to-end open-domain question answering (QA) system.

Unlike most QA or reading comprehension models, which are best described as rerankers or extractors since they assume as input relatively small amounts of text (an article, top k sentences or passages, etc.), our system operates directly on a large corpus of Wikipedia articles. We integrate best practices from the information retrieval community with BERT to produce an end-to-end system, and experiments on a standard benchmark

* equal contribution

test collection show large improvements over previous work. Our results show that fine-tuning pretrained BERT with SQuAD (Rajpurkar et al., 2016) is sufficient to achieve high accuracy in identifying answer spans. The simplicity of this design is one major feature of our architecture. We have deployed BERTserini as a chatbot that users can interact with on diverse platforms, from laptops to mobile phones.

2 Background and Related Work

While the origins of question answering date back to the 1960s, the modern formulation can be traced to the Text Retrieval Conferences (TRECs) in the late 1990s (Voorhees and Tice, 1999). With roots in information retrieval, it was generally envisioned that a QA system would comprise pipeline stages that select increasingly finer-grained segments of text (Tellex et al., 2003): document retrieval to identify relevant documents from a large corpus, followed by passage ranking to identify text segments that contain answers, and finally answer extraction to identify the answer spans.

As NLP researchers became increasingly interested in QA, they placed greater emphasis on the later stages of the pipeline to emphasize various aspects of linguistic analysis. Information retrieval techniques receded into the background and became altogether ignored. Most popular QA benchmark datasets today—for example, TrecQA (Yao et al., 2013), WikiQA (Yang et al., 2015), and MSMARCO (Bajaj et al., 2016)—are best characterized as answer selection tasks. That is, the system is given the question as well as a candidate list of sentences to choose from. Of course, those candidates have to come from *somewhere*, but their source lies outside the problem formulation. Similarly, reading comprehension datasets such as SQuAD (Rajpurkar et al., 2016)

Proceedings of NAACL-HLT 2019: Demonstrations, pages 72–77
Minneapolis, Minnesota, June 2 - June 7, 2019. ©2019 Association for Computational Linguistics

eschew retrieval entirely, since there is only a single document from which to extract answers.

In contrast, what we refer to as "end-to-end" question answering begins with a large corpus of documents. Since it is impractical to apply inference exhaustively to all documents in a corpus with current models (mostly based on neural networks), this formulation necessarily requires some type of term-based retrieval technique to restrict the input text under consideration—and hence an architecture quite like the pipelined systems from over a decade ago. Recently, there has been a resurgence of interest in this task, the most notable of which is Dr.QA (Chen et al., 2017). Other recent papers have examined the role of retrieval in this end-to-end formulation (Wang et al., 2017; Kratzwald and Feuerriegel, 2018; Lee et al., 2018), some of which have, in essence, rediscovered ideas from the late 1990s and early 2000s.

For a wide range of applications, researchers have recently demonstrated the effectiveness of neural models that have been pretrained on a language modeling task (Peters et al., 2018; Radford et al., 2018); BERT (Devlin et al., 2018) is the latest refinement of this idea. Our work tackles end-to-end question answering by combining BERT with Anserini, an IR toolkit built on top of the popular open-source Lucene search engine. Anserini (Yang et al., 2017, 2018) represents recent efforts by researchers to bring academic IR into better alignment with the practice of building real-world search applications, where Lucene has become the *de facto* platform used in industry. Through an emphasis on rigorous software engineering and regression testing for replicability, Anserini codifies IR best practices today. Recently, Lin (2018) showed that a well-tuned Anserini implementation of a query expansion model proposed over a decade ago still beats two recent neural models for document ranking. Thus, BERT and Anserini represent solid foundations on which to build an end-to-end question answering system.

3 System Architecture

The architecture of BERTserini is shown in Figure 1 and is comprised of two main modules, the Anserini retriever and the BERT reader. The retriever is responsible for selecting segments of text that contain the answer, which is then passed to the reader to identify an answer span. To facilitate

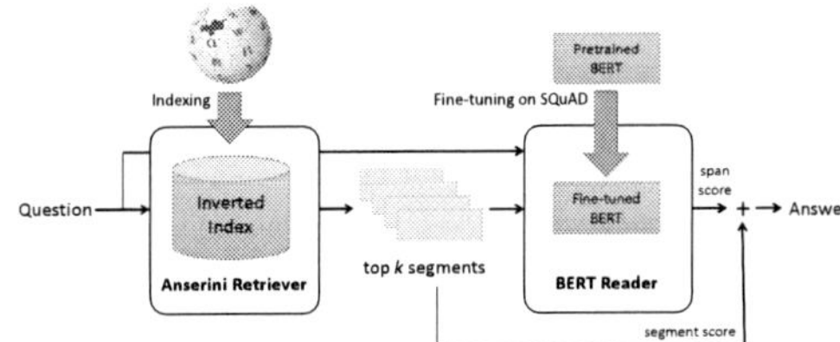

Figure 1: Architecture of BERTserini.

comparisons to previous work, we use the same Wikipedia corpus described in Chen et al. (2017) (from Dec. 2016) comprising 5.08M articles. In what follows, we describe each module in turn.

3.1 Anserini Retriever

For simplicity, we adopted a single-stage retriever that directly identifies segments of text from Wikipedia to pass to the BERT reader—as opposed to a multi-stage retriever that first retrieves documents and then ranks passages within. However, to increase flexibility, we experimented with different granularities of text at indexing time:

Article: The 5.08M Wikipedia articles are directly indexed; that is, an article is the unit of retrieval.

Paragraph: The corpus is pre-segmented into 29.5M paragraphs and indexed, where each paragraph is treated as a "document" (i.e., the unit of retrieval).

Sentence: The corpus is pre-segmented into 79.5M sentences and indexed, where each sentence is treated as a "document".

At inference time, we retrieve k text segments (one of the above conditions) using the question as a "bag of words" query. We use a post-v0.3.0 branch of Anserini,[1] with BM25 as the ranking function (Anserini's default parameters).

3.2 BERT Reader

Text segments from the retriever are passed to the BERT reader. We use the model in Devlin et al. (2018), but with one important difference: to allow comparison and aggregation of results from different segments, we remove the final softmax layer over different answer spans; cf. (Clark and Gardner, 2018).

Our BERT reader is based on Google's reference implementation[2] (TensorFlow 1.12.0). For

---

[1] http://anserini.io/
[2] https://github.com/google-research/bert

Model	EM	F1	R
Dr.QA (Chen et al., 2017)	27.1	-	77.8
Dr.QA + Fine-tune	28.4	-	-
Dr.QA + Multitask	29.8	-	-
R^3 (Wang et al., 2017)	29.1	37.5	-
Kratzwald and Feuerriegel (2018)	29.8	-	-
Par. R. (Lee et al., 2018)	28.5	-	83.1
Par. R. + Answer Agg.	28.9	-	-
Par. R. + Full Agg.	30.2	-	-
MINIMAL (Min et al., 2018)	34.7	42.5	64.0
BERTserini (Article, $k = 5$)	19.1	25.9	63.1
BERTserini (Paragraph, $k = 29$)	36.6	44.0	75.0
BERTserini (Sentence, $k = 78$)	34.0	41.0	67.5
BERTserini (Paragraph, $k = 100$)	**38.6**	**46.1**	**85.8**

Table 1: Results on SQuAD development questions.

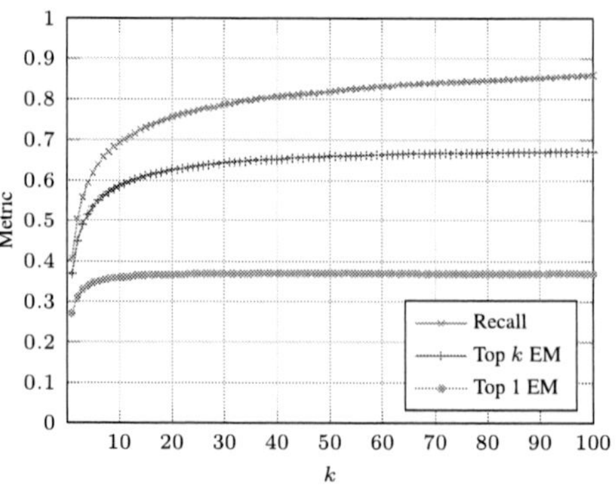

Figure 2: Model effectiveness with different numbers of retrieved paragraphs.

training, we begin with the BERT-Base model (uncased, 12-layer, 768-hidden, 12-heads, 110M parameters) and then fine tune the model on the training set of SQuAD (v1.1). All inputs to the reader are padded to 384 tokens; the learning rate is set to 3×10^{-5} and all other defaults settings are used.

At inference time, for retrieved articles, we apply the BERT reader paragraph by paragraph. For retrieved paragraphs, we apply inference over the entire paragraph. For retrieved sentences, we apply inference over the entire sentence. In all cases, the reader selects the best text span and provides a score. We then combine the reader score with the retriever score via linear interpolation:

$$S = (1 - \mu) \cdot S_{\text{Anserini}} + \mu \cdot S_{\text{BERT}}$$

where $\mu \in [0, 1]$ is a hyperparameter. We tune μ on 1000 randomly-selected question-answer pairs from the SQuAD training set, considering all values in tenth increments.

4 Experimental Results

We adopt exactly the same evaluation methodology as Chen et al. (2017), which was also used in subsequent work. Test questions come from the development set of SQuAD; since our answers come from different texts, we only evaluate with respect to the SQuAD answer spans (i.e., the passage context is ignored). Our evaluation metrics are also the same as Chen et al. (2017): exact match (EM) score and F1 score (at the token level). In addition, we compute recall (R), the fraction of questions for which the correct answer appears in *any* retrieved segment; this is what Chen

et al. (2017) call the document retrieval results. Note that this recall is *not* the same as the token-level recall component in the F1 score.

Our main results are shown in Table 1, where we report metrics with different Anserini retrieval conditions (article, paragraphs, and sentences). We compare article retrieval at $k = 5$, paragraph retrieval at $k = 29$, and sentence retrieval at $k = 78$. The article setting matches the retrieval condition in Chen et al. (2017). The values of k for the paragraph and sentence conditions are selected so that the reader considers approximately the same amount of text: each paragraph contains 2.7 sentences on average, and each article contains 5.8 paragraphs on average. The table also copies results from previous work for comparison.

We see that article retrieval underperforms paragraph retrieval by a large margin: the reason, we believe, is that articles are long and contain many non-relevant sentences that serve as distractors to the BERT reader. Sentences perform reasonably but not as well as paragraphs because they often lack the context for the reader to identify the answer span. Paragraphs seem to represent a "sweet spot", yielding a large improvement in exact match score over previous results.

Our next experiment examined the effects of varying k, the number of text segments considered by the BERT reader. Here, we focus only on the paragraph condition, with $\mu = 0.5$ (the value learned via cross validation). Figure 2 plots three metrics with respect to k: recall, top k exact match, and top exact match. Recall measures the fraction of questions for which the correct answer appears in *any* retrieved segment, exactly as in Table 1. Top k exact match represents a lenient condition where the system receives credit for a correctly-identified span in *any* retrieved segment. Finally, top exact match is evaluated with respect to the top-scoring span, comparable to the results reported in Table 1. Scores for the paragraph condition at $k = 100$ are also reported in the table: we note that the exact match score is substantially higher than the previously-published best result that we are aware of.

We see that, as expected, scores increase with larger k values. However, the top exact match score doesn't appear to increase much after around $k = 10$. The top k exact match score continues growing a bit longer but also reaches saturation. Recall appears to continue increasing all the way up to $k = 100$, albeit more slowly as k increases. This means that the BERT reader is unable to take advantage of these additional answer passages that appear in the candidate pool.

These curves also provide a failure analysis: The top recall curve (in blue) represents the upper bound with the current Anserini retriever. At $k = 100$, it is able to return at least one relevant paragraph around 86% of the time, and thus we can conclude that passage retrieval does not appear to be the bottleneck in overall effectiveness in the current implementation.

The gap between the top blue recall curve and the top k exact match curve (in red) quantifies the room for improvement with the BERT reader; these represent cases in which the reader did not identify the correct answer in *any* paragraph. Finally, the gap between the red curve and the bottom top exact match curve (in purple) represents cases where BERT *did* identify the correct answer, but not as the top-scoring span. This gap can be characterized as failures in scoring or score aggregation, and it seems to be the biggest area for improvement—suggesting that our current approach (weighted interpolation between the BERT and Anserini scores) is insufficient. We are exploring reranking models that are capable of integrating more relevance signals.

One final caveat: this error analysis is based on the SQuAD ground truth. Although our answers might not match the SQuAD answer spans, they may nevertheless be acceptable (for example, different answers to time-dependent questions). In future work we plan on manually examining a sample of the errors to produce a more accurate classification of the failures.

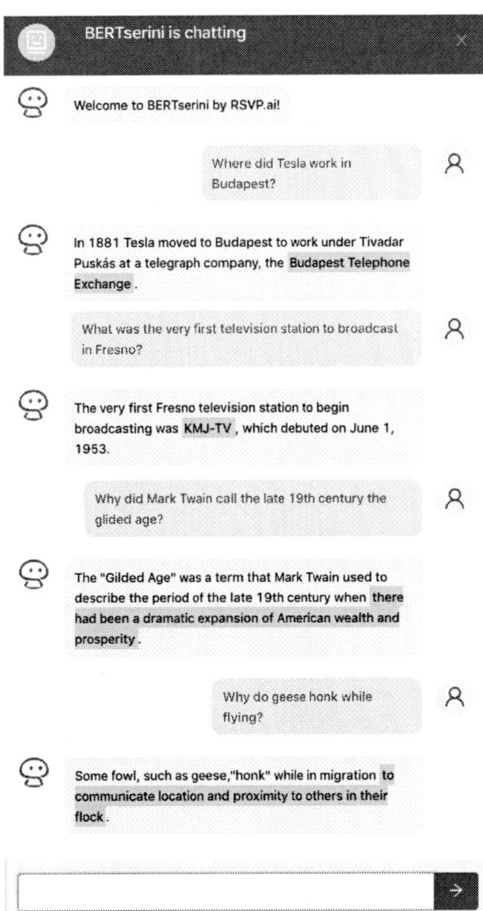

Figure 3: A screenshot of BERTserini in RSVP.ai's chatbot interface. These samples from SQuAD illustrate the range of questions that the system can answer.

5 Demonstration

We have deployed BERTserini as a chatbot that users can interact with in two different ways: a Slackbot and RSVP.ai's intelligent platform that allows businesses to construct natural dialogue services easily and quickly. However, both use the same backend services. A screenshot of the RSVP.ai chat platform is shown in Figure 3. The current interface uses the paragraph indexing condition, but we return only the sentence containing the answer identified by the BERT reader. The answer span is highlighted in the response (Lin et al., 2003). In the screenshot we can see the diversity of questions that BERTserini can handle— different types of named entities as well as queries whose answers are not noun phrases.

One important consideration in an operational

system is the latency of the responses. Informed by the analysis in Figure 2, in our demonstration system we set $k = 10$ under the paragraph condition. While this does not give us the maximum possible accuracy, it represents a good cost/quality tradeoff. To quantify processing time, we randomly selected 100 questions from SQuAD and recorded average latencies; measurements were taken on a machine with an Intel Xeon E5-2620 v4 CPU (2.10GHz) and a Tesla P40 GPU. Anserini retrieval (on the CPU) averages 0.5s per question, while BERT processing time (on the GPU) averages 0.18s per question.

6 Conclusion

We introduce BERTserini, our end-to-end open-domain question answering system that integrates BERT and the Anserini IR toolkit. With a simple two-stage pipeline architecture, we are able to achieve large improvements over previous systems. Error analysis points to room for improvement in retrieval, answer extraction, and answer aggregation—all of which represent ongoing efforts. In addition, we are also interested in expanding the multilingual capabilities of our system.

References

Payal Bajaj, Daniel Campos, Nick Craswell, Li Deng, Jianfeng Gao, Xiaodong Liu, Rangan Majumder, Andrew McNamara, Bhaskar Mitra, Tri Nguyen, Mir Rosenberg, Xia Song, Alina Stoica, Saurabh Tiwary, and Tong Wang. 2016. MS MARCO: A human generated MAchine Reading COmprehension dataset. *arXiv:1611.09268*.

Danqi Chen, Adam Fisch, Jason Weston, and Antoine Bordes. 2017. Reading Wikipedia to answer open-domain questions. In *Proceedings of the 55th Annual Meeting of the Association for Computational Linguistics (Volume 1: Long Papers)*, pages 1870–1879.

Christopher Clark and Matt Gardner. 2018. Simple and effective multi-paragraph reading comprehension. In *Proceedings of the 56th Annual Meeting of the Association for Computational Linguistics (Volume 1: Long Papers)*, pages 845–855.

Jacob Devlin, Ming-Wei Chang, Kenton Lee, and Kristina Toutanova. 2018. BERT: Pre-training of deep bidirectional transformers for language understanding. *arXiv:1810.04805*.

Bernhard Kratzwald and Stefan Feuerriegel. 2018. Adaptive document retrieval for deep question answering. In *Proceedings of the 2018 Conference on Empirical Methods in Natural Language Processing*, pages 576–581.

Jinhyuk Lee, Seongjun Yun, Hyunjae Kim, Miyoung Ko, and Jaewoo Kang. 2018. Ranking paragraphs for improving answer recall in open-domain question answering. In *Proceedings of the 2018 Conference on Empirical Methods in Natural Language Processing*, pages 565–569.

Jimmy Lin. 2018. The neural hype and comparisons against weak baselines. *SIGIR Forum*, 52(2):40–51.

Jimmy Lin, Dennis Quan, Vineet Sinha, Karun Bakshi, David Huynh, Boris Katz, and David R. Karger. 2003. The role of context in question answering systems. In *Extended abstracts of the 2003 Conference on Human Factors in Computing Systems (CHI 2003)*, pages 1006–1007.

Sewon Min, Victor Zhong, Richard Socher, and Caiming Xiong. 2018. Efficient and robust question answering from minimal context over documents. In *Proceedings of the 56th Annual Meeting of the Association for Computational Linguistics (Volume 1: Long Papers)*, pages 1725–1735.

Rodrigo Nogueira and Kyunghyun Cho. 2019. Passage re-ranking with BERT. *arXiv:1901.04085*.

Matthew Peters, Mark Neumann, Mohit Iyyer, Matt Gardner, Christopher Clark, Kenton Lee, and Luke Zettlemoyer. 2018. Deep contextualized word representations. In *Proceedings of the 2018 Conference of the North American Chapter of the Association for Computational Linguistics: Human Language Technologies, Volume 1 (Long Papers)*, pages 2227–2237.

Alec Radford, Karthik Narasimhan, Tim Salimans, and Ilya Sutskever. 2018. Improving language understanding by generative pre-training. Technical report.

Pranav Rajpurkar, Jian Zhang, Konstantin Lopyrev, and Percy Liang. 2016. SQuAD: 100,000+ questions for machine comprehension of text. In *Proceedings of the 2016 Conference on Empirical Methods in Natural Language Processing*, pages 2383–2392.

Stefanie Tellex, Boris Katz, Jimmy Lin, Gregory Marton, and Aaron Fernandes. 2003. Quantitative evaluation of passage retrieval algorithms for question answering. In *Proceedings of the 26th Annual International ACM SIGIR Conference on Research and Development in Information Retrieval (SIGIR 2003)*, pages 41–47.

Ellen M. Voorhees and Dawn M. Tice. 1999. The TREC-8 Question Answering Track evaluation. In *Proceedings of the Eighth Text REtrieval Conference (TREC-8)*, pages 83–106.

Shuohang Wang, Mo Yu, Xiaoxiao Guo, Zhiguo Wang, Tim Klinger, Wei Zhang, Shiyu Chang, Gerald Tesauro, Bowen Zhou, and Jing Jiang. 2017. R^3:

Reinforced reader-ranker for open-domain question answering. *arXiv:1709.00023*.

Peilin Yang, Hui Fang, and Jimmy Lin. 2017. Anserini: Enabling the use of Lucene for information retrieval research. In *Proceedings of the 40th Annual International ACM SIGIR Conference on Research and Development in Information Retrieval (SIGIR 2017)*, pages 1253–1256.

Peilin Yang, Hui Fang, and Jimmy Lin. 2018. Anserini: Reproducible ranking baselines using Lucene. *Journal of Data and Information Quality*, 10(4):Article 16.

Yi Yang, Wen-tau Yih, and Christopher Meek. 2015. WikiQA: A challenge dataset for open-domain question answering. In *Proceedings of the 2015 Conference on Empirical Methods in Natural Language Processing*, pages 2013–2018.

Xuchen Yao, Benjamin Van Durme, Chris Callison-burch, and Peter Clark. 2013. Answer extraction as sequence tagging with tree edit distance. In *Proceedings of the 2013 Conference of the North American Chapter of the Association for Computational Linguistics: Human Language Technologies*, pages 858–867.

FAKTA: An Automatic End-to-End Fact Checking System

Moin Nadeem, Wei Fang, Brian Xu, Mitra Mohtarami, James Glass
MIT Computer Science and Artificial Intelligence Laboratory
Cambridge, MA, USA
{mnadeem, weifang, bwxu, mitram, glass}@mit.edu

Abstract

We present FAKTA which is a unified framework that integrates various components of a fact checking process: document retrieval from media sources with various types of reliability, stance detection of documents with respect to given claims, evidence extraction, and linguistic analysis. FAKTA predicts the factuality of given claims and provides evidence at the document and sentence level to explain its predictions.

1 Introduction

With the rapid increase of fake news in social media and its negative influence on people and public opinion (Mihaylov et al., 2015; Mihaylov and Nakov, 2016; Vosoughi et al., 2018), various organizations are now performing *manual* fact checking on suspicious claims. However, manual fact-checking is a time consuming and challenging process. As an alternative, researchers are investigating *automatic* fact checking which is a multi-step process and involves: (*i*) retrieving potentially relevant documents for a given claim (Mihaylova et al., 2018; Karadzhov et al., 2017), (*ii*) checking the reliability of the media sources from which documents are retrieved, (*iii*) predicting the stance of each document with respect to the claim (Mohtarami et al., 2018; Xu et al., 2018), and finally (*iv*) predicting factuality of given claims (Mihaylova et al., 2018). While previous works separately investigated individual components of the fact checking process, in this work, we present a unified framework titled FAKTA that integrates these components to not only predict the factuality of given claims, but also provide evidence at the document and sentence level to explain its predictions. To the best of our knowledge, FAKTA is the only system that offers such a capability.

2 FAKTA

Figure 1 illustrates the general architecture of FAKTA. The system is accessible via a Web browser and has two sides: client and server. When a user at the client side submits a textual claim for fact checking, the server handles the request by first passing it into the document retrieval component to retrieve a list of top-K relevant documents (see Section 2.1) from four types of sources: Wikipedia, highly-reliable, mixed reliability and low reliability mainstream media (see Section 2.2). The retrieved documents are passed to the re-ranking model to refine the retrieval result (see Section 2.1). Then, the stance detection component detects the stance/perspective of each relevant document with respect to the claim, typically modeled using labels such as *agree*, *disagree* and *discuss*. This component further provides rationales at the sentence level for explaining model predictions (see Section 2.3). Each document is also passed to the linguistic analysis component to analyze the language of the document using different linguistic lexicons (see Section 2.4). Finally, the aggregation component combines the predictions of stance detection for all the relevant documents and makes a final decision about the factuality of the claim (see Section 2.5). We describe the components below.

2.1 Document Retrieval & Re-ranking Model

We first convert an input claim to a query by only considering its verbs, nouns and adjectives (Potthast et al., 2013). Furthermore, claims often contain named entities (e.g., names of persons and organizations). We use the NLTK package to identify named entities in claims, and augment the initial query with all named entities from the claim's text. Ultimately, we generate queries of 5–10 tokens, which we execute against a search engine. If the search engine does not retrieve any results for

Proceedings of NAACL-HLT 2019: Demonstrations, pages 78–83
Minneapolis, Minnesota, June 2 - June 7, 2019. ©2019 Association for Computational Linguistics

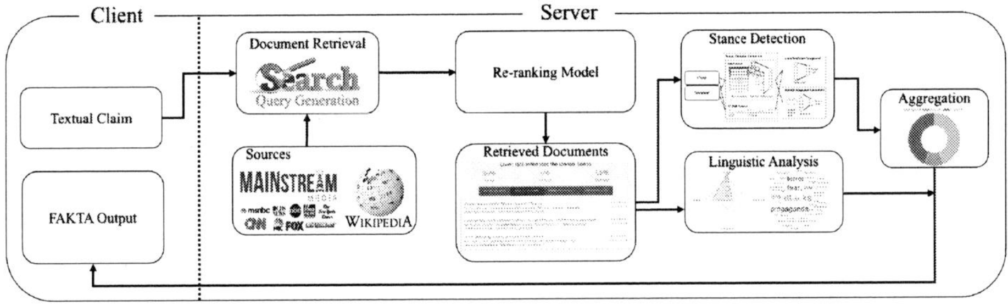

Figure 1: The architecture of our FAKTA system.

the query, we iteratively relax the query by dropping the final tokens one at a time. We also use Apache Lucene[1] to index and retrieve relevant documents from the 2017 Wikipedia dump (see our experiments in Section 3). Furthermore, we use the Google API[2] to search across three pre-defined lists of media sources based on their factuality and reliability as explained in Section 2.2. Finally, the re-ranking model of Lee et al. (2018) is applied to select the top-K relevant documents. This model uses all the POS tags in a claim that carry high discriminating power (NN, NNS, NNP, NNPS, JJ, CD) as keywords. The re-ranking model is defined as follows:

$$f_{rank} = \frac{|match|}{|claim|} \times \frac{|match|}{|title|} \times score_{init}, \quad (1)$$

where $|claim|$, $|title|$, and $|match|$ are the counts of such POS tags in the claim, title of a document, both claim and title respectively, and $score_{init}$ is the initial ranking score computed by Lucene or ranking from Google API.

2.2 Sources

While current search engines (e.g., Google, Bing, Yahoo) retrieve relevant documents for a given query from any media source, we retrieve relevant documents from four types of sources: Wikipedia, and high, mixed and low factual media. Journalists often spend considerable time verifying the reliability of their information sources (Popat et al., 2017; Nguyen et al., 2018), and some fact-checking organizations have been producing lists of unreliable online news sources specified by their journalists. FAKTA utilizes information about news media listed on the Media Bias/Fact Check (MBFC) website[3], which contains manual annotations and analysis of the factuality of $2,500$ news websites. Our list from MBFC includes $1,300$ websites annotated by journalists as *high* or *very high*, 700 websites annotated as *low* and *low-questionable*, and 500 websites annotated as *mixed* (i.e., containing both factually true and false information). Our document retrieval component retrieves documents from these three types of media sources (i.e., *high*, *mixed* and *low*) along with Wikipedia that mostly contains factually-true information.

2.3 Stance Detection & Evidence Extraction

In this work, we use our best model presented in (Xu et al., 2018) for stance detection. To the best of our knowledge, this model is the current state-of-the-art system on the Fake News Challenge (FNC) dataset.[4] Our model combines Bag of Words (BOW) and Convolutional Neural Networks (CNNs) in a two-level *hierarchy* scheme, where the first level predicts whether the label is *related* or *unrelated* (see Figure 2, the top-left pie chart in FAKTA), and then related documents are passed to the second level to determine their stances, *agree*, *disagree*, and *discuss* labels (see Figure 2, the bottom-left pie chart in FAKTA). Our model is further supplemented with an adversarial domain adaptation technique which helps it overcome the limited size of labeled data when training through different domains.

To provide rationales for model prediction, FAKTA further processes each sentence in the document with respect to the claim and computes a stance score for each sentence. The relevant sentences in the document are then highlighted and color coded with respect to stance labels (see Figure 2). FAKTA provides the option for re-ordering these rationales according to a specific stance label.

---

[1] https://lucene.apache.org
[2] https://developers.google.com/custom-search
[3] https://mediabiasfactcheck.com

[4] http://www.fakenewschallenge.org

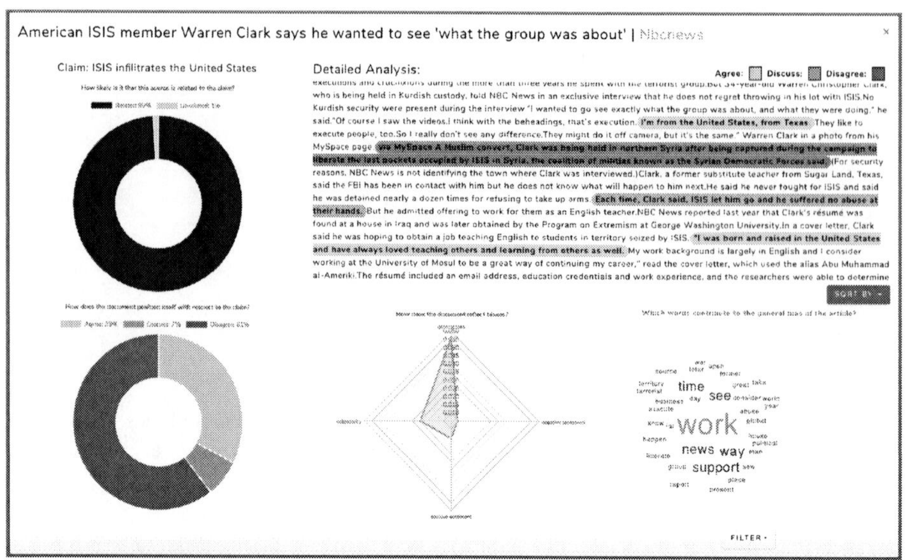

Figure 2: Screenshot of FAKTA for a document retrieved for the claim "ISIS infilitrates the United States."

2.4 Linguistic Analysis

We analyze the language used in documents using the following linguistic markers:

—*Subjectivity lexicon* (Riloff and Wiebe, 2003): which contains weak and strong subjective terms (we only consider the strong subjectivity cues),

—*Sentiment cues* (Liu et al., 2005): which contains *positive* and *negative* sentiment cues, and

—*Wiki-bias lexicon* (Recasens et al., 2013): which involves bias cues and controversial words (e.g., *abortion* and *execute*) extracted from the Neutral Point of View Wikipedia corpus (Recasens et al., 2013).

Finally, we compute a score for the document using these cues according to Equation (2), where for each lexicon type L_i and document D_j, the frequency of the cues for L_i in D_j is normalized by the total number of words in D_j:

$$L_i(D_j) = \frac{\sum\limits_{cue \in L_i} count(cue, D_j)}{\sum\limits_{w_k \in D_j} count(w_k, D_j)} \qquad (2)$$

These scores are shown in a radar chart in Figure 2. Furthermore, FAKTA provides the option to see a lexicon-specific word cloud of frequent words in each documents (see Figure 2, the right side of the radar chart which shows the word cloud of Sentiment cues in the document).

2.5 Aggregation

Stance Detection and Linguistic Analysis components are executed in parallel against all documents

retrieved by our document retrieval component from each type of sources. All the stance scores are averaged across these documents, and the aggregated scores are shown for each *agree*, *disagree* and *discuss* categories at the top of the ranked list of retrieved documents. Higher agree score indicates the claim is factually true, and higher disagree score indicates the claim is factually false.

3 Evaluation and Results

We use the Fact Extraction and VERification (FEVER) dataset (Thorne et al., 2018) to evaluate our system. In FEVER, each claim is assigned to its relevant Wikipedia documents with agree/disagree stances to the claim, and claims are labeled as *supported* (SUP, i.e. factually true), *refuted* (REF, i.e. factually false), and *not enough information* (NEI, i.e., there is not any relevant document for the claim in Wikipedia). The data includes a total of 145K claims, with around 80K, 30K and 35K SUP, REF and NEI labels respectively.

Document Retrieval: Table 1 shows results for document retrieval. We use various search and ranking algorithms that measure the similarity between each input claim as query and Web documents. Lines 1–11 in the table show the results when we use Lucene to index and search the data corpus with the following retrieval models: BM25 (Robertson et al., 1994) (Line 1), Classic based on the TF.IDF model (Line 2), and Divergence from Independence (DFI) (Kocabaş et al.,

	Model	R@1	R@5	R@10	R@20
1.	BM25	28.84	38.66	62.34	70.10
2.	Classic	9.14	23.10	31.65	40.70
3.	DFI	40.93	66.98	74.84	81.22
4.	DFR_{H3}	43.67	71.18	78.32	83.16
5.	DFR_z	43.14	71.17	78.60	83.88
6.	IB_{LL}	41.86	68.02	75.46	81.13
7.	IB_{SPL}	42.27	69.55	77.03	81.99
8.	LMDirichlet	39.00	68.86	77.39	83.04
9.	$LMJelinek_{0.05}$	37.39	59.75	67.58	74.15
10.	$LMJelinek_{0.10}$	37.30	59.85	67.58	74.44
11.	$LMJelinek_{0.20}$	37.01	59.60	67.60	74.62
	using Query Generation				
12.	$Lucene_{DFR_z}$	40.70	68.48	76.21	81.93
13.	Google API	56.62	71.92	73.86	74.89
	using Re-ranking Model				
14.	$Lucene_{DFR_z}$	**62.37**	**78.12**	**80.84**	**82.11**
15.	Google API	57.80	72.10	74.15	74.89

Table 1: Results of document retrieval on FEVER.

	Model	Settings	$F_{1(SUP/REF/NEI)}$	$F_{1(Macro)}$	Acc.
1.	MLP	3lbl/RS	-	-	40.63
2.	FAKTA	L/3lbl/RS	41.33/23.55/44.79	36.56	38.76
3.	FAKTA	G/3lbl/RS	47.49/43.01/28.17	39.65	41.21
4.	FAKTA	L/2lbl	58.33/57.71/-	58.02	58.03
5.	FAKTA	G/2lbl	58.96/59.74/-	59.35	59.35

Table 2: FAKTA full pipeline Results on FEVER.

2014) (Line 3). We also use Divergence from Independence Randomness (DFR) (Amati and Van Rijsbergen, 2002) with different term frequency normalization, such as the normalization provided by Dirichlet prior (DFR_{H_3}) (Line 4) or a Zipfian relation prior (DFR_z) (Line 5). We also consider Information Based (IB) models (Clinchant and Gaussier, 2010) with Log-logistic (IB_{LL}) (Line 6) or Smoothed power-law (IB_{SPL}) (Line 7) distributions. Finally, we consider LMDirichlet (Zhai and Lafferty, 2001) (Line 8), and LMJelinek (Zhai and Lafferty, 2001) with different settings for its hyperparameter (Lines 9–11). According to the resulting performance at different ranks $\{1$–$20\}$, we select the ranking algorithm DFR_z ($Lucene_{DFR_z}$) as our retrieval model.

In addition, Lines 12–13 show the results when claims are converted to queries as explained in Section 2.1. The results (Lines 5 and 12) show that Lucene performance decreases with query generation. This might be because the resulting queries become more abstract than their corresponding claims which may introduce some noise to the intended meaning of claims. However, Lines 14–15 show that our re-ranking model, explained in Section 2.1, can improve both Lucene and Google results.

FAKTA Full Pipeline: The complete pipeline consists of document retrieval and re-ranking model (Section 2.1), stance detection and rationale extraction[5] (Section 2.3) and aggregation model (Section 2.5). Table 2 shows the results for the full pipeline. Lines 1–3 show the results for all three SUP, REF, and NEI labels (3lbl) and Ran-

domly Sampled (RS) documents from Wikipedia for the NEI label. We label claims as NEI if the most relevant document retrieved has a retrieval score less than a threshold, which was determined by tuning on development data. Line 1 is the multi-layer perceptron (MLP) model presented in (Riedel et al., 2017). Lines 2–3 are the results for our system when using Lucene (L) and Google API (G) for document retrieval. The results show that our system achieves the highest performance on both $F_{1(Macro)}$ and accuracy (Acc) using Google as retrieval engine. We repeat our experiments when considering only SUP and REF labels (2lbl) and the results are significantly higher than the results with 3lbl (Lines 4–5).

4 The System in Action

The current version of FAKTA[6] and its short introduction video[7] and source code[8] are available online. FAKTA consists of three views:

—The text entry view: to enter a claim to be checked for factuality.

—Overall result view: includes four lists of retrieved documents from four factuality types of sources: Wikipedia, and high-, mixed-, and low-factuality media (Section 2.2). For each list, the final factuality score for the input claim is shown at the top of the page (Section 2.5), and the stance detection score for each document appears beside it.

—Document result view: when selecting a retrieved document, FAKTA shows the text of the document and highlights its important sentences according to their stance scores with respect to the claim. The stance detection results for the document are further shown as pie chart at the left side of the view (Section 2.3), and the linguistic analysis is shown at the bottom of the view (Section 2.4).

5 Related Work

Automatic fact checking (Xu et al., 2018) centers on evidence extraction for given claims, re-

---

[5] We used Intel AI's Distiller (Zmora et al., 2018) to compress the model.

[6] http://fakta.mit.edu
[7] http://fakta.mit.edu/video
[8] https://github.com/moinnadeem/fakta

liability evaluation of media sources (Baly et al., 2018a), stance detection of documents with respect to claims (Mohtarami et al., 2018; Xu et al., 2018; Baly et al., 2018b), and fact checking of claims (Mihaylova et al., 2018). These steps correspond to different Natural Language Processing (NLP) and Information Retrieval (IR) tasks including information extraction and question answering (Shiralkar et al., 2017). Veracity inference has been mostly approached as text classification problem and mainly tackled by developing linguistic, stylistic, and semantic features (Rashkin et al., 2017; Mihaylova et al., 2018; Nakov et al., 2017), as well as using information from *external* sources (Mihaylova et al., 2018; Karadzhov et al., 2017).

These steps are typically handled in isolation. For example, previous works (Wang, 2017; OBrien et al., 2018) proposed algorithms to predict factuality of claims by mainly focusing on only input claims (i.e., step (*iv*)) and their metadata information (e.g., the speaker of the claim). In addition, recent works on the Fact Extraction and VERification (FEVER) (Thorne et al., 2018) has focused on a specific domain (e.g., Wikipedia).

To the best of our knowledge, there is currently no end-to-end systems for fact checking which can search through Wikipedia and mainstream media sources across the Web to fact check given claims. To address these gaps, our FAKTA system covers all fact-checking steps and can search across different sources, predict the factuality of claims, and present a set of evidence to explain its prediction.

6 Conclusion

We have presented FAKTA–an online system for automatic end-to-end fact checking of claims. FAKTA can assist individuals and professional fact-checkers to check the factuality of claims by presenting relevant documents and rationales as evidence for its predictions. In future work, we plan to improve FAKTA's underlying components (e.g., stance detection), extend FAKTA to cross-lingual settings, and incorporate temporal information for fact checking.

Acknowledgments

We thank anonymous reviewers for their insightful comments, suggestions, and feedback. This research was supported in part by HBKU Qatar Computing Research Institute (QCRI), DSTA of Singapore, and Intel AI.

References

Gianni Amati and Cornelis Joost Van Rijsbergen. 2002. Probabilistic models of information retrieval based on measuring the divergence from randomness. *ACM Transactions on Information Systems (TOIS)*, 20(4):357–389.

Ramy Baly, Georgi Karadzhov, Dimitar Alexandrov, James Glass, and Preslav Nakov. 2018a. Predicting factuality of reporting and bias of news media sources. In *Proceedings of the 2018 Conference on Empirical Methods in Natural Language Processing*, pages 3528–3539. Association for Computational Linguistics.

Ramy Baly, Mitra Mohtarami, James Glass, Lluís Màrquez, Alessandro Moschitti, and Preslav Nakov. 2018b. Integrating stance detection and fact checking in a unified corpus. In *Proceedings of the 16th Annualw Conference of the North American Chapter of the Association for Computational Linguistics*, NAACL-HLT '18, New Orleans, LA, USA.

Stéphane Clinchant and Eric Gaussier. 2010. Information-based models for ad hoc ir. In *Proceedings of the 33rd International ACM SIGIR Conference on Research and Development in Information Retrieval*, SIGIR'10, pages 234–241, New York, NY, USA. ACM.

Georgi Karadzhov, Preslav Nakov, Lluís Màrquez, Alberto Barrón-Cedeño, and Ivan Koychev. 2017. Fully automated fact checking using external sources. In *Proceedings of the International Conference Recent Advances in Natural Language Processing, RANLP 2017*, pages 344–353. INCOMA Ltd.

İlker Kocabaş, Bekir Taner Dinçer, and Bahar Karaoğlan. 2014. A nonparametric term weighting method for information retrieval based on measuring the divergence from independence. *Inf. Retr.*, 17(2):153–176.

Nayeon Lee, Chien-Sheng Wu, and Pascale Fung. 2018. Improving large-scale fact-checking using decomposable attention models and lexical tagging. In *Proceedings of the 2018 Conference on Empirical Methods in Natural Language Processing*, pages 1133–1138. Association for Computational Linguistics.

Bing Liu, Minqing Hu, and Junsheng Cheng. 2005. Opinion observer: Analyzing and comparing opinions on the web. In *Proceedings of the 14th International Conference on World Wide Web*, pages 342–351, Chiba, Japan.

Todor Mihaylov, Georgi Georgiev, and Preslav Nakov. 2015. Finding opinion manipulation trolls in news community forums. In *Proceedings of the Nineteenth Conference on Computational Natural Language Learning*, pages 310–314. Association for Computational Linguistics.

Todor Mihaylov and Preslav Nakov. 2016. Hunting for troll comments in news community forums. In *Proceedings of the 54th Annual Meeting of the Association for Computational Linguistics*, pages 399–405, Berlin, Germany.

Tsvetomila Mihaylova, Preslav Nakov, Lluis Marquez, Alberto Barron-Cedeno, Mitra Mohtarami, Georgi Karadzhov, and James Glass. 2018. Fact checking in community forums. In *Proceedings of the Thirty-Second AAAI Conference on Artificial Intelligence*, pages 5309–5316, New Orleans, LA, USA.

Mitra Mohtarami, Ramy Baly, James Glass, Preslav Nakov, Lluís Màrquez, and Alessandro Moschitti. 2018. Automatic stance detection using end-to-end memory networks. In *Proceedings of the 16th Annualw Conference of the North American Chapter of the Association for Computational Linguistics*, NAACL-HLT '18, New Orleans, LA, USA.

Preslav Nakov, Tsvetomila Mihaylova, Lluıs Marquez, Yashkumar Shiroya, and Ivan Koychev. 2017. Do not trust the trolls: Predicting credibility in community question answering forums. In *Proceedings of the International Conference Recent Advances in Natural Language Processing (RANLP)*, pages 551–560.

An Nguyen, Aditya Kharosekar, Matthew Lease, and Byron Wallace. 2018. An interpretable joint graphical model for fact-checking from crowds. In *AAAI Conference on Artificial Intelligence*.

Nicole OBrien, Sophia Latessa, Georgios Evangelopoulos, and Xavier Boix. 2018. The language of fake news: Opening the black-box of deep learning based detectors. In *Proceedings of the Thirty-second Annual Conference on Neural Information Processing Systems (NeurIPS)–AI for Social Good*.

Kashyap Popat, Subhabrata Mukherjee, Jannik Strötgen, and Gerhard Weikum. 2017. Where the truth lies: Explaining the credibility of emerging claims on the web and social media. In *Proceedings of the 26th International Conference on World Wide Web Companion*, WWW '17 Companion, pages 1003–1012, Republic and Canton of Geneva, Switzerland.

Martin Potthast, Matthias Hagen, Tim Gollub, Martin Tippmann, Johannes Kiesel, Paolo Rosso, Efstathios Stamatatos, and Benno Stein. 2013. Overview of the 5th international competition on plagiarism detection. In *Working Notes for CLEF 2013 Conference , Valencia, Spain, September 23-26, 2013*.

Hannah Rashkin, Eunsol Choi, Jin Yea Jang, Svitlana Volkova, and Yejin Choi. 2017. Truth of varying shades: Analyzing language in fake news and political fact-checking. In *Proceedings of the 2017 Conference on Empirical Methods in Natural Language Processing*, pages 2921–2927.

Marta Recasens, Cristian Danescu-Niculescu-Mizil, and Dan Jurafsky. 2013. Linguistic models for analyzing and detecting biased language. In *Proceedings of the 51st Annual Meeting of the Association for Computational Linguistics*, pages 1650–1659, Sofia, Bulgaria.

Benjamin Riedel, Isabelle Augenstein, Georgios P. Spithourakis, and Sebastian Riedel. 2017. A simple but tough-to-beat baseline for the fake news challenge stance detection task. *CoRR*, abs/1707.03264.

Ellen Riloff and Janyce Wiebe. 2003. Learning extraction patterns for subjective expressions. In *Proceedings of the Conference on Empirical Methods in Natural Language Processing*, pages 105–112, Sapporo, Japan.

Stephen E. Robertson, Steve Walker, Susan Jones, Micheline Hancock-Beaulieu, and Mike Gatford. 1994. Okapi at trec-3. In *TREC*, pages 109–126. National Institute of Standards and Technology (NIST).

Prashant Shiralkar, Alessandro Flammini, Filippo Menczer, and Giovanni Luca Ciampaglia. 2017. Finding streams in knowledge graphs to support fact checking. *arXiv preprint arXiv:1708.07239*.

James Thorne, Andreas Vlachos, Christos Christodoulopoulos, and Arpit Mittal. 2018. Fever: a large-scale dataset for fact extraction and verification. In *Proceedings of the 2018 Conference of the North American Chapter of the Association for Computational Linguistics (HLT-NAACL)*, pages 809–819.

Soroush Vosoughi, Deb Roy, and Sinan Aral. 2018. The spread of true and false news online. *Science*, 359(6380):1146–1151.

William Yang Wang. 2017. "liar, liar pants on fire": A new benchmark dataset for fake news detection. In *Proceedings of the 55th Annual Meeting of the Association for Computational Linguistics (Volume 2: Short Papers)*, pages 422–426. Association for Computational Linguistics.

Brian Xu, Mitra Mohtarami, and James Glass. 2018. Adversarial doman adaptation for stance detection. In *Proceedings of the Thirty-second Annual Conference on Neural Information Processing Systems (NeurIPS)–Continual Learning*.

Chengxiang Zhai and John Lafferty. 2001. A study of smoothing methods for language models applied to ad hoc information retrieval. In *Proceedings of the 24th Annual International ACM SIGIR Conference on Research and Development in Information Retrieval*, SIGIR'01, pages 334–342, New York, NY, USA. ACM.

Neta Zmora, Guy Jacob, and Gal Novik. 2018. Neural network distiller. Available at https://doi.org/10.5281/zenodo.1297430.

iComposer: An Automatic Songwriting System for Chinese Popular Music

Hsin-Pei Lee
Institute of
Information Science,
Academia Sinica
`hhpslily`
`@iis.sinica.edu.tw`

Jhih-Sheng Fan
Institute of
Information Science,
Academia Sinica
`fann1993814`
`@iis.sinica.edu.tw`

Wei-Yun Ma
Institute of
Information Science,
Academia Sinica
`ma`
`@iis.sinica.edu.tw`

Abstract

In this paper, we introduce *iComposer*, an interactive web-based songwriting system designed to assist human creators by greatly simplifying music production. *iComposer* automatically creates melodies to accompany any given text. It also enables users to generate a set of lyrics given arbitrary melodies. *iComposer* is based on three sequence-to-sequence models, which are used to predict melody, rhythm, and lyrics, respectively. Songs generated by *iComposer* are compared with human-composed and randomly-generated ones in a subjective test, the experimental results of which demonstrate the capability of the proposed system to write pleasing melodies and meaningful lyrics at a level similar to that of humans.

1 Introduction

Music is a universal language. There is no human society that does not, at some point, have a musical heritage and tradition. Over the past few years, many computer science researchers have worked on music information retrieval, focusing on genre recognition, symbolic melodic similarity, melody extraction, mood classification, etc.

With respect to computational creativity, tasks such as automatic music composition or lyrics generation have been discussed for decades. However, a relatively new topic—the relationship between lyrics and melody—remains somewhat mysterious. It is difficult to explain how music and spoken words fit together and why the pairing of these two creates an emotionally compelling experience; we believe this merits a deeper investigation.

Inspired by work on text-to-image synthesis and image caption generation, we propose *iComposer*, a simple and effective bi-directional songwriting system that automatically generates melody from text and vice versa. We believe that *iComposer*

has value in capturing relationships between lyrics and melody. Moreover, *iComposer* makes it possible for more people, both professional and amateur musicians, to enjoy and benefit from this creative activity.

An LSTM (long short-term memory) based model is especially suitable for this task as it is structured to use historical information to predict the next value in the sequence. Our architecture consists of three subnetworks, each of which is a sequence-to-sequence model. These three subnetworks generate the pitch, duration, and lyrics for each note, and jointly learn the structure of Chinese popular music.

Choi, Fazekas, and Sandler (2016) use text-based LSTM for automatic music composition, Potash, Romanov, and Rumshisky (2015) demonstrate the effectiveness of LSTM on rap lyrics generation, and Watanabe et al. (2018) propose an RNN-based lyrics language model conditioned on melodies of Japanese songs. Bao et al. (2018) propose a sequence-to-sequence neural network model that composes melody from lyrics. However, to the best of our knowledge, *iComposer* is the first songwriting system that utilizes a sequence-to-sequence model in generating both melody and Chinese lyrics that match each other perfectly.

In addition to self-evaluation, we designed an experiment to evaluate the quality of the generated songs. Thirty subjects were asked to subjectively rate the aesthetic value of 10 selections, a mixture of original songs and computer-generated songs. The experimental results indicate that *iComposer* composes compelling songs that are quite similar to those composed by humans, and are much better than those generated by the baseline method.

2 Methodology

In this section, we briefly introduce our data gathering and pre-processing techniques, and then de-

Proceedings of NAACL-HLT 2019: Demonstrations, pages 84–88
Minneapolis, Minnesota, June 2 - June 7, 2019. ©2019 Association for Computational Linguistics

scribe the proposed network architecture and provide a system overview.

2.1 Dataset

For the purpose of this study, music sheets with vocal lines and their accompanying lyrics are necessary. Moreover, files with a single instrument corresponding to the melody are favored for better performance in the LSTM model. However, as far as we know there is no such dataset available, and most state-of-the-art melody extraction tools are still unsatisfactory.

We collected 1000 Chinese popular music pieces in MIDI format and extracted feature information using `pretty_midi`, a Python module for creating, manipulating, and analyzing MIDI files (Raffel and Ellis, 2014). Musical notes are represented by MIDI note numbers from 0 to 127, where 60 is defined as middle C. Note durations are represented by numbers in the range from 0.1 to 3.0 seconds.

We then recruited 20 people with at least five years of experience playing instruments to isolate the main melodies from polyphonic music and align the lyrics to their corresponding notes, as shown in Figure 1. The dataset consists of approximately 300,000 character-note pairs, of which we partitioned 80% as the training set and used the rest for testing. Note that the correspondence between notes and characters is not always one-to-one. A single sung character can be composed of multiple notes (i.e. one-to-many alignment).

```
1  我  以  為  要  是  唱  得  用  心  良  苦
2  74  76  78  76  74  73  69  74  73  74  69
3  妳  總  會  對  我  多  點  在  乎
4  74  73  74  69  74  74  73  74  76
5  我  以  為  雖  然  愛  情
6  74  76  78  76  74  73  69

1  我  以  為  要  是  唱  得  用  心  良  苦
2  0.3 0.3 0.6 0.3 0.3 0.6 0.6 0.6 0.3 0.3 1.2
3  妳  總  會  對  我  多  點  在  乎
4  0.3 0.3 0.6 0.3 0.3 0.6 0.6 0.6 0.3
5  我  以  為  雖  然  愛  情
6  0.3 0.3 0.6 0.3 0.3 0.6 0.6
```

Figure 1: Results of character-note alignment . Every character is bound to its corresponding note number and note duration.

2.2 Network Architecture

LSTM networks, introduced by Hochreiter and Schmidhuber (1997), have been shown effective for a wide variety of sequence-based tasks, including machine translation and speech recognition. They consist of a chain of memory cells that store state through multiple time steps to mitigate the vanishing gradient problem of recurrent neural networks.

The neural network proposed in this paper is a sequence-to-sequence model with a single layer and 100 nodes in both the encoder and decoder LSTM. Since music and lyrics both can be represented as a sequence of events, the generating process can be thought of as estimating the conditional probability

$$p(y_1, ..., y_n | x_1, ..., x_m) = \prod_{t=1}^{n} p(y_t | v, y_1, ..., y_{t-1})$$

where $x_1, ..., x_m$ is the input sequence, $y_1, ..., y_n$ is the output sequence, and v is the fixed-dimensional representation of the input sequence.

All the code for this system was written in Python using Pytorch as a backend, and was trained using stochastic gradient descent (batch size = 4), Adam optimization, and a learning rate of 0.001. The initial weights were randomly initialized with a range between -0.1 and 0.1.

2.2.1 Melody Generation

The melody is generated using two sequence-to-sequence models. The first predicts the note number, and the second predicts the note duration. As both models take the same text as input, it makes no difference which is run first. Once the pitch and duration of the notes are generated, we synthesize the data as audio using `pretty_midi`.

2.2.2 Lyrics Generation

In contrast to the melody generation process mentioned above, generating lyrics requires only one sequence-to-sequence model. We first extract note numbers from the given MIDI file, and then feed a sequence of pitches into the LSTM encoder. Then lyrics are automatically generated by the LSTM decoder.

3 Evaluation

In this section, we illustrate the behavior of the proposed system with an analysis of some generated lyrics and melodies. After this, we provide and discuss details about the subjective test.

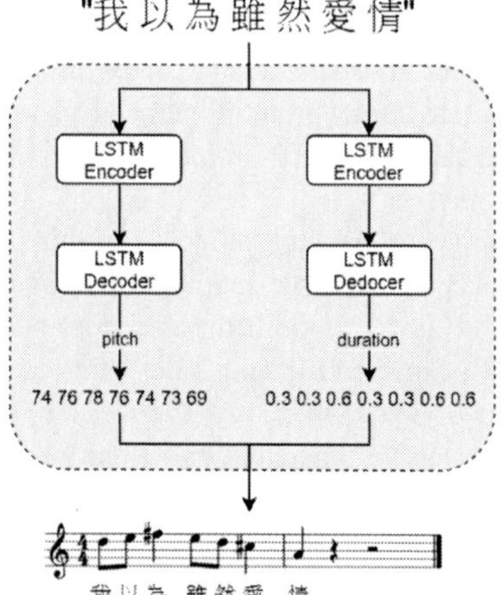

Figure 2: Melody generation model. Take the lyrics – "I thought that although love..." in Chinese as an example.

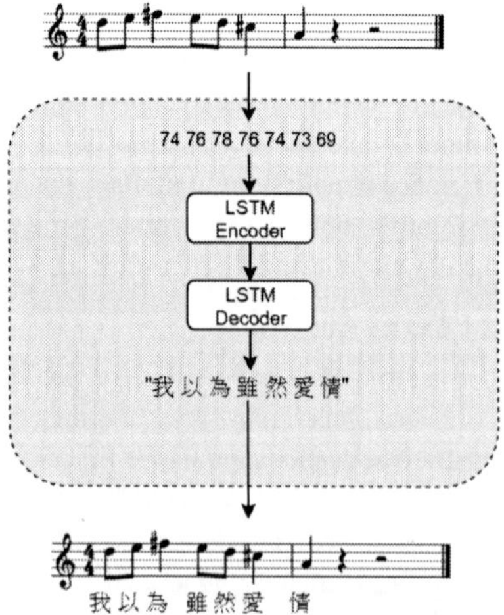

Figure 3: Lyrics generation model. Take the lyrics – "I thought that although love..." in Chinese as an example.

3.1 Analysis

The quality of the generated lyrics can be evaluated based on the variety of words. Here, we focus on this trait to show our model is learning and improving in a general sense.

According to our statistics on all the generated lyrics, only 1154 words are being used in epoch 10. In epoch 50, the variety of words increases to 1386. Finally, in epoch 100, there are 1646 different words in total. As the number of epoch increases, we could consistently see a noticeable improvement in lyrics.

Figure 4 presents some examples of generated lyrics from a certain melody. We can see that many words are repeated in the sequence in epoch 10. However, after epochs of training, the variety of words become greater. In epoch 100, there is no adjacent repeated words occur.

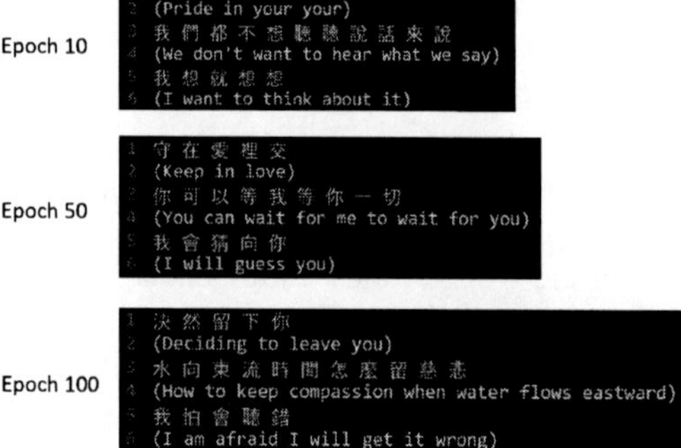

Figure 4: Lyrics generated from the same melody at different epochs. (Sentences in the parentheses are the English translation generated by Google Translation.)

3.2 Subjective Test

Since it is challenging to objectively evaluate the quality of songs, we evaluate the success of *iComposer* with experiments conducted using 30 human participants. All the subjects were college students aged 18 to 25, as the primary consumers of popular music are in this age group. In addition, we required our subjects to have as least five years of instrument playing or songwriting experience to ensure the reliability of our survey feedback.

The questionnaire contained 10 question groups, each with 3 melody clips or 3 sets of lyrics generated by either humans, *iComposer*, or the baseline model. These three types of songs are arranged in random order, and each is approximately 15 seconds in length. None of the thirty chosen melodies and lyrics appeared in the training set, and were thus unseen to the model. In each case, an attempt was made to find less commonly known songs, so that the generated melodies and lyrics could be more fairly compared to the original ones.

For our baseline method, random notes were selected from MIDI note numbers 60–80, as pitch appears more frequently in this range according to the note distribution chart of our dataset shown in Figure 5 . The randomly-generated lyrics were chosen from 1000 most frequently used words in the dataset.

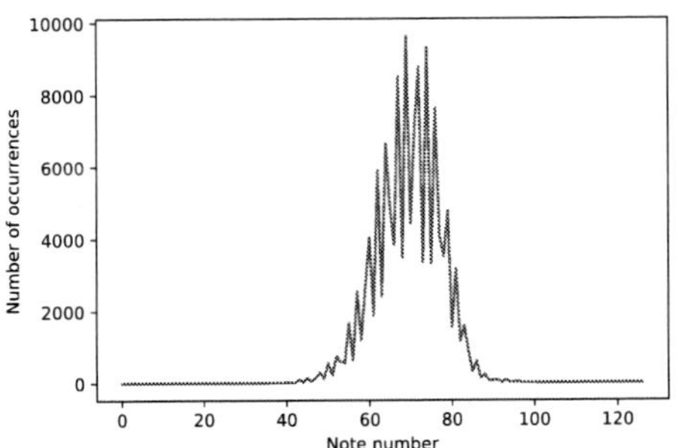

Figure 5: Frequency distribution of notes in the dataset

Survey participants were asked to listen to a mixture of melodies and lyrics generated by humans, *iComposer*, and our baseline model. It was not until the completion of the experiment that subjects were informed that some selections were computer-generated. During the experiment, subjects were asked to subjectively rate the melodies and lyrics from 1 to 10 in terms of the following standards (larger scores indicate better quality) :

- **Melody**
  How smooth are the melodies?

- **Lyrics**
  How meaningful are the lyrics?

- **Overall**
  How well do the melodies fit with the lyrics?

Table 1: Subjective Test Results

Model	Melody	Lyrics	Overall
baseline	3.12	2.43	3.24
iComposer	6.23	6.38	5.72
human	7.55	6.90	7.69

Table 1 shows the average responses to each question on the questionnaire mentioned above. According to the results, *iComposer* outperforms the baseline model in all three metrics, indicating its ability to generate songs in a more natural way. Moreover, melodies and lyrics generated by *iComposer* are rated slightly lower than human creations, which further suggests its effectiveness in songwriting. We can also observe from Table 1 that subjects give significantly lower scores to baseline model on **Lyrics** metrics. This may be due to the obvious grammatical errors the model made that make the rest two look a lot better. In contrast, an unexpected melody sometimes still demonstrate an acceptable level of melodic pleasantness and singability. Therefore, the gap between random-generated melody and the one created by *iComposer* is not that huge.

We also provide the average score of every question groups rated by 30 subjects. As shown in Figure 6 our model is capable of creating songs that are close to human creations in most cases. The model even produces better lyrics in lyrics set number 1 and 5.

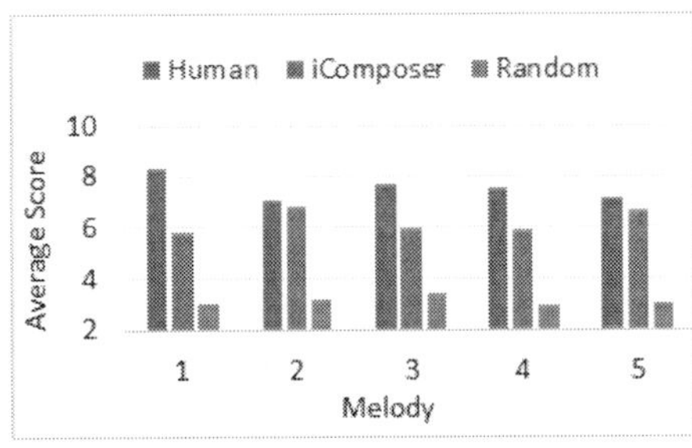

(a) Average score of each melody

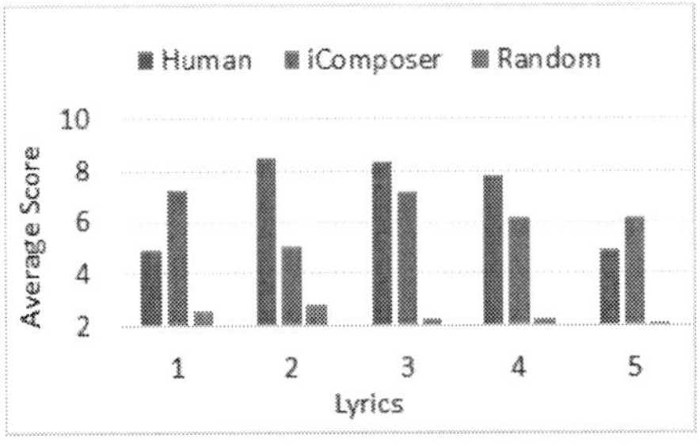

(b) Average score of each lyrics segment

Figure 6: Average aesthetic score of 15 melody clips and 15 sets of lyrics as rated by 30 human participants

4 Discussion

Our goal in this preliminary study is to build an artificial artist. The survey feedback illustrates that *iComposer* is promising.

Learning the structure of Chinese popular music is merely our first attempt: there are still a multitude of related issues that merit further exploration. For example, in Chinese the same syllable can be pronounced in four different tones: high, rising, rising then falling, and falling. Therefore, we could rate the fluidity of a song taking into account its conformity between flowing pitches and tones. Another novel task that interests us is the distinction between verse and chorus, namely, what particular features distinguish between verse and chorus. Taking these issues into account would dramatically improve our current work.

5 User Interface

iComposer is accessible via a web interface that allows users either to enter text data or to upload MIDI files. Once the text or melody has been given, users click the submit button to automatically compose songs.

Figure 7: A web interface that allows users either to enter text data or to upload MIDI files.

After submission, users are directed to the music player interface. The lyrics shown on the page scroll down automatically in sync to the music. The system would play the music and also highlight the lyrics being sung. If users want to save the song, *iComposer* provides the songs in MIDI format for downloading.

Figure 8: Music player interface. It would play the music and highlight the lyrics being sung.

Our *iComposer* interface is accessible at: `http://ckip.iis.sinica.edu.tw/service/iComposer`

The demonstration video is posted on youtube at: `https://www.youtube.com/watch?v=Gstzqls2f4A`

The source code is available at: `https://github.com/hhpslily/iComposer`

References

Hangbo Bao, Shaohan Huang, Furu Wei, Lei Cui, Yu Wu, Chuanqi Tan, Songhao Piao, and Ming Zhou. 2018. Neural melody composition from lyrics. In *arXiv preprint arXiv:1809.04318*.

Keunwoo Choi, George Fazekas, and Mark Sandler. 2016. Text-based lstm networks for automatic music composition. In *Proceedings of the 1st Conference on Computer Simulation of Musical Creativity*.

Sepp Hochreiter and Jürgen Schmidhuber. 1997. Long short-term memory. *Neural Computation*, 9(8):1735–1780.

Peter Potash, Alexey Romanov, and Anna Rumshisky. 2015. Ghost-writer: Using an lstm for automatic rap lyric generation. In *Proceedings of the 2015 Conference on Empirical Methods in Natural Language Processing*, pages 1919–1924.

Colin Raffel and Daniel P. W. Ellis. 2014. Intuitive analysis, creation and manipulation of midi data with `pretty_midi`. In *Proceedings of the 15th International Society for Music Information Retrieval Conference Late Breaking and Demo Papers*, pages 84–93.

Kento Watanabe, Yuichiroh Matsubayashi, Satoru Fukayama, Masataka Goto, Kentaro Inui, and Tomoyasu Nakano. 2018. A melody-conditioned lyrics language model. In *Proceedings of the 2018 Conference of the North American Chapter of the Association for Computational Linguistics: Human Language Technologies*.

Plan, Write, and Revise: an Interactive System
for Open-Domain Story Generation

Seraphina Goldfarb-Tarrant[12], Haining Feng[1], Nanyun Peng[1]
[1] Information Sciences Institute, University of Southern California
[2] University of Washington
`serif@uw.edu, haining@usc.edu, npeng@isi.edu`

Abstract

Story composition is a challenging problem for machines and even for humans. We present a neural narrative generation system that interacts with humans to generate stories. Our system has different levels of human interaction, which enables us to understand at what stage of story-writing human collaboration is most productive, both to improving story quality and human engagement in the writing process. We compare different varieties of interaction in *story-writing*, *story-planning*, and *diversity controls* under time constraints, and show that increased types of human collaboration at both planning and writing stages results in a 10-50% improvement in story quality as compared to less interactive baselines. We also show an accompanying increase in user engagement and satisfaction with stories as compared to our own less interactive systems and to previous turn-taking approaches to interaction. Finally, we find that humans tasked with collaboratively improving a particular characteristic of a story are in fact able to do so, which has implications for future uses of human-in-the-loop systems.

1 Introduction

Collaborative human-machine story-writing has had a recent resurgence of attention from the research community (Roemmele and Swanson., 2017; Clark and Smith, 2018). It represents a frontier for AI research; as a research community we have developed convincing NLP systems for some generative tasks like machine translation, but lag behind in creative areas like open-domain storytelling. Collaborative open-domain storytelling incorporates human interactivity for one of two aims: to improve human creativity via the aid of a machine, or to improve machine quality via the aid of a human. Previously existing approaches treat the former aim, and have shown that storytelling systems are not yet developed enough to help human writers. We attempt the latter, with the goal of investigating at what stage human collaboration is most helpful.

Swanson and Gordon (2009) use an information retrieval based system to write by alternating turns between a human and their system. Clark and Smith (2018) use a similar turn-taking approach to interactivity, but employ a neural model for generation and allow the user to edit the generated sentence before accepting it. They find that users prefer a full-sentence collaborative setup (vs. shorter fragments) but are mixed with regard to the system-driven approach to interaction. Roemmele and Swanson. (2017) experiment with a user-driven setup, where the machine doesn't generate until the user requests it to, and then the user can edit or delete at will. They leverage user-acceptance or rejection of suggestions as a tool for understanding the characteristics of a helpful generation. All of these systems involve the user in the *story-writing* process, but lack user involvement in the *story-planning* process, and so they lean on the user's ability to knit a coherent overall story together out of locally related sentences. They also do not allow a user to control the novelty or "unexpectedness" of the generations, which Clark and Smith (2018) find to be a weakness. Nor do they enable iteration; a user cannot revise earlier sentences and have the system update later generations. We develop a system[1] that allows a user to interact in all of these ways that were limitations in previous systems; it enables involvement in planning, editing, iterative revising, and control of novelty. We conduct experiments to understand which types of interaction are most effective for improving stories and for making users satisfied and engaged.

We have two main interfaces that enable hu-

---

[1] The live demo is at `http://cwc-story.isi.edu`, with a video at `https://youtu.be/-hGd2399dnA`. Code and models are available at `https://github.com/seraphinatarrant/plan-write-revise`.

89

Proceedings of NAACL-HLT 2019: Demonstrations, pages 89–97
Minneapolis, Minnesota, June 2 - June 7, 2019. ©2019 Association for Computational Linguistics

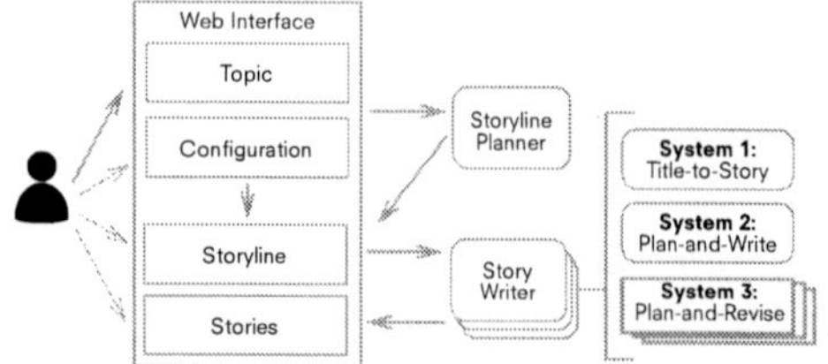

Figure 1: Diagram of human-computer interaction mediated by the the demo system. The dotted arrows represent optional interactions that the user can take. Depending on the set-up, the user may choose to interact with one or all story models.

man interaction with the computer. There is *cross-model* interaction, where the machine does all the composition work, and displays three different versions of a story written by three distinct models for a human to compare. The user guides generation by providing a topic for story-writing and by tweaking decoding parameters to control novelty, or *diversity*. The second interface is *intra-model* interaction, where a human can select the model to interact with (potentially after having chosen it via *cross-model*), and can collaborate at all stages to jointly create better stories. The full range of interactions available to a user is: select a model, provide a topic, change diversity of content, collaborate on the planning for the story, and collaborate on the story sentences. It is entirely user-driven, as the users control how much is their own work and how much is the machine's at every stage. It supports revision; a user can modify an earlier part of a written story or of the story plan at any point, and observe how this affects later generations.

2 System Description

2.1 System Overview

Figure 1 shows a diagram of the interaction system. The dotted arrows represent optional user interactions.

Cross-model mode requires the user to enter a *topic*, such as "the not so haunted house", and can optionally vary the *diversity* used in the STORYLINE PLANNER or the STORY WRITER. *Diversity* numbers correspond directly to softmax temperatures, which we restrict to a reasonable range, determined empirically. The settings are sent to the STORYLINE PLANNER module, which generates a storyline for the story in the form of a sequence of phrases as per the method of Yao et al. (2019). Everything is then sent to the STORY WRITER,

which will return three stories.

Intra-model mode enables advanced interactions with one story system of the user's choice. The STORYLINE PLANNER returns either one storyline phrase or many, and composes the final storyline out of the combination of phrases the system generated, the user has written, and edits the user has made. These are sent to the STORY WRITER, which returns either a single sentence or a full story as per user's request. The process is flexible and iterative. The user can choose how much or little content they want to provide, edit, or re-generate, and they can return to any step at any time until they decide they are done.

Pre-/Post-processing and OOV handling To enable interactive flexibility, the system must handle open-domain user input. User input is lowercased and tokenized to match the model training data via spaCy[2]. Model output is naively detokenized via Moses (Koehn et al., 2007) based on feedback from users that this was more natural. User input OOV handling is done via WordNet (Miller, 1995) by recursively searching for hypernyms and hyponyms (in that order) until either an in-vocabulary word is found or until a maximum distance from the initial word is reached.[3] We additionally experimented with using cosine similarity to GloVe vectors (Pennington et al., 2014), but found that to be slower and not qualitatively better for this domain.

2.2 Web Interface

Figure 2 shows screenshots for both the *cross-model* and *intra-model* modes of interaction. Figure 2a shows that the *cross-model* mode makes clear the differences between different model generations for the same topic. Figure 2b shows the variety of interactions a user can take in *intra-model* interaction, and is annotated with an example-in-action. User inserted text is underlined in blue, generated text that has been removed by the user is in grey strike-through. The *refresh* symbol marks areas that the user re-generated to get a different sentence (presumably after being unhappy with the first result). As can be seen in this example, minor user involvement can result in a significantly better story.

---

[2]`spacy.io`
[3]*distance* is difference og levels in the WordNet hierarchy, and was set empirically to 10.

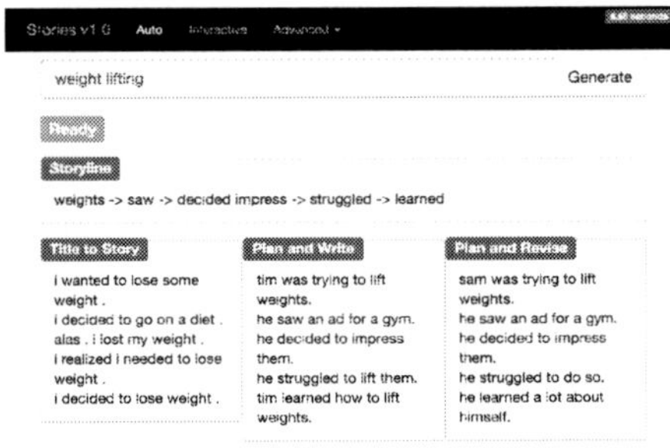

(a) cross-model interaction, comparing three models with advanced options to alter the storyline and story diversities.

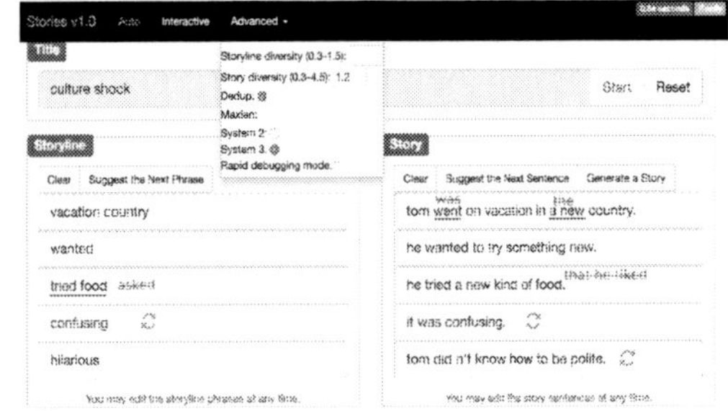

(b) intra-model interaction, showing advanced options and annotated with user interactions from an example study.

Figure 2: Screenshots of the demo user interface

2.3 Model Design

All models for both the STORYLINE PLANNER and STORY WRITER modules are conditional language models implemented with LSTMs based on Merity et al. (2018). These are 3-stacked LSTMs that include weight-dropping, weight-tying, variable length back propagation with learning rate adjustment, and Averaged Stochastic Gradient Descent (ASGD). They are trained on the ROC dataset (Mostafazadeh et al., 2016), which after lowercasing and tokenization has a vocabulary of 38k. Storyline Phrases are extracted as in Yao et al. (2019) via the RAKE algorithm (Rose et al., 2010) which results in a slightly smaller Storyline vocabulary of 31k. The STORYLINE PLANNER does decoding via sampling to encourage creative exploration. The STORY WRITER has an option to use one or all three systems, all of which decode via beamsearch and are detailed below.

The *Title-to-Story* system is a baseline, which generates directly from topic.

The *Plan-and-Write* system adopts the static model in Yao et al. (2019) to use the storyline to supervise story-writing.

Plan-and-Revise is a new system that combines the strengths of Yao et al. (2019) and Holtzman et al. (2018). It supplements the Plan-and-Write model by training two discriminators on the ROC data and using them to re-rank the LSTM generations to prefer increased *creativity* and *relevance*.[4] Thus the decoding objective of this system becomes $f_\lambda(x, y) = log(P_{lm}(y|x)) + \sum_k \lambda_k s_k(x, y)$ where P_{lm} is the conditional language model probability of the LSTM, s_k is the discriminator scoring function, and λ_k is the

learned weight of that discriminator. At each timestep all live beam hypotheses are scored and re-ranked. Discriminator weights are learnt by minimizing Mean Squared Error on the difference between the scores of gold standard and generated story sentences.

3 Experiments

We experiment with six types of interaction: five variations created by restricting different capabilities of our system, and a sixth turn-taking baseline that mimics the interaction of the previous work (Clark and Smith, 2018; Swanson and Gordon, 2009). We choose our experiments to address the research questions: What type of interaction is most engaging? Which type results in the best stories? Can a human tasked with correcting for certain weaknesses of a model successfully do so? The variations on interactions that we tested are:

1. Machine only: no human-in-loop.
2. Diversity only: user can compare and select models but only diversity is modifiable.
3. Storyline only: user collaborates on storyline but not story.
4. Story only: user collaborates on story but not storyline.
5. All: user can modify everything.
6. Turn-taking: user and machine take turns writing a sentence each (user starts). user can edit the machine-generations, but once they move on to later sentences, previous sentences are read-only.[5]

We expand experiment 5 to answer the question of whether a human-in-the-loop interactive sys-

---

[4]Holtzman et al. (2018) use four discriminators, but based on ablation testing we determined these two to perform best on our dataset and for our task.

[5]This as closely matches the previous work as possible with our user interface. This model does not use a storyline.

tem can address specific shortcomings of generated stories. We identify three types of weaknesses common to generation systems – *Creativity*, *Relevance*, and *Causal & Temporal Coherence*, and conduct experiments where the human is instructed to focus on improving specifically one of them. The targeted human improvement areas intentionally match the *Plan-and-Revise* discriminators, so that, if successful, the "human discriminator" data can assist in training the machine discriminators. All experiments (save experiment 2, which lets the user pick between models) use the *Plan-and-Revise* system.

3.1 Details

We recruit 30 Mechanical Turk workers per experiment (270 unique workers total) to complete story writing tasks with the system.[6] We constrain them to ten minutes of work (five for writing and five for a survey) and provide them with a fixed *topic* to control this factor across experiments. They co-create a story and complete a questionnaire which asks them to self-report on their engagement, satisfaction, and perception of story quality.[7] For the additional focused error-correction experiments, we instruct Turkers to try to improve the machine-generated stories with regard to the given aspect, under the same time constraints. As an incentive, they are given a small bonus if they are later judged to have succeeded.

We then ask a separate set of Turkers to rate the stories for overall quality and the three improvement areas. All ratings are on a five-point scale. We collect two ratings per story, and throw out ratings that disagree by more than 2 points. A total of 11% of ratings were thrown out, leaving four metrics across 241 stories for analysis.

4 Results

User Engagement Self-reported scores are relatively high across the board, as can be seen in Table 1, with the majority of users in all experiments saying they would like to use the system again. The lower scores in the *Diversity only* and *Storyline only* experiments are elucidated by qualitative comments from users of frustration at the inability to sufficiently control the generations with influence over only those tools. *Storyline only* is low-

---

Experiment	E	Q	S	Use Again
Diversity only	3.77	2.90	3.27	1.40
Storyline only	4.04	3.36	3.72	1.27
Story only	**4.50**	3.17	3.60	1.60
All	4.41	3.55	3.76	1.55
All + Creative	4.00	3.27	3.70	**1.70**
All + Relevant	4.20	3.47	3.83	1.57
All + C-T	4.30	**3.77**	**4.30**	1.53
Turn-taking	4.31	3.38	3.66	1.52

Table 1: User self-reported scores, from 1-5. E: Entertainment value, Q: Quality of Story, S: Satisfaction with Story. Note that the final column *Use Again* is based on converting "no" to 0, "conditional" to 1, and "yes" to 2.

Experiment	Overall	Creative	Relevant	C-T
Machine	2.34	2.68	2.46	2.54
Diversity only	2.50	2.96	2.75	2.81
Storyline only	3.21	3.27	3.88	3.65
Story only	3.70*	**4.04***	3.96*	**4.24***
All	3.54	3.62	3.93*	3.83
All + Creative	**3.73***	3.96*	3.98*	3.93*
All + Relevant	3.53*	3.52	4.05	3.91*
All + C-T	3.62*	3.88*	4.00*	3.98*
Turn-taking	3.55*	3.68	**4.27***	3.81

Table 2: Results for all experiments, from 1-5. Best scores per metric are bolded, scores not significantly different ($\alpha = 0.1$, per Wilcoxon Signed-Rank Test) are starred. C-T stands for Causal-Temporal Coherence, the + experiments are the extensions where the user focuses on improving a particular quality.

est for *Use Again*, which can be explained by the model behavior when dealing with unlikely storyline phrases. Usually, the most probable generated story will contain all storyline phrases (exact or similar embeddings) in order, but there is no mechanism that strictly enforces this. When a storyline phrase is uncommon, the story model will often ignore it. Many users expressed frustration at the irregularity of their ability to guide the model when collaborating on the storyline, for this reason.

Users were engaged by collaboration; all experiments received high scores on being entertaining, with the collaborative experiments rated more highly than *Diversity only*. The pattern is repeated for the other scores, with users being more satisfied and feeling their stories to be higher quality for all the more interactive experiments. The *Turn-taking* baseline fits into this pattern; users prefer it more than the less interactive *Diversity only* and *Storyline only*, but often (though not always) less than the more interactive *Story only, All, All+* experiments. Interestingly, user perception of the quality of their stories does not align well with independent rankings. Self-reported quality is low in the *Story only* experiment, which contrasts with it being highest rated independently (as discussed below). Self-reported scores also suggest that users judge their stories to be much better when they have been focusing on causal-temporal coherence, though this focus carries over to a smaller improvement in independent rankings. While it is clear that additional interactivity is a good idea, the disjunct between user perception of their writing and reader perception under different experiment conditions is worthwhile to consider for future interactive systems.

Story Quality As shown in Table 2, human involvement of *any kind* under tight constraints helps story quality across all metrics, with mostly better results the more collaboration is allowed. The exception to this trend is *Story only* collaboration, which performs best or close to best across the board. This was unexpected; it is possible that these users benefited from having to learn to control only *one* model, instead of both, given the limited time. It is also possible that being forced to be reliant on system storylines made these users more creative.

Turn-taking Baseline The turn-taking baseline performs comparably in overall quality and relevance to other equally interactive experiments (*Story only, All, All+*). It achieves highest scores in relevance, though the top five systems for relevance are not statistically significantly different. It is outperformed on creativity and causal-temporal coherence by the strong *Story only* variation, as well as the *All, All+* systems. This suggests that local sentence-level editing is sufficient to keep a story on topic and to write well, but that creativity and causal-temporal coherence require some degree of global cohesion that is assisted by iterative editing. The same observation as to the strength of *Story only* over *All* applies here as well; turn-taking is the least complex of the interactive systems, and may have boosted performance from being simpler since time was constrained and users used the system only once. Thus a turn-based system is a good choice for a scenario where users use a system infrequently or only once, but the comparative performance may decrease in future experiments with more relaxed time constraints or where users use the system repeatedly.

Targeted Improvements The results within the *All* and *All +* setups confirm that stories can be improved with respect to a particular metric. The diagonal of strong scores displays this trend, where the creativity-focused experiment has high creativity, etc. An interesting side effect to note is that focusing on *anything* tends to produce better stories, reflected by higher overall ratings. *All + Relevance* is an exception which does not help creativity or overall (perhaps because relevance instantly becomes very high as soon a human is involved), but apart from that *All +* experiments are better across all metrics than *All*. This could mean a few things: that when a user improves a story in one aspect, they improve it along the other axes, or that users reading stories have trouble rating aspects entirely independently.

5   Conclusions and Future Work

We have shown that all levels of human-computer collaboration improve story quality across all metrics, compared to a baseline computer-only story generation system. We have also shown that flexible interaction, which allows the user to return to edit earlier text, improves the specific metrics of creativity and causal-temporal coherence above previous rigid turn-taking approaches. We find that, as well as improving story quality, more interaction makes users more engaged and likely to use the system again. Users tasked with collaborating to improve a specific story quality were able to do so, as judged by independent readers.

As the demo system has successfully used an ensemble of collaborative discriminators to improve the same qualities that untrained human users were able to improve even further, this suggests promising future research into human-collaborative stories as training data for new discriminators. It could be used both to strengthen existing discriminators and to develop novel ones, since discriminators are extensible to arbitrarily many story aspects.

Acknowledgments

We thank the anonymous reviewers for their feedback, as well as the members of the PLUS lab for their thoughts and iterative testing. This work is supported by Contract W911NF-15- 1-0543 with the US Defense Advanced Research Projects Agency (DARPA).

References

Anne Spencer Ross Chenhao Tan Yangfeng Ji Clark, Elizabeth and Noah A. Smith. 2018. Creative writing with a machine in the loop: Case studies on slogans and stories. In *23rd International Conference on Intelligent User Interfaces (IUI)*.

Ari Holtzman, Jan Buys, Maxwell Forbes, Antoine Bosselut, David Golub, and Yejin Choi. 2018. Learning to write with cooperative discriminators. In *Proceedings of ACL*.

Philipp Koehn, Hieu Hoang, Alexandra Birch, Chris Callison-Burch, Marcello Federico, Nicola Bertoldi, Brooke Cowan, Wade Shen, Christine Moran, Richard Zens, et al. 2007. Moses: Open source toolkit for statistical machine translation. In *Proceedings of the 45th annual meeting of the ACL on interactive poster and demonstration sessions*, pages 177–180. Association for Computational Linguistics.

Stephen Merity, Nitish Shirish Keskar, and Richard Socher. 2018. Regularizing and optimizing lstm language models. In *Proceedings of the Sixth International Conference on Learning Representations (ICLR)*.

George A. Miller. 1995. Wordnet: A lexical database for english. In *Communications of the ACM Vol. 38*.

Nasrin Mostafazadeh, Nathanael Chambers, Xiaodong He, Devi Parikh, Dhruv Batra, Lucy Vanderwende, Pushmeet Kohli, and James Allen. 2016. A corpus and cloze evaluation for deeper understanding of commonsense stories. In *Proceedings of NAACL-HLT*, pages 839–849.

Jeffrey Pennington, Richard Socher, and Christopher D. Manning. 2014. Glove: Global vectors for word representation. In *Empirical Methods in Natural Language Processing (EMNLP)*, pages 1532–1543.

Andrew S. Gordon Roemmele, Melissa and Reid Swanson. 2017. Evaluating story generation systems using automated linguistic analyses. In *SIGKDD 2017 Workshop on Machine Learning for Creativity*.

Stuart Rose, Dave Engel, Nick Cramer, and Wendy Cowley. 2010. Automatic keyword extraction from individual documents. In *Text Mining: Applications and Theory*.

Reid Swanson and Andrew S. Gordon. 2009. Say anything: A demonstration of open domain interactive digital storytelling. In *Joint International Conference on Interactive Digital Storytelling*.

Lili Yao, Nanyun Peng, Weischedel Ralph, Kevin Knight, Dongyan Zhao, and Rui Yan. 2019. Plan-and-write: Towards better automatic storytelling. In *Proceedings of the thirty-third AAAI Conference on Artificial Intelligence (AAAI)*.

A Demo Video

The three-minute video demonstrating the interaction capabilities of the system can be viewed at `https://youtu.be/-hGd2399dnA`. (Same video as linked in the paper footnote).

B Training and Decoding Parameters

B.1 Decoding

Default diversity (Softmax Temperature) for Storyline Planner is *0.5*, for Story Writer it is *None* (as beamsearch is used an thus can have but does not require a temperature). Beam size for all Story Writer models is *5*. Additionally, Storyline Phrases are constrained to be unique (unless a user duplicates them), and Beamsearch is not normalized by length (both choices determined empirically).

B.2 Training

We follow the parameters used in Yao et al. (2019) and Merity et al. (2018).

Parameter	Storyline Model	Story Models
Embedding Dim	500	1000
Hidden Layer Dim	1000	1500
Input Embedding Dropout	0.4	0.2
Hidden Layer Dropout	0.1	01
Batch Size	20	20
BPTT	20	75
Learning Rate	10	10
Vocabulary size	31,382	37,857
Total Model Parameters	32,489,878	80,927,858
Epochs	50	120

Table 3: Training parameters for models used in demo.

C User Study

C.1 Questionnaire

Post Story Generation Questionnaire
How satisfied are you with the final story?
What do you think is the overall quality of the final story?
Was the process entertaining?
Would you use the system again?

Table 4: Questionnaire for user self-reporting, range 1 to 5 (1 low).

C.2 Mechanical Turk Materials

Following are examples of the materials used in doing Mechanical Turk User Studies. Figure 3 is an example of the *All + Creative* focused experiment for *story-writing*. The instructions per experiment differ across all, but the template is the same. Figure 4 is the survey for ranking stories across various metrics. This remains constant save that story order was shuffled every time to control for any effects of the order a story was read in.

Figure 3: Template & Instructions for Writing Stories in the *All + Creative* experiment.

Instructions

Hello! We are academic researchers studying different methods of story writing.

Please take a few minutes to read the instructions for our website and get used to the interface. It should be quick and will help you get a quality bonus.

The objective is for you to take about five minutes and co-write a story with our system and try to improve the Creativity of the story. Our system works by generating a storyline, and then a story based on it, and you collaborate with it.

If your final story is judged to have improved Creativity, you will get a bonus.

Note:

- **We need unique Workers, so you are only allowed to do one of these.** Please do not auto-accept the next one.
- Only **five** sentences. Please do collaborate as well - if you just write a story yourself we will know and reject the HIT.

This is an example of a story:

bobby and his friends were fascinated by the dark.
they dared each other to get close to a haunted house.
bobby heard a noise coming from the window.
he ran to the house to see what it was.
it was a scary, scary house.

Steps:

1. You will be given a **Title**
2. Go to our website http://cwc-story.isi.edu:5002/interactive.html (http://cwc-story.isi.edu:5002/interactive.html), enter the title into the text box, and click **Start.**
3. Now in the **Storyline** section you can click *Suggest the Next Phrase* or enter your own.
4. A storyline phrase is one or more words that help define the content of the corresponding sentence. For example, "apprehensive" or "fun time" or "charged sentenced prison".
5. Once you have five phrases, you can go to the **Story** section and click *Suggest the Next Sentence*, or enter your own
6. In both sections, you can switch between writing and suggesting, and you can delete, make edits to your work or the computer's work, or replace or re-suggest at any time. Do this as many times as you want.
7. *Clear* clears the entire storyline or story section.
8. If you want, under the **Advanced** menu, you can change **storyline diversity** and **story diversity** to make the system more creative. After you do, click **Reset**, enter the title, and **Start** again.
9. Take *5 minutes* and try to get the best story you can. Change any Advanced options or storyline or story phrases, but keep the *same* title.
10. When you're done, paste the sentences of your choice into the text box below, and then answer a few questions about your experience. The questions are required, but you are not judged on your answers, so answer honestly.

Details:

1. **storyline diversity** and **story diversity** both control how creative the system will be. Lower numbers mean it is more conservative, or "normal", and higher numbers mean it is more creative or "experimental". There is some element of randomness, so sometimes you'll get the same result with different numbers, or a different result with the same numbers.
2. When **diversity** is > 1, sometimes the generations can become strange (nonsense, or less than 5 sentences/phrases). Just lower the diversity and try again, or just re-suggest or add your own till it's 5, or edit it and use it as inspiration for your work.
3. Sometimes punctuation or other things come out weird, don't worry about it.
4. If you want the system to do everything for the first round, you can click *Generate a Story* and it will fill everything out so you can start changing.

Rules:

1. Stories will later be judged, and you will receive a **$0.50 bonus** if your story is judged as having improved creativity.
2. We do review **every** HIT, so if you break the rules above or have not actually tried the system, we will reject it.

Title:

${title}

1. Enter the text of your pick for final most Creative story here.

Figure 4: Template & Instructions for Ranking Stories

Survey Instructions

We are a group of researchers conducting research about storytelling.

In this survey, you will be provided with a **title** and **eight stories** about that title.

Please compare and rank them according to the given criteria.

1. Please read all the stories carefully, and give a score to each story based on: **Relevance, Creativity, Overall Quality, and Event Coherence (we will explain these).**
2. Multiple stories **can** receive the same score. However, please do read all the story versions before rating them and consider them in relation to each other.
3. Briefly **explain** why you made the decisions you did for each story. Just basic thoughts or bullet points is fine, but this is required.
4. Don't worry about punctuation and spelling of the stories, those don't matter
5. We do review **every** HIT response, and will reject it if your answers make no sense and you don't give any reasoning.

Explanation of metrics:

- **Relevance:** Is the story relevant to the title, i.e. is it on topic?
- **Creativity:** Is the story unusual and interesting, in either vocabulary or content?
- **Overall Quality:** How good do you think the story is?
- **Event Coherence:** Do the things that happen in the story make sense together and are they in the right order? For example, for the sentences: "the ice cream tasted delicious. she tasted the ice cream" the events make sense, but are in the wrong order and should get a lower rating. For the sentences: "jim's boss yelled at him. jim had a great day" the ordering is fine but the events don't go together. Events that go together and are in the right order should have a higher rating, as in: "jim's boss yelled at him. jim went home exhausted and unhappy."

An Example:

title: *haunted house*

a) bobby and his friends were fascinated by the dark. they dared each other to get close to a haunted house. bobby heard a noise coming from the window. he ran to the house to see what it was. it was a scary, scary house.

Relevance	◯ 1. terrible	◯ 2. bad	◯ 3. neutral	◯ 4. good	◉ 5. great
Creativity	◯ 1. terrible	◯ 2. bad	◯ 3. neutral	◯ 4. good	◉ 5. great
Event Coherence	◯ 1. terrible	◯ 2. bad	◯ 3. neutral	◉ 4. good	◯ 5. great
Overall Quality	◯ 1. terrible	◯ 2. bad	◯ 3. neutral	◉ 4. good	◯ 5. great

Briefly explain why you made your decisions:

The story was on topic, and made sense, and was good, but the last sentence didn't really fit perfectly with earlier events.

LT Expertfinder: An Evaluation Framework
for Expert Finding Methods

Tim Fischer   **Steffen Remus**   **Chris Biemann**

Language Technology Group
Department of Informatics
Universität Hamburg, Germany
`{5fischer,lastname}@informatik.uni-hamburg.de`

Abstract

Expert finding is the task of ranking persons for a predefined topic or search query. Most approaches to this task are evaluated in a supervised fashion, which depends on predefined topics of interest as well as gold standard expert rankings. However, manually ranking experts can be considered highly subjective and small variants in rankings are hardly distinguishable. Particularly for dynamic systems, where topics are not predefined but formulated as a search query, we believe a more informative approach is to perform user studies for directly comparing different methods in the same view. In order to accomplish this in a user-friendly way, we present the LT Expertfinder web application, which is equipped with various query-based expert finding methods that can be easily extended, a detailed expert profile view, detailed evidence in form of relevant documents and statistics, and an evaluation component that allows a qualitative comparison between different rankings.

1 Introduction

Human expertise is one of the noteworthy resources in the world. However, true experts may be rare and their expertise difficult to quantify due to multiple continuously changing factors. The goal of *expert finding* is to rank people regarding their knowledge about a certain topic, which is a challenging, yet rewarding task with many real-world applications. Just to name a few, some applications might be: Companies may require highly trained specialists whose consultancies can be requested for specific problems (Balog et al., 2006), conference organizers may need to assign submissions to reviewers which best match their expertise (Fang and Zhai, 2007), recruiters may search for talented employees and emerging experts in a particular field (Serdyukov et al., 2008).

1.1 Problem statement

While it is common to cast approaches to expert finding in a supervised learning framework, this requires respective datasets, necessarily limited to a narrow set of topics. Some of such datasets are: the enriched versions of DBLP[1] provided by the ArnetMiner project (Tang et al., 2008), used by e.g. Deng et al. (2008); Yang et al. (2009); Moreira et al. (2011), or the W3C Corpus[2] of TREC[3], used by e.g. Balog et al. (2006). Obviously, however, the subjective nature of attributed expertise makes expert ranking quality hard to quantify. A certain value of an evaluation measure based on gold standard dataset comparison with respect to supervised or unsupervised system outputs does not necessarily guarantee a better or worse performance of one system compared to another. Also, depending on the targeted domain, a supervised setting might not be a viable option for evaluation. In real-world settings, where underlying data changes dynamically and expert finding is rather an interactive approach than a one-shot query evaluation, we find it more adequate to facilitate an evaluation procedure based on user studies, where alternative approaches are comparatively judged.

1.2 Motivation & Contribution

In this paper, we address this issue and present the LT Expertfinder web application, which is equipped with several query-based expert finding methods and can be easily extended. A detailed expert profile helps users to eventually select one expert in favor of another. Methodological evidence, in form of relevant documents and various

---

[1] `https://aminer.org/lab-datasets/expertfinding/`

[2] `https://tides.umiacs.umd.edu/webtrec/trecent/parsed_w3c_corpus.html`

[3] TextREtrieval Conference: `https://trec.nist.gov/`

98

Proceedings of NAACL-HLT 2019: Demonstrations, pages 98–104
Minneapolis, Minnesota, June 2 - June 7, 2019. ©2019 Association for Computational Linguistics

statistics, as well as a view of the query-dependent citation graph, is provided. Finally, we added an evaluation component that allows the qualitative comparison between different rankings. To the best of our knowledge, this is the first tool that provides evidences and a direct comparison to multiple expert rankings. We apply our system to the *ACL Anthology Network*[4] in order to find experts on various computational linguistics topics.

2 Related Work

Early expert finding systems relied on manually crafted, and manually queried, databases. Maintaining these databases is obviously a time consuming and complex task on the administrative and user side. Early automatic expert finding systems usually focused on specific domains like email (Campbell et al., 2003) or software documentation (Mockus and Herbsleb, 2002). One of the first approaches that automatically extracts expertise from any kind of document was the P@NOPTIC system by Craswell et al. (2001).

Shared tasks, such as the *Enterprise Track* of TREC (Craswell et al., 2005; Soboroff et al., 2006; Bailey et al., 2007; Balog et al., 2008) resulted in many automatic methods for predefined topics. Those systems can be grouped into four major categories: *a)* generative models (Balog et al., 2006; Fang and Zhai, 2007; Deng et al., 2008), *b)* voting models (Macdonald and Ounis, 2006), *c)* graph-based models (Serdyukov et al., 2008; Campbell et al., 2003; Jurczyk and Agichtein, 2007; Zhang et al., 2007), and *d)* discriminative models (Hashemi et al., 2013). For an extensive survey on expert finding methods, we refer to Lin et al. (2017).

Hawking (2004) highlights the importance of expert profiling mainly because the results should provide more information than simply a ranked list of person names. Balog and De Rijke (2007) emphasizes the importance of the social network, i.e. colleagues and collaborators contribute greatly to the value of an expert.

Thus, systems, such as the ArnetMiner[5] tool (Tang et al., 2008), aim at modeling entire academic social networks by automatically extracting researcher profiles from the Web. Moreover, ArnetMiner models topical aspects of papers, au-

thors, and publication venues. The CareerMap[6] (Wu et al., 2018), which is now a component of ArnetMiner, visualizes a scholar's career trajectory, which is extracted from ArnetMiner's publication database. The CL Scholar[7] system (Singh et al., 2018) mines textual and network information for knowledge graph construction and question answering using natural language or keywords. CSSeer[8] (Chen et al., 2013) is a keyphrase-based recommendation system for expert finding based on the CiteSeerX[9] digital library and Wikipedia. It extracts keyphrases from the title and abstract of documents in CiteSeerX and utilizes this information to infer the author's expertise. The Expert2Bólè system (Yang et al., 2009) features generic expert finding as well as bólè search, which aims at identifying the top supervisors in a given field. The authors argue that generic expert finding methods are insufficient for finding specific experts for different purposes. In their application, bólè search, it is for example more important to find persons who are able to judge and nuture other experts than to assess their own expertise. Hence, generic expert finding methods cannot be applied to this problem.

3 LT Expertfinder

The LT Expertfinder features detailed expert profiles and various expert finding methods in an extendible framework. Moreover, it provides user-friendly evaluation methods: a view of the query-dependent citation graph, an evaluation view combining different results and provenances in form of relevant documents and related statistics.

3.1 Dataset

For the purpose of this paper, we use the *ACL Anthology Network* (AAN, Radev et al., 2013) as our underlying corpus, but note that it can be easily exchanged. The application is not limited to this particular data source. The AAN is based on papers in *ACL*[10] *Anthology* – a digital archive of conference and journal papers about natural language processing and computational linguistics – and provides citation and collaboration information. In its current version from December 2016, the AAN in-

---

[4] http://tangra.cs.yale.edu/newaan/
[5] https://aminer.org/

[6] https://aminer.org/
mostinfluentialscholar/ml
[7] https://github.com/CLScholar
[8] http://csseer.ist.psu.edu/
[9] http://citeseerx.ist.psu.edu
[10] Association of Computational Linguistics

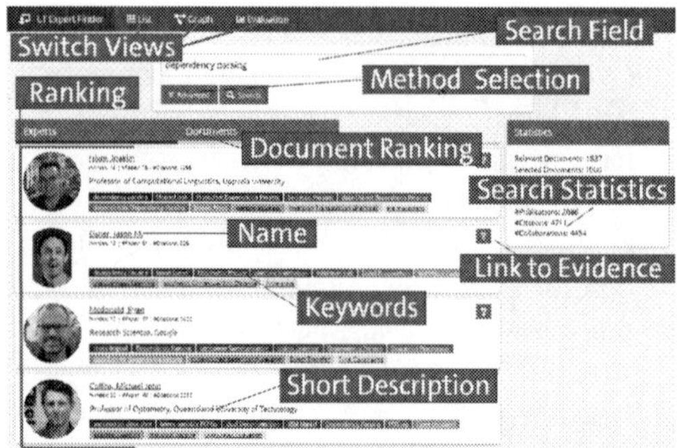

(a) List view: select a ranking method in the 'Advanced' tab, is-sue a search query, and get the results in a list view with concise author information as well as detailed result set statistics.

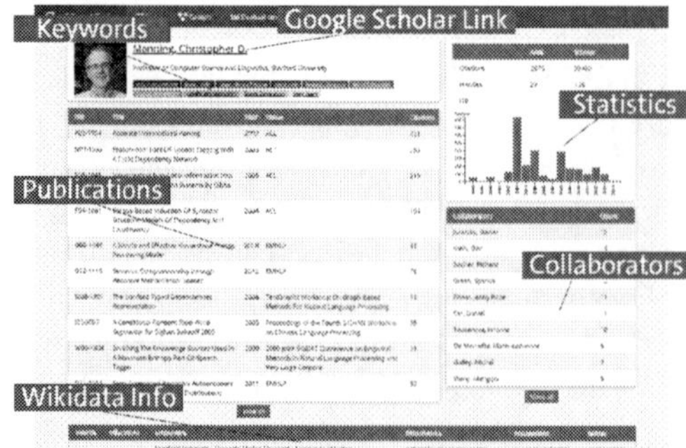

(b) Profile view: list all publications ranked by number of cita-tions, view collaboration information and external information from Wikidata as well as Google Scholar (if available) and link to the respective source pages.

Figure 1: LT Expertfinder Application

cludes more than 23K papers including their full text, 18K authors, 124K citations and 142K distinct co-authorship relations.

We further enriched the data with more detailed author information by heuristic Wikidata and Google Scholar entity page look-ups that match an author's name. Note that not every author has a Wikidata or Google Scholar entry, and some authors have multiple entries. In total we count approximately 9K authors with a matching Google Scholar entity, and 14K authors with matching Wikidata entities, of which 1.5K authors can be linked to exactly one Wikidata entity. Our heuristic does not distinguish between Wikidata entities and shows them all, whereas only the first Google Scholar entity is selected.

3.2 Application

The main contributions of this tool are to provide different expert search methods, detailed expert profiles and evidence features, which support a user's decision making process. The application's main page is shown in Figure 1a, which contains a simple search field for query input and a list of the retrieved ranked list of experts. The ranked expert list consists of condensed expert profiles showing the name, an image, a description, statistics and keywords representing expertise areas. The result is obtained by the particular method that is selected beforehand from a range of different expert finding methods.

The profile view (cf. Figure 1b) can be accessed by clicking on an expert's name (anywhere in the application). It shows publications as well as collaborators, various statistics like citations, cita-

tions over time, h-index and i10-index, and more. Keywords are extracted for each document in the corpus using a keyword extractor tool (Wiedemann et al., 2018)[11], which provides results as a ranked list of keywords[12]. In order to provide keywords for each author, the keywords of each document that an author has written are aggregated and ranked by document frequency. Lastly, the profile view shows information such as awards, educational degrees, employers (current and previous) as extracted from Wikidata.

3.3 Expert Finding Methods

We implemented three initial expert finding methods for the LT Expertfinder.

3.3.1 Model2

The document generation model by Balog et al. (2012) is widely used as a baseline to compare expert finding methods. In their original paper, Balog et al. (2012) present two models: Model1, the candidate generation model and Model2, the document generation model. Their experiments reveal that Model2 performs better.

The main challenge of the expert finding task is the accurate estimation of $p(q|c_i)$ as a ranking function of a candidate expert $c_i \in C$ and query terms q (Balog et al., 2012). The probability $p(q|c_i)$ is estimated by using a simple generative process: Given a candidate c_i, select a document d associated with c_i and generate the query q with the probability $p(q|d, c_i)$, which is obtained

---

[11]`https://github.com/uhh-lt/lt-keyterms`
[12]We only keep the top ten multi-term keywords per document.

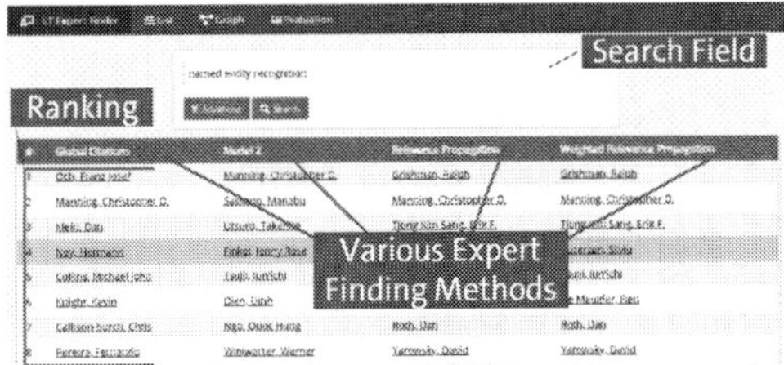

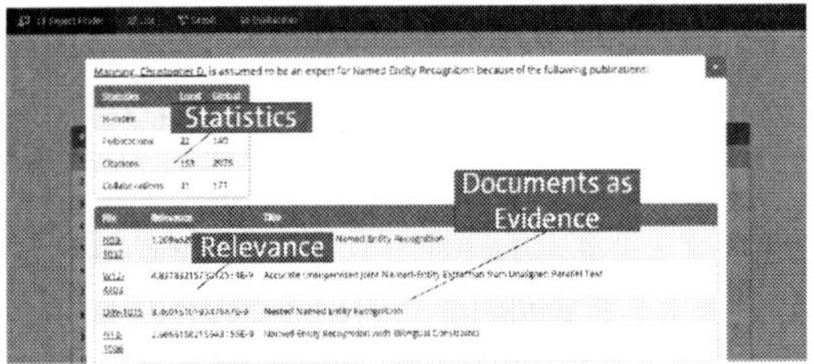

(a) Evaluation view: in this example, four different methods rank experts for the query "Named Entity Recognition". Click-ing authors opens the evidence view (cf. Figure 2b).

(b) Evidence view: this view is opened from the evaluation view (cf. Figure 2a). It shows the author, which is linked to the au-thor profile, several query dependent statistics and, and relevant documents (which open via a click).

Figure 2: Evaluation with LT Expertfinder

using a language modeling approach $p(q|d, c_i) \approx p(q|d)$.

3.3.2 Relevance Propagation (RP)

Serdyukov et al. (2008) proposed graph-based approaches to expert finding. They introduced so-called expertise graphs, which consist of candidate experts and documents connected by authorship relations. Expertise graphs are query-dependent, as they are constructed from the relevant documents that are retrieved by a standard document retrieval for a given query. Serdyukov et al. model expert finding as a random walk through the expertise graph where authors are ranked by the 'number of visits' of the random walker. In their paper, they present different random walk techniques, with incremental improvements. We re-implemented the k-step random walk as well as the infinite random walk. The infinite random walk is based on the assumption that the walk to find experts is a non-stop process. This technique is run iteratively until the expert rankings converge as opposed to the k-step random walk, which applies the calculations a fixed number of times.

3.3.3 Weighted Relevance Propagation

We further improve RP by introducing additional edges and edge weights. We include document citations, co-authorship relations and various weighting schemes for every edge type. Document citations are weighted by recency since we argue that a random user will most likely decide to read the most recent paper. Co-authorship relations are weighted by the number of total co-authorships, i.e. all outgoing edges to other author nodes. Authorships are weighted by a combination of the local and and the global h-index, where the local h-index refers to the h-index that is computed on the current result set of documents, and the global h-index refers to the to corpus wide h-index. As the h-index represents both the number of publications as well as the number of citations per publication, it is a suitable choice for determining the query-independent relevance of an author. Finally, the expert ranking is obtained by an infinite random walk through the weighted expertise graph. The main difference to RP is, that this method's infinite random walk is applied with respect to the calculated weightings of the expertise graph.

3.3.4 Other methods

The tool also supports several other methods. It includes basic ranking methods based on simple statistics like h-index and citation count. These methods basically find all authors that dealt with the query topic and then rank the authors by their global or local h-index or citation count. In addition to that, the tool includes PageRank (Page et al., 1999), which ranks authors based on their incoming citations and co-authorships. Lastly, the tool contains a ranking method based on relevance scores obtained from a document retrieval on the query topic. Simply put, this method utilizes the sum of the relevance scores of an author's documents to create an expert ranking.

3.4 Comparison & Evidence

One of the major contributions of our tool is to provide a user-friendly comparison method. The evaluation view (cf. Figure 2a) executes the major expert finding methods and presents columnar results. With this view, it is easy to identify differences as well as to qualitatively compare the results. Clicking on an expert's name in this component will open the evidence view (cf. Figure 2b) for further investigation. It shows the documents

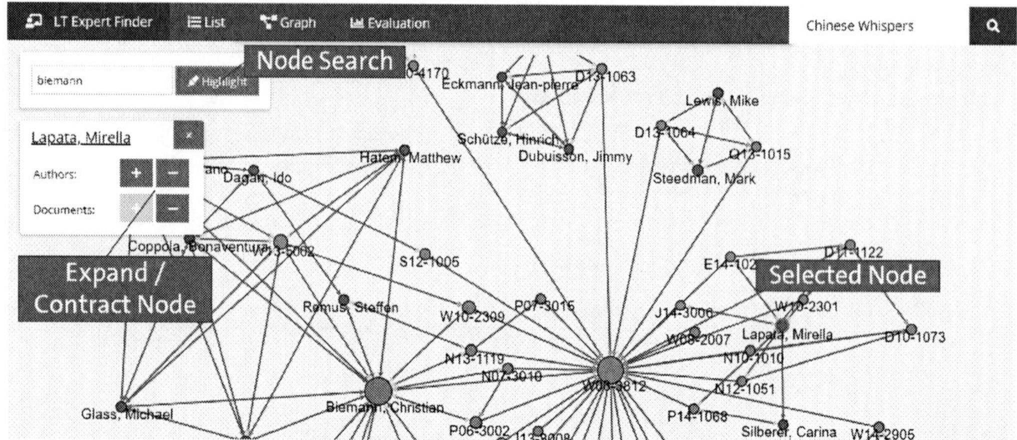

Figure 3: Graph view: authors are rendered as blue nodes, documents are rendered as green nodes, the highlighted node is rendered in red. The size of a node reflects its relevance. The graph is initially filtered by relevance to reduce cognitive overload and can be expanded or reduced for particular nodes.

that are relevant to the query and written by the candidate expert including their document relevance score calculated by the respective method, and several query dependent statistics such as h-index, number of citations, etc.

The graph view, which is shown in Figure 3 visualizes the query-based citation network for a particular method. Documents and authors are rendered as nodes whereas citations, authorship relations and co-authorship relations are represented as edges. Thus, it allows a quick peek into the data and an even better understanding of the results.

4 Conclusion

We presented the LT Expertfinder, a user-friendly tool for expert search, expert profiling, and most of all it enables the qualitative comparison of different ranking approaches and provides evidence for the ranking process. We implemented several ranking methods that can be easily extended with more methods. Also, it provides detailed expert profiles, which are linked to Wikidata and Google Scholar. Additionally, an explorable graph view is provided, which helps for further analysis of the results. This combination of features in a single tool is, to the best of our knowledge, still unexplored and helpful for the community for further development and evaluation of expert finding methods. For the future, we plan to expand our corpus using automatic crawling methods of scientific papers, which are analyzed and indexed

on a daily basis. Crawling the ACL Anthology has already been successfully performed by Singh et al. (2018) with the help of their PDF Extraction tool OCR++ (Singh et al., 2016), which we also intend to use. Further, we plan to utilize the LT Expertfinder to develop methods for finding emerging experts in a field. We release the LT Expertfinder as freely available, open source application, under a permissive license.[13,14,15,16] A short demonstration video is also available[17].

References

Peter Bailey, Arjen P. De Vries, Nick Craswell, and Ian Soboroff. 2007. Overview of the TREC 2007 Enterprise Track. In *Proceedings of the Sixteenth Text REtrieval Conference*, Gaithersburg, MD, USA.

Krisztian Balog, Leif Azzopardi, and Maarten de Rijke. 2006. Formal Models for Expert Finding in Enterprise Corpora. In *Proceedings of the 29th Annual International ACM SIGIR Conference on Research and Development in Information Retrieval*, pages 43–50, Seattle, WA, USA.

Krisztian Balog and Maarten De Rijke. 2007. Determining Expert Profiles (with an Application to Expert Finding). In *Proceedings of the 20th Inter-*

---

[13]Demo: `http://ltdemos.informatik.uni-hamburg.de/lt-expertfinder/ui/`
[14]Docker: `https://cloud.docker.com/u/uhhlt/repository/docker/uhhlt/xpertfinder`
[15]Source Code: `https://github.com/uhh-lt/lt-expertfinder`
[16]License: Apache License, Version 2.0
[17]`https://youtu.be/A4yRZezWUvE`

national Joint Conference on Artifical Intelligence, pages 2657–2662, Hyderabad, India.

Krisztian Balog, Yi Fang, Maarten de Rijke, Pavel Serdyukov, and Luo Si. 2012. Expertise Retrieval. *Foundations and Trends in Information Retrieval*, 6(2):127–256.

Krisztian Balog, Paul Thomas, Nick Craswell, Ian Soboroff, Peter Bailey, and Arjen P. De Vries. 2008. Overview of the TREC 2008 Enterprise Track. In *Proceedings of the Eighteenth Text REtrieval Conference*, Gaithersburg, MD, USA.

Christopher S. Campbell, Paul P. Maglio, Alex Cozzi, and Byron Dom. 2003. Expertise Identification Using Email Communications. In *Proceedings of the 12th ACM International Conference on Information and Knowledge Management*, pages 528–531, New Orleans, LA, USA.

Hung-Hsuan Chen, Pucktada Treeratpituk, Prasenjit Mitra, and C. Lee Giles. 2013. CSSeer: An Expert Recommendation System Based on CiteseerX. In *Proceedings of the 13th ACM/IEEE-CS Joint Conference on Digital Libraries*, pages 381–382, Indianapolis, IN, USA.

Nick Craswell, Arjen P. De Vries, and Ian Soboroff. 2005. Overview of the TREC 2005 Enterprise Track. In *Proceedings of the Fourteenth Text REtrieval Conference*, pages 199–205, Gaithersburg, MD, USA.

Nick Craswell, David Hawking, Anne-Marie Vercoustre, and Peter Wilkins. 2001. P@NOPTIC expert: Searching for experts not just for documents. In *Ausweb Poster Proceedings*, pages 21–25, Coffs Harbour, Queensland, Australia.

H. Deng, I. King, and M. R. Lyu. 2008. Formal Models for Expert Finding on DBLP Bibliography Data. In *Proceedings of the Eighth International Conference on Data Mining*, pages 163–172, Pisa, Italy.

Hui Fang and ChengXiang Zhai. 2007. Probabilistic models for expert finding. In *Proceedings of the 29th European Conference on Information Retrieval Research*, pages 418–430, Rome, Italy.

Seyyed Hadi Hashemi, Mahmood Neshati, and Hamid Beigy. 2013. Expertise retrieval in bibliographic network: A topic dominance learning approach. In *Proceedings of the 22nd ACM International Conference on Information & Knowledge Management*, pages 1117–1126, San Francisco, CA, USA.

David Hawking. 2004. Challenges in Enterprise Search. In *Proceedings of the 15th Australasian Database Conference*, pages 15–24, Dunedin, New Zealand.

Pawel Jurczyk and Eugene Agichtein. 2007. Discovering Authorities in Question Answer Communities by Using Link Analysis. In *Proceedings of the 16th ACM International Conference on Information and Knowledge Management*, pages 919–922, Lisbon, Portugal.

Shuyi Lin, Wenxing Hong, Dingding Wang, and Tao Li. 2017. A survey on expert finding techniques. *Journal of Intelligent Information Systems*, 49(2):255–279.

Craig Macdonald and Iadh Ounis. 2006. Voting for Candidates: Adapting Data Fusion Techniques for an Expert Search Task. In *Proceedings of the 15th ACM International Conference on Information and Knowledge Management*, pages 387–396, Arlington, VA, USA.

Audris Mockus and James D. Herbsleb. 2002. Expertise Browser: A Quantitative Approach to Identifying Expertise. In *Proceedings of the 24th International Conference on Software Engineering*, pages 503–512, Orlando, FL, USA.

Catarina Moreira, Bruno Martins, and Pável Calado. 2011. Using Rank Aggregation for Expert Search in Academic Digital Libraries. In *Simpósio de Informática, INForum*, Portugal.

Lawrence Page, Sergey Brin, Rajeev Motwani, and Terry Winograd. 1999. The PageRank citation ranking: Bringing order to the web. Technical report, Stanford InfoLab.

Dragomir R. Radev, Pradeep Muthukrishnan, Vahed Qazvinian, and Amjad Abu-Jbara. 2013. The ACL Anthology Network corpus. *Language Resources and Evaluation*, 47(4):919–944.

Pavel Serdyukov, Henning Rode, and Djoerd Hiemstra. 2008. Modeling Multi-step Relevance Propagation for Expert Finding. In *Proceedings of the 17th ACM International Conference on Information and Knowledge Management*, pages 1133–1142, Napa Valley, CA, USA.

Mayank Singh, Barnopriyo Barua, Priyank Palod, Manvi Garg, Sidhartha Satapathy, Samuel Bushi, Kumar Ayush, Krishna Sai Rohith, Tulasi Gamidi, Pawan Goyal, and Animesh Mukherjee. 2016. OCR++: A Robust Framework For Information Extraction from Scholarly Articles. In *Proceedings of COLING 2016, the 26th International Conference on Computational Linguistics: Technical Papers*, pages 3390–3400, Osaka, Japan.

Mayank Singh, Pradeep Dogga, Sohan Patro, Dhiraj Barnwal, Ritam Dutt, Rajarshi Haldar, Pawan Goyal, and Animesh Mukherjee. 2018. CL Scholar: The ACL Anthology Knowledge Graph Miner. In *Proceedings of the 2018 Conference of the North American Chapter of the Association for Computational Linguistics: Demonstrations*, pages 16–20, New Orleans, LA, USA.

Ian Soboroff, Arjen P. De Vries, and Nick Craswell. 2006. Overview of the TREC 2006 Enterprise Track. In *Proceedings of the Fifteenth Text REtrieval Conference*, Gaithersburg, MD, USA.

Jie Tang, Jing Zhang, Limin Yao, Juanzi Li, Li Zhang, and Zhong Su. 2008. ArnetMiner: Extraction and Mining of Academic Social Networks. In *Proceedings of the 14th International Conference on Knowledge Discovery and Data Mining*, pages 990–998, Las Vegas, NV, USA.

Gregor Wiedemann, Seid Muhie Yimam, and Chris Biemann. 2018. A Multilingual Information Extraction Pipeline for Investigative Journalism. In *Proceedings of the 2018 Conference on Empirical Methods in Natural Language Processing: System Demonstrations*, pages 78–83, Brussels, Belgium.

Kan Wu, Jie Tang, Zhou Shao, Xinyi Xu, Bing Gao, and Shu Zhao. 2018. CareerMap: Visualizing career trajectory. *Science China Information Sciences*, 61:1–3.

Zi Yang, Jie Tang, Bo Wang, Jingyi Guo, Juanzi Li, and Songcan Chen. 2009. Expert2Bólè : From Expert Finding to Bólè Search. In *Proceedings of the 15th International Conference on Knowledge Discovery and Data Mining*, Paris, France.

Jun Zhang, Mark S. Ackerman, and Lada Adamic. 2007. Expertise Networks in Online Communities: Structure and Algorithms. In *Proceedings of the 16th International Conference on World Wide Web*, pages 221–230, Banff, AB, Canada.

SkillBot: Towards Automatic Skill Development via User Demonstration

Yilin Shen, Avik Ray, Hongxia Jin, Sandeep Nama
Samsung Research America, Mountain View, CA, USA
`{yilin.shen,avik.r,hongxia.jin,s.nama}@samsung.com`

Abstract

We present SkillBot that takes the first step to enable end users to teach new skills in personal assistants (PA). Unlike existing PA products that need software developers to build new skills via IDE tools, an end user can use SkillBot to build new skills just by naturally demonstrating the task on device screen. SkillBot automatically develops a natural language understanding (NLU) engine and implements the action without the need of coding. On both benchmark and in-house datasets, we validate the competitive performance of SkillBot automatically built NLU. We also observe that it only takes a few minutes for an end user to build a new skill using SkillBot.

1 Introduction

Artificially intelligent voice-enabled personal assistants (PA) have been emerging in our daily life, such as Alexa, Google Assistant, Siri, Bixby, etc. Existing off-the-shelf personal assistants serve different domains, in which each domain has a large number of capabilities, called *skills*. A skill refers to the understanding of various utterances about one intent/task and the execution of this intent/task.

Existing industrial PA products completely rely on software developers to build new skills by manually developing NLU engine and implementing action fulfillment. On one hand, while recent work CRUISE (Shen et al., 2018a) and SliQA-I (Shen et al., 2019) have introduced automatic training utterance and question generation approaches with lightweight human workload, they still require the involvement of software developers for NLU development through IDE tools. Another line of research is to personalize NLU engine in existing skills (Azaria et al., 2016; Ray et al., 2018; Shen et al., 2018b;

Wang et al., 2018a), yet they cannot support building new skills. On the other hand, developers need to write a significant amount of code in order to fulfill a sequence of operations to carry out the task (DialogFlow, 2018; Alexa, 2018).

However, in practice, it is infeasible for software developers to pre-build all possible skills that satisfy all users' needs. First, the pre-collected training corpus usually cannot exhaustively cover all possible varieties of utterances. Second, due to the heavy workload on fulfillment implementation, many actions are not implemented to be supported in PA. Thus, it is critically desirable to design an easy to use system that can facilitate *end users* to quickly build high quality new skills. Unlike existing IDE for skill development, such system needs to be more friendly and natural to ordinary end users without any complex interfaces.

In this paper, we take the first step to present SkillBot that enables end users to initialize building PA skills. An ordinary user, without either natural language expertise or software development background, only needs to demonstrate the task on his daily device screen. SkillBot, without a complex IDE interface, automatically learns the action by tracking user operations and develops the NLU engine by automatically generating training utterances based on pre-built skills. Since users intend to use spoken language to interact with PA, we follow most industrial products (DialogFlow, 2018; Alexa, 2018) to use spoken language understanding (SLU) as our NLU engine, which understands user query by detecting its intent (skill) and extracting semantic slots (slot filling) (Liu and Lane, 2016; Kim et al., 2017; Wang et al., 2018b). Even though our fully automated SkillBot only aims to satisfy each user's personal needs rather than understand all various expressions

Proceedings of NAACL-HLT 2019: Demonstrations, pages 105–109
Minneapolis, Minnesota, June 2 - June 7, 2019. ©2019 Association for Computational Linguistics

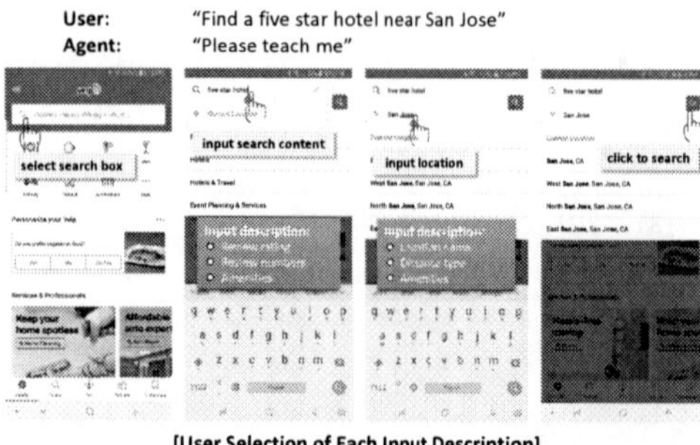

(a) Learning via Demonstration: When PA asks for teaching, the user operates step by step accordingly in Yelp app. For each user input, SkillBot prompts to ask user to select the most relevant description of this input.

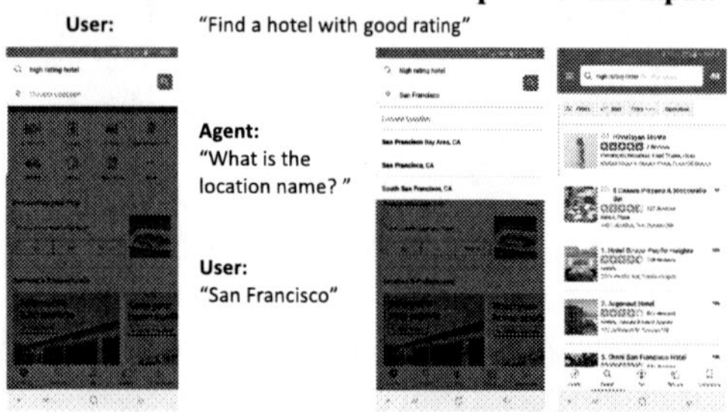

(b) Automatic Execution: After parsing the utterance using NLU, PA executes the learned action step by step. When finding a missing input, PA prompts for user input.

Figure 1: SkillBot Running Example: Learning and executing new skill "find hotel" in Yelp

from any user, we show the competitive NLU performance of SkillBot built skills in later experiments. More importantly, in most cases it only takes a user several minutes to build a new skill using SkillBot. As such, SkillBot leverages the existing skills to help end users automatically and quickly build high quality skills to meet their personal needs.

2 SkillBot System Overview

2.1 Our Settings

To satisfy user personalized needs in PA, SkillBot aims to enable end users to build their own (long-tail) skills *only by demonstration on screen*. That said, an end user only *naturally* uses their device as usual to build a new skill. In this first work, we assume that there exist a set of pre-built popular (head) skills in the ecosystem and these skills contain both annotated training utterances and a text description for each slot. In addition, we target on teaching and executing actions on the same mobile apps.

Figure 1 shows a running example in which

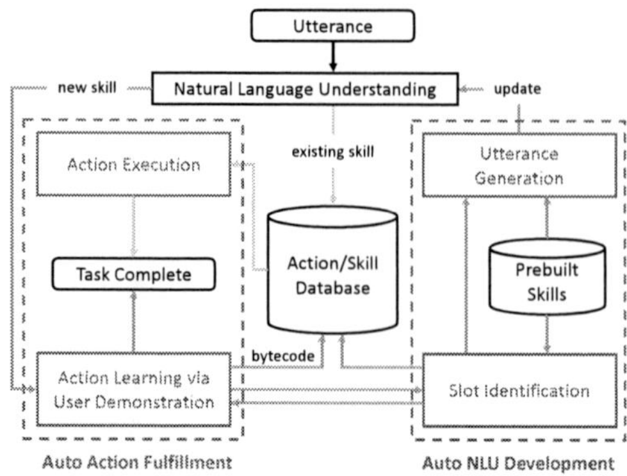

Figure 2: SkillBot Architecture & Workflow: When learning via demonstration (green arrows), automatic action fulfillment (runs as a system service on each user's device) first tracks and captures system level event sequence based on user operations. It outputs a bytecode file with learned event sequence for this skill and saves in database for future execution. After each user input operation, automatic NLU development identifies the list of possible slot descriptions for user to select and then generates more training utterances by leveraging existing training utterances in pre-built skills. At last, the NLU engine is updated using all generated utterances. When executing an existing skill (orange arrows), based on the parsed skill from NLU, the corresponding bytecode is retrieved to automatically execute all saved steps.

SkillBot helps an end user to build the new "find hotel" skill in Yelp. For an end user, he uses PA as usual via voice utterances. SkillBot prompts the user to teach when PA cannot understand and execute the user utterance correctly. As in Figure 1a, all the end user needs to do is to demonstrate on screen step by step how he wants PA to execute. After each user input, SkillBot identifies possible slot descriptions and asks user to select the most relevant one. SkillBot then automatically builds the new skill and outputs a well-trained NLU engine and an action executable file. A user could teach a new skill multiple times where each skill is considered to have the same on-screen operation sequence. Next time, in Figure 1b, PA can correctly understand this user's different expressions of this intent and execute the right action.

2.2 System Design

Recall that our target is to facilitate the end users who have neither natural language expertise nor software development knowledge. Thus, SkillBot is designed to support these two automation respectively. Specifically, SkillBot consists of two main components, *automatic action fulfillment*

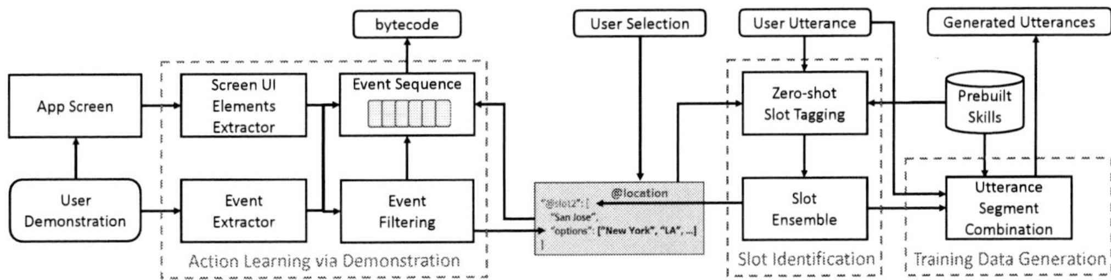

Figure 3: New Skill Learning in SkillBot

and *automatic NLU development*. In addition, SkillBot also has an action/skill database to save the mapping between learned actions and corresponding skills. Figure 2 shows SkillBot architecture and work flow. Since we use the off-the-shelf NLU models in this paper, auto NLU development focuses on generating annotated training utterances.

3 Learning via Demonstration

3.1 Action Learning

Action learning module has two main threads, as shown in the left part of Figure 3. Following user demonstration, at each screen, screen UI element extractor collects all UI elements in the format of a DOM tree on the current screen that the user is operating. In the meanwhile, event extractor collects all events from user operates in this screen.

Since there are typically a lot of system services running on device, the extracted events usually include many irrelevant ones that is not from user demonstrated actions, such as 'windows change', 'window state change', 'system or other app notifications', etc. In order to filter the irrelevant events, we first prune all events out of the current front end app based on their event package name. To further ensure some unexpected events within app (e.g., location permission request in Yelp app), we allow user to teach again at any point when user sees any unusual popups or notifications. At last, a bytecode is outputted including the event sequence in which each event contains its UI element information and the required slot value input based on the identified slot in Section 3.2.1.

3.2 Automatic NLU Development

The key idea of training utterance generation is to identify the slots in the user utterance and then use them to generate more training utterances based on the training utterances in existing pre-built skills.

3.2.1 Slot Identification

This module is invoked after each user input during demonstration. As shown in the middle part (blue) of Figure 3, after user inputs "San Jose" in the example of Figure 1a, it receives the user utterance and the optional values (e.g., "New York", "LA", etc.) extracted from dropdown list of the user input box (Yelp location textbox) during action learning.

Taking the above input, we first construct the set of natural language utterances by replacing the input values with other optional values. For each utterance, zero-shot slot tagging module extracts its semantic slots based on each slot description using the zero-shot model in (Bapna et al., 2017) trained on pre-built skills. Slot ensemble module performs a joint slot detection across all constructed utterances by combining the likelihood scores of each slot. The descriptions of identified top ranked slots are sent to the user to select the most relevant one.

3.2.2 Utterance Generation

In this first work, we assume that each training utterance in pre-built skills has been decomposed into segments by human expert or our proposed CRUISE approach (Shen et al., 2018a). Each segment contains a slot tag (two examples are shown in the right side of Figure 4). We only use the subset of segments associated with the aforementioned identified slots.

We generate the utterance by combining identified segments into long utterances by concatenating them together (middle part in Figure 4). To do so, we first use the off-the-shelf Stanford parser to identify the verb and main object in user utterance. In the sample utterance of Figure 1, "find" and "hotel" are marked as verb and object based on the parser tree. As

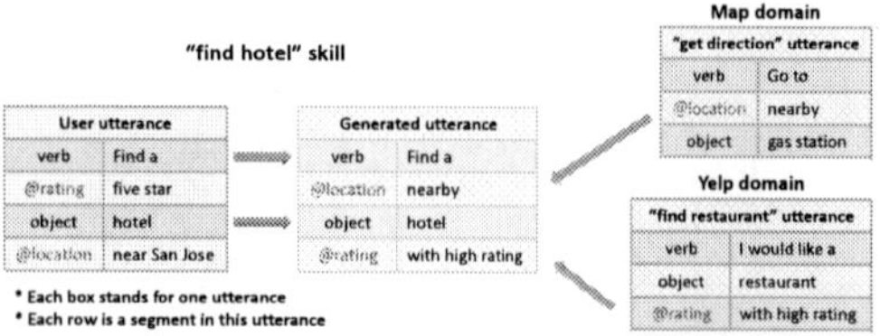

Figure 4: Utterance Generation Example

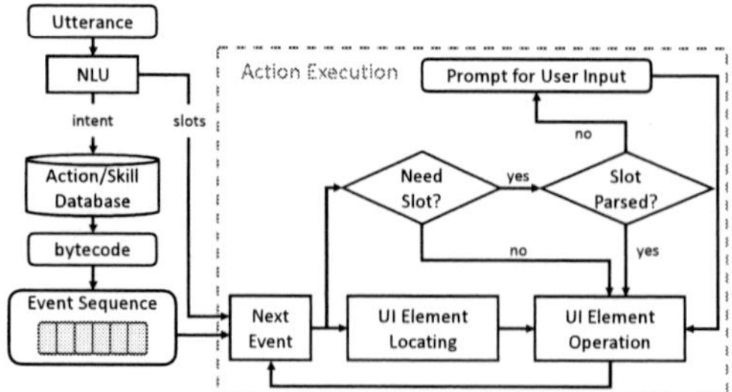

Figure 5: Automatic Skill Execution in SkillBot

the arrows show in Figure 4, we next generate the permutations of segments before and after the object based on their places in original utterances with non-overlapping slots.

4 Automatic Execution

Figure 5 shows the flow of automatic execution of a skill. NLU first parses the utterance and outputs its intent and slots. The intent class is used to query the action/skill database to retrieve the bytecode of the corresponding action. SkillBot executes the events one by one following the sequence. For each event, the execution consists of the following two threads: One thread determines if this event requires a slot input based on the saved meta data during learning. If so, we extract on the slot results parsed by NLU. If this information is missing in utterance or NLU fails to parse, we prompt the follow-up question to ask user. The other thread first locates the UI element based on its saved coordinates. It then inputs slot values and simulates the user operation by using gesture control based on the element coordinates (e.g., MotionEvent in Android devices).

5 Experiments

In this section, we focus on evaluating SkillBot built NLU engine given that auto action learning and execution are restricted to the same app.

We test on both benchmark and in-house datasets/domains: (1) *ATIS* (4978 training, 893 test) with 17 intent labels and 79 slot labels (Hemphill et al., 1990); (2) *In-house Yelp* (1968 training, 911 test) with 5 intents and 10 slots. To evaluate both datasets which are not generated by CRUISE, we segment each utterance using dependency parser and slot annotations (each segment ends with a slot). The noisy segments are further removed by human experts. In the experiment, we assume that user always select the correct slot description after each input to ensure the correct slot identification. We use the

benchmark BiRNN based joint NLU model (Liu and Lane, 2016).

In each dataset (with k intents), for each intent I, we assume the user teaches this intent I given the remaining $k - 1$ intents as pre-built skills. Let $\mathcal{T}_I$ be the subset of training data w.r.t. intent I, and $\mathcal{T}_I^c$ be utterances w.r.t. the remaining $k - 1$ intents. Our baseline NLU engine is trained on this training set $\mathcal{T}_I^c$ of remaining $k - 1$ intents. Next, we randomly sample 5 user utterances (assuming a user teaches the new intent 5 times) from set $\mathcal{T}_I$, and use our utterance generation algorithm to auto generate dataset A_I for intent I. Our SkillBot built NLU (called *SkillBot NLU*) is trained on the combined training data $\mathcal{T}_I^c \cup A_I$. Both the NLU engines are tested on the original test dataset (having all k intents).

Table 1 presents the results. For ATIS, we show the results for top 8 intents, which contain at least 0.9% of the overall training utterances (the third column displays this fraction). SkillBot NLU achieves a large gain in intent accuracy over the baseline in both datasets. Moreover, we observe that the accuracy gain is also roughly correlated to the fraction of all test utterances in each intent. This indicates that the SkillBot NLU can correctly learn most of the test utterances in the newly added intent. SkillBot NLU also improves the slot filling F1 score in most intents. In cases when SkillBot NLU completely misses a slot, it can directly ask a follow-up question to allow user provide the slot value before action fulfillment. Therefore, SkillBot with follow-up user clarification further improves the F1 score and obtains performance gain in last column.

6 Discussion & Future Work

We present the first SkillBot that enables end users to build skills in PA. SkillBot automates both action fulfillment and NLU development. In

Table 1: SkillBot NLU Experimental Results

Domain	Intent/Skill	Train Size(%)	Intent (Accuracy)			Slot Filling (F1 Score)			
			Baseline	SkillBot	Gain (%)	Baseline	SkillBot	SkillBot+Follow-up	Gain (%)
ATIS	atis_flight	74.34	27.00	**60.40**	33.40	85.13	**87.45**	**89.37**	4.24
	atis_airfare	8.59	90.40	**92.40**	2.00	97.43	96.96	97.39	-0.04
	atis_ground_service	5.13	92.40	**97.20**	4.80	96.69	**96.99**	97.36	0.67
	atis_airline	3.14	94.00	**96.40**	2.40	97.43	**97.54**	97.98	0.55
	atis_abbreviation	2.90	94.20	**95.60**	1.40	97.04	**97.45**	97.88	0.84
	atis_aircraft	1.56	94.80	**96.40**	1.60	97.54	97.46	**97.92**	0.38
	atis_flight_time	1.00	95.40	**97.60**	2.20	97.07	**97.37**	98.06	0.99
	atis_quantity	0.91	95.40	**97.20**	1.80	97.37	97.05	**97.56**	0.19
Yelp	search_restaurant	23.23	78.16	**88.04**	9.88	92.50	**92.85**	**94.71**	2.21
	get_directions	24.20	72.78	**85.40**	12.62	93.29	92.10	**94.36**	1.07
	bookmark	22.75	76.73	**84.96**	8.23	94.13	**94.90**	**96.90**	2.77
	reservation	12.53	89.13	**95.06**	5.93	93.53	**94.06**	**96.15**	2.62
	call_restaurant	16.60	82.66	**92.54**	9.88	93.31	92.12	**94.46**	1.15

future work, we will evaluate SkillBot in more real and larger-scale scenarios: allow end users to teach more naturally with less clarification by improving the accuracy of slot identification; support building a brand new domain by enabling slot identification to map more varieties of slots in other domains; incorporate with other non-CRUISE pre-built skills without pre-segmented utterances; enhance the robustness of action learning to tackle the dynamics in mobile device system; expand cross app action teaching in which we will design machine learning algorithms for event filtering and UI semantic mapping.

Acknowledgments

The authors would like to thank Abhishek Patel and Xiangyu Zeng for useful discussion and their help of demo implementation and video shooting.

References

Amazon Alexa. 2018. https://developer.amazon.com/docs/custom-skills/handle-requests-sent-by-alexa.html.

Amos Azaria, Jayant Krishnamurthy, and Tom M Mitchell. 2016. Instructable intelligent personal agent. In *AAAI*, pages 2681–2689.

Ankur Bapna, Gokhan Tür, Dilek Hakkani-Tür, and Larry Heck. 2017. Towards zero-shot frame semantic parsing for domain scaling. In *Interspeech*, pages 2476–2480.

DialogFlow. 2018. https://dialogflow.com/.

Charles T Hemphill, John J Godfrey, George R Doddington, et al. 1990. The atis spoken language systems pilot corpus. In *Proceedings of the DARPA speech and natural language workshop*, pages 96–101.

Young-Bum Kim, Sungjin Lee, and Karl Stratos. 2017. ONENET: joint domain, intent, slot prediction for spoken language understanding. In *ASRU*, pages 547–553.

Bing Liu and Ian Lane. 2016. Attention-based recurrent neural network models for joint intent detection and slot filling. *arXiv preprint arXiv:1609.01454*.

Avik Ray, Yilin Shen, and Hongxia Jin. 2018. Learning out-of-vocabulary words in intelligent personal agents. In *IJCAI*, pages 4309–4315.

Yilin Shen, Avik Ray, Abhishek Patel, and Hongxia Jin. 2018a. CRUISE: cold-start new skill development via iterative utterance generation. In *ACL, System Demonstrations*, pages 105–110.

Yilin Shen, Yu Wang, Abhishek Patel, and Hongxia Jin. 2019. Sliqa-i: Towards cold-start development of end-to-end spoken language interface for question answering. In *ICASSP*.

Yilin Shen, Xiangyu Zeng, Yu Wang, and Hongxia Jin. 2018b. User information augmented semantic frame parsing using progressive neural networks. In *Interspeech*, pages 3464–3468.

Yu Wang, Abhishek Patel, Yilin Shen, and Hongxia Jin. 2018a. A deep reinforcement learning based multimodal coaching model (dcm) for slot filling in spoken language understanding(slu). In *Interspeech*, pages 3444–3448.

Yu Wang, Yilin Shen, and Hongxia Jin. 2018b. A bi-model based RNN semantic frame parsing model for intent detection and slot filling. In *NAACL-HLT*, pages 309–314.

Multilingual Entity, Relation, Event and Human Value Extraction

Manling Li[1], Ying Lin[1], Joseph Hoover[3], Spencer Whitehead[1],
Clare R. Voss[2], Morteza Dehghani[3], Heng Ji[1]
[1] Rensselaer Polytechnic Institute, Troy, NY, USA
{lim22,liny9,whites5,jih}@rpi.edu
[2] US Army Research Laboratory, Adelphi, MD, USA
clare.r.voss.civ@mail.mil
[3] University of Southern California, Los Angeles, CA, USA
{jehoover,mdehghan}@usc.edu

Abstract

This paper demonstrates a state-of-the-art end-to-end multilingual (English, Russian, and Ukrainian) knowledge extraction system that can perform entity discovery and linking, relation extraction, event extraction, and coreference. It extracts and aggregates knowledge elements across multiple languages and documents as well as provides visualizations of the results along three dimensions: temporal (as displayed in an event timeline), spatial (as displayed in an event heatmap), and relational (as displayed in entity-relation networks). For our system to further support users' analyses of causal sequences of events in complex situations, we also integrate a wide range of human moral value measures, independently derived from region-based survey, into the event heatmap. This system is publicly available as a docker container and a live demo,[1,2] with a video demonstrating the system [3].

1 Introduction

Knowledge extraction aims to convert unstructured texts into structured entities, relations and events. Recently, we have developed a state-of-the-art multilingual knowledge extraction system for three languages including English, Russian, and Ukrainian (Zhang et al., 2018). However, individual extraction components lack the ability to aggregate knowledge from multiple languages and documents. For example, complementary salient information about the *Ukraine crisis* may be extracted from English, Ukrainian, and Russian news documents. We develop a novel framework, as illustrated in Figure 1, to aggregate knowledge elements from multiple documents in multiple languages and visualize these knowledge elements

in three interfaces (temporal, spatial, and entity-relation networks) which support effective multi-dimensional search and filtering. The system is publicly available as a series of docker containers and it can be easily run via a single script. We also provide a live demo of the system that efficiently extracts knowledge elements from user input text.

The system improves the ease and speed with which users may discover inter-connections among knowledge elements from multiple languages and documents, so users can isolate subsets of activity that warrant further attention. The complementary dimensions of the three visualization interfaces provide distinct yet comprehensive views of the entities, relations, and events as well as, most notably, their implicit connections.

For example, in the *Ukraine crisis*, a *Transport-Person* event in an *airport* in *Kramatorsk* is part of the *Attack* event in *Sloviansk*. A causal relation between these two events may be discovered both in the event heat-map interface, where the former event in *Kramatorsk* is located near the latter event in *Sloviansk*, and in the event timeline interface, where these two events both occur in *April 2014*. Furthermore, the entity-relation network interface enables users to retrieve and relate entities of interest while reasoning about such events. The interface displays each retrieved entity with its one-hop relations to other entities, which then allows the user to retrieve one-hop relations for any of those entities, thereby traversing the network and discovering information. We see this in traversing the network following the *Leadership* relation from *Donbass People's militia* to *Pro-Russian separatists* and then the *Sponsorship* relation from *Pro-Russian separatists* to *Russia*, suggesting the *Donbass People's militia* is sponsored by *Russia*.

Other types of implicit knowledge that are not readily discovered by traditional methods of knowledge extraction, such as human values, play

---

[1]System: http://nlp.cs.rpi.edu/demo/aida_pipeline-master.zip

[2]Demo: http://nlp.cs.rpi.edu/software/

[3]Video: https://youtu.be/cQPHaxGLn8k

Proceedings of NAACL-HLT 2019: Demonstrations, pages 110–115
Minneapolis, Minnesota, June 2 - June 7, 2019. ©2019 Association for Computational Linguistics

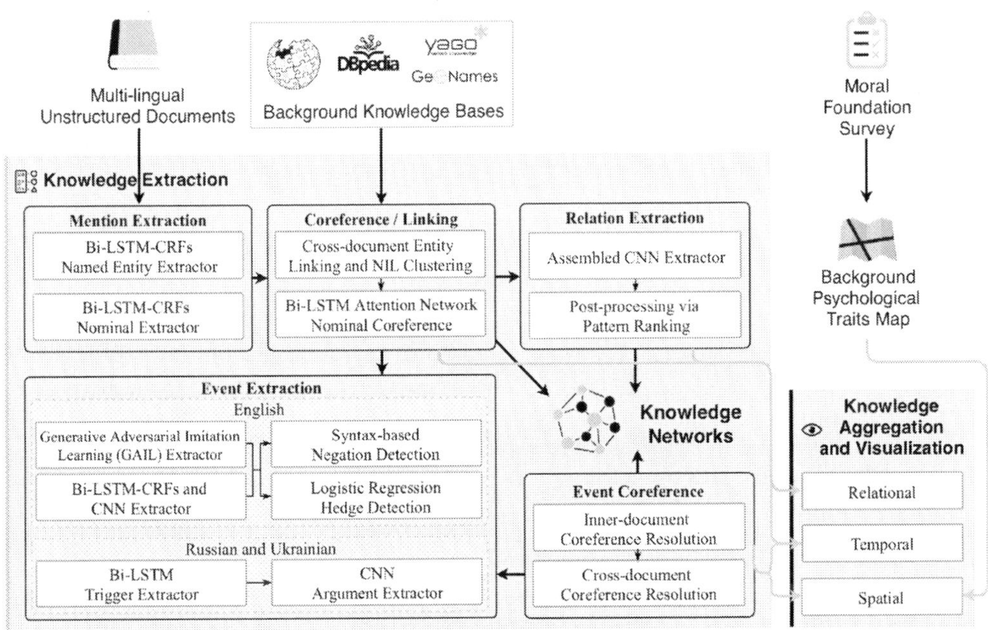

Figure 1: System overview.

a major role in social functioning and motivation (Rai and Fiske, 2011; Haidt, 2012; Graham et al., 2013; Schwartz, 2017). Numerous studies suggest that human values are often central motivating factors for protests, conflicts, and violence (Ginges and Atran, 2009; Fiske et al., 2014; Mooijman and Van Dijk, 2015; Skitka et al., 2017). Therefore, we integrate region-specific estimates of dominant psychological characteristics into the spatial event heat-map, which provides an additional layer of information that can be used to understand geo-spatial event patterns.

2 Multilingual Knowledge Extraction

The overall architecture of our multilingual knowledge extraction system is illustrated in Figure 1. The system performs entity discovery and linking (Pan et al., 2017; Lin et al., 2018), time expression extraction and normalization (Manning et al., 2014), relation extraction (Shi et al., 2018), event extraction (Zhang et al., 2017, 2019), and event coreference (Zhang et al., 2015). The system supports the extraction of 7 entity types, 23 relations, and 47 event types, as defined in the DARPA AIDA ontology.[4] Table 1 shows the main types.

For Russian and Ukrainian text input, we did

Entity	Person, Organization, Geopolitical Entity, Facility, Location, Weapon, Vehicle
Relation	Physical, Part-Whole, Personal-Social, Measurement, Organization-Affiliation, General-Affiliation
Event	Life, Movement, Business, Conflict, Contact, Manufacture, Personnel, Justice, Transaction, Government, Inspection, Existence

Table 1: Main types of knowledge elements

not adopt the alternative approach of translating the source documents into English and then applying English knowledge extraction system due to the low-quality of state-of-the-art machine translation and word alignment for these two languages.

Once within-document knowledge elements for each language are extracted, the system performs cross-lingual entity linking to Wikipedia, cross-document entity clustering for unlinkable mentions, and cross-document event coreference resolution for cross-lingual information fusion. Further details of each component are described in (Zhang et al., 2018). Currently, each main component in the system outperforms the best reported results in the literature, as shown in Table 2.

---

[4]`https://www.darpa.mil/program/`
`active-interpretation-of-disparate-alternatives`

Components	Ours	State-of-the-art
Name Tagging	91.8%	91.4% (Liu et al., 2018)
Relation Extraction	66.4%	65.2% (Fu et al., 2017)
Event Trigger Labeling	72.9%	69.6% (Sha et al., 2018)
Event Argument Labeling	59.0%	57.2% (Sha et al., 2018)

Table 2: F1 score comparisons of our approach vs. state-of-the-art for English knowledge extraction.

3 Knowledge Aggregation and Visualization

To demonstrate the capabilities of our aforementioned system, we process 10,984 documents about the Ukraine-Russia conflict scenario from the DARPA AIDA program, including 7,415 in English, 2,307 in Russian, and 929 in Ukrainian.

We organize the extracted events in our interfaces, as described below, along the temporal and spatial dimensions in order to assist users both in gaining a comprehensive view of the evolving situations in this scenario and in detecting shared patterns of occurrence and possible connections among events of interest over time and space.

3.1 Event Timeline

We extract and normalize time arguments to construct an event timeline in Figure 2 using TimelineJS for visualization.[5] There are three zones in the web-enabled timeline interface. By clicking on an event in the timeline (*i.e.*, the gray area at the bottom of the screen), the pertinent context sentence for that event is displayed in the middle of the screen with the trigger and arguments highlighted in color, along with a link to the sentence's source document (Figure 3). Clicking on the source document link retrieves the document with full inline annotations and its publication date, to support inference of the absolute date(s) from relative time expressions in the text (*e.g.*, "*two days ago*"). Additionally, at the top of the interface, users may search and filter with multiple criteria (*entity name*, *event type*, *event subtype*, *argument role*, and *time period*) to narrow down the results to a particular query of interest.

Figure 2: Example of the event timeline interface.

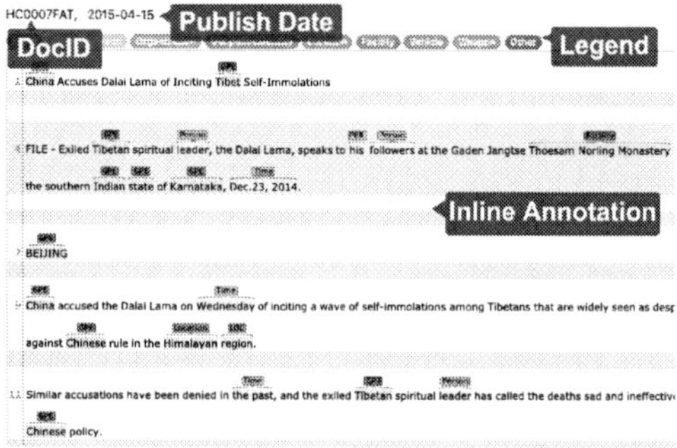

Figure 3: Example source document with inline annotation retrieved from the link in the event timeline interface.

3.2 Event and Human Value Heatmap

We link event locations to the GeoNames database (Vatant and Wick, 2012) via the entity linking component and visualize involved events on a world map using Mapbox for visualization, as Figure 4 illustrates.[6] Each event is displayed as a dot or, when zooming in, an icon on the map. The color of a dot indicates the language of the source sentence, while the icon denotes the event type. Users can apply filters to the map to view the events of a certain type or language.

In addition to events, we also integrate regional estimates of human values into the heatmap. Specifically, the system encodes the geographic variations of 10 distinct dimensions of the human values in Table 3. These values are proposed in the Schwartz Basic Theory of Human Values (Schwartz, 2012) as a culturally universal taxonomy of human values.

The human values estimates are derived from the European Social Survey (ESS) (Round, 5, 6,

---

[5] https://timeline.knightlab.com/

[6] https://www.mapbox.com/

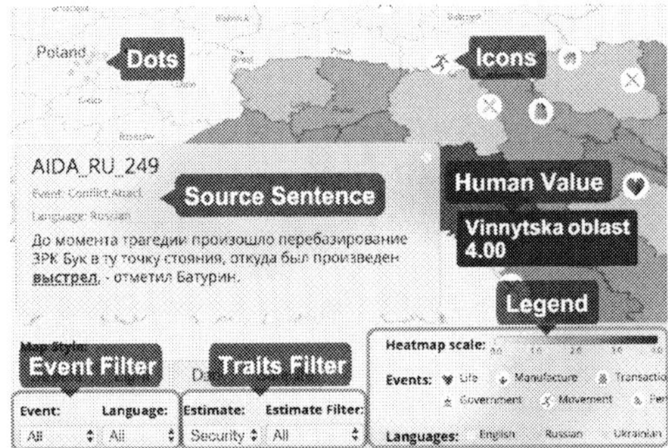

Figure 4: Example event heatmap with events and human values by region.

Human Values	Achievement, Benevolence, Conformity, Hedonism, Power, Security, Self-direction, Simulation, Tradition, Universalism
Age Filter	15-29, 30-44, 45-59, 60+
Gender Filter	Female, Male

Table 3: Human values. In the heatmap, the estimates for these values are displayed by region.

7), a nationally representative survey administered throughout the European Union. While the ESS data is sufficient for directly estimating *national* human values, it cannot be used to directly derive Oblast-level estimates because it is not representative at the Oblast-level.[7] To resolve this issue, we employ a state-of-the-art approach to survey adjustment and small-area estimation called Multilevel Regression and Synthetic Post-stratification with Spatial Smoothing (MrsP-SM) (Park et al., 2004; Selb and Munzert, 2011; Leemann and Wasserfallen, 2017; Hoover and Dehghani, 2018). This involves a model-based approach to post-stratification in which a hierarchical regression model is used to model person-level responses to a survey item as a function of demographic characteristics, region-level factors, and geographic indicators. Then, the model is used to generate predictions for each combination of demographic variables and geographic region. Finally, the predictions are weighted by the demographic population proportions within each region, yielding a set of regularized regional estimates that are adjusted for representativeness. To obtain regional human values estimates in the event heatmap, we estimate

MrsP-SM models for each of the 10 Schwartz Human Values domains.

Human values have close ties to the intentions underlying events. A *Demonstration* event may result in violence, property destruction and involvement of extremist groups. The values of *Benevolence*, *Hedonism*, and *Conformity* among authority figures may impact their response to a protest. Additionally, people in areas where *Conflict* events are common may have higher values for *Security* and lower values for *Achievement*.

3.3 Entity-relation Networks

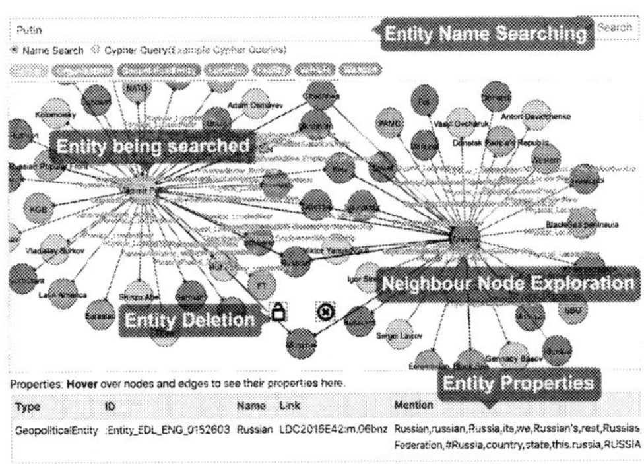

Figure 5: Entity-relation network.

A critical task for users gaining an understanding of complex scenarios is to explore implicit entity relations beyond the scope of traditional in-line document annotation. Our interface provides interactive knowledge graph exploration, using Neo4j[8] (Figure 5), where entities can be searched by name and a sub-graph for each entity with its one-hop neighbors and their relations is returned, with entity properties displayed at the bottom of the interface. Users may either explore each retrieved neighbour by double clicking on it for its subgraph, or reduce their search graph by deleting entities no longer of interest. Thus, users can construct a multi-hop entity-relation graph, discovering variable length paths between entities. Each entity is labeled with its canonical name mention, while the entities without name mentions are removed from the network.

4 Conclusions and Future Work

In this paper, we demonstrate a comprehensive multi-lingual knowledge extraction, aggregation

---

[7]Our regional unit of analysis is the Oblast, of which there are 24 in Ukraine.

[8]https://neo4j.com/

and visualization system which can effectively discover and synthesize knowledge elements from multiple data sources, and present them to users in multiple dimensions. In the future, we plan to conduct utility experiments with users to compare and evaluate the quality and speed of generating summary reports with and without using our interfaces.

Acknowledgments

This work was supported by the U.S. ARL NSCTA No. W911NF-09-2-0053 and DARPA AIDA Program No. FA8750-18-2-0014. The views and conclusions contained in this document are those of the authors and should not be interpreted as representing the official policies, either expressed or implied, of the U.S. Government. The U.S. Government is authorized to reproduce and distribute reprints for Government purposes notwithstanding any copyright notation here on.

References

A P Fiske, T S Rai, and S Pinker. 2014. *Virtuous Violence: Hurting and Killing to Create, Sustain, End, and Honor Social Relationships*. Cambridge University Press.

Lisheng Fu, Thien Huu Nguyen, Bonan Min, and Ralph Grishman. 2017. Domain adaptation for relation extraction with domain adversarial neural network. In *Proceedings of the Eighth International Joint Conference on Natural Language Processing (Volume 2: Short Papers)*, volume 2, pages 425–429.

Jeremy Ginges and Scott Atran. 2009. What motivates participation in violent political action. *Annals of the New York Academy of Sciences*, 1167(1):115–123.

Jesse Graham, Jonathan Haidt, Sena Koleva, Matt Motyl, Ravi Iyer, Sean P Wojcik, and Peter H Ditto. 2013. Moral foundations theory: The pragmatic validity of moral pluralism. In *Advances in experimental social psychology*, volume 47, pages 55–130. Elsevier.

Jonathan Haidt. 2012. *The righteous mind: Why good people are divided by politics and religion*. Vintage.

J Hoover and M Dehghani. 2018. The big, the bad, and the ugly: Geographic estimation with flawed psychological data. *PsyArXiv. October*.

Lucas Leemann and Fabio Wasserfallen. 2017. Extending the use and prediction precision of subnational public opinion estimation: EXTENDING USE AND PRECISION OF MrP. *American journal of political science*, 61(4):1003–1022.

Ying Lin, Shengqi Yang, Veselin Stoyanov, and Heng Ji. 2018. A multi-lingual multi-task architecture for low-resource sequence labeling. In *Proceedings of the 56th Annual Meeting of the Association for Computational Linguistics (Volume 1: Long Papers)*, volume 1, pages 799–809.

Liyuan Liu, Jingbo Shang, Xiang Ren, Frank Fangzheng Xu, Huan Gui, Jian Peng, and Jiawei Han. 2018. Empower sequence labeling with task-aware neural language model. In *Thirty-Second AAAI Conference on Artificial Intelligence*.

Christopher Manning, Mihai Surdeanu, John Bauer, Jenny Finkel, Steven Bethard, and David McClosky. 2014. The stanford corenlp natural language processing toolkit. In *Proceedings of 52nd annual meeting of the association for computational linguistics: system demonstrations*, pages 55–60.

Marlon Mooijman and Wilco W Van Dijk. 2015. The self in moral judgement: How self-affirmation affects the moral condemnation of harmless sexual taboo violations. *Cognition and Emotion*, 29(7):1326–1334.

Xiaoman Pan, Boliang Zhang, Jonathan May, Joel Nothman, Kevin Knight, and Heng Ji. 2017. Cross-lingual name tagging and linking for 282 languages. In *Proceedings of the 55th Annual Meeting of the Association for Computational Linguistics (Volume 1: Long Papers)*, volume 1, pages 1946–1958.

David K Park, Andrew Gelman, and Joseph Bafumi. 2004. Bayesian multilevel estimation with post-stratification: State-Level estimates from national polls. *Political analysis: an annual publication of the Methodology Section of the American Political Science Association*, 12(4):375–385.

Tage Shakti Rai and Alan Page Fiske. 2011. Moral psychology is relationship regulation: moral motives for unity, hierarchy, equality, and proportionality. *Psychological review*, 118(1):57–75.

ESS Round. 5. 5: European social survey round 4 data (2010). *Data file edition*, 5.

ESS Round. 6. 6: European social survey round 6 data (2012). *Data file edition*, 6.

ESS Round. 7. 7: European social survey round 7 data (2014). *Data file edition*, 7.

Shalom H Schwartz. 2012. An overview of the schwartz theory of basic values. *Online Readings in Psychology and Culture*, 2(1):11.

Shalom H Schwartz. 2017. The refined theory of basic values. In Sonia Roccas and Lilach Sagiv, editors, *Values and Behavior: Taking a Cross Cultural Perspective*, pages 51–72. Springer International Publishing, Cham.

P Selb and S Munzert. 2011. Estimating constituency preferences from sparse survey data using auxiliary geographic information. *Political analysis: an annual publication of the Methodology Section of the American Political Science Association.*

Lei Sha, Feng Qian, Baobao Chang, and Zhifang Sui. 2018. Jointly extracting event triggers and arguments by dependency-bridge rnn and tensor-based argument interaction. In *Thirty-Second AAAI Conference on Artificial Intelligence.*

Ge Shi, Chong Feng, Lifu Huang, Boliang Zhang, Heng Ji, Lejian Liao, and Heyan Huang. 2018. Genre separation network with adversarial training for cross-genre relation extraction. In *Proceedings of the 2018 Conference on Empirical Methods in Natural Language Processing*, pages 1018–1023.

Linda J Skitka, Brittany E Hanson, and Daniel C Wisneski. 2017. Utopian hopes or dystopian fears? exploring the motivational underpinnings of moralized political engagement. *Personality & social psychology bulletin*, 43(2):177–190.

Bernard Vatant and Marc Wick. 2012. Geonames ontology. *Dostupné online:¡ http://www. geonames. org/ontology/ontology_v3*, 1.

Boliang Zhang, Di Lu, Xiaoman Pan, Ying Lin, Halidanmu Abudukelimu, Heng Ji, and Kevin Knight. 2017. Embracing non-traditional linguistic resources for low-resource language name tagging. In *Proceedings of the Eighth International Joint Conference on Natural Language Processing (Volume 1: Long Papers)*, volume 1, pages 362–372.

Tongtao Zhang, Heng Ji, and Avirup Sil. 2019. Joint entity and event extraction with generative adversarial imitation learning. *Data Intelligence.*

Tongtao Zhang, Hongzhi Li, Heng Ji, and Shih-Fu Chang. 2015. Cross-document event coreference resolution based on cross-media features. In *Proceedings of the 2015 Conference on Empirical Methods in Natural Language Processing*, pages 201–206.

Tongtao Zhang, Ananya Subburathinam, Ge Shi, Lifu Huang, Di Lu, Xiaoman Pan, Manling Li, Boliang Zhang, Qingyun Wang, Spencer Whitehead, Heng Ji, Alireza Zareian, Hassan Akbari, Brian Chen, Ruiqi Zhong, Steven Shao, Emily Allaway, Shih-Fu Chang, Kathleen McKeown, Dongyu Li, Xin Huang, Kexuan Sun, Xujun Peng, Ryan Gabbard, Marjorie Freedman, Mayank Kejriwal, Ram Nevatia, Pedro Szekely, T.K. Satish Kumar, Ali Sadeghian, Giacomo Bergami, Sourav Dutta, Miguel Rodriguez, and Daisy Zhe Wang. 2018. Gaia - a multi-media multi-lingual knowledge extraction and hypothesis generation system. In *Proceedings of TAC KBP 2018, the 25th International Conference on Computational Linguistics: Technical Papers.*

Litigation Analytics: Extracting and querying motions and orders from US federal courts

Thomas Vacek, Dezhao Song, Hugo Molina-Salgado,
Ronald Teo, Conner Cowling and Frank Schilder
Thomson Reuters R&D
610 Opperman Drive
Eagan, MN 55123, USA
`FirstName.LastName@ThomsonReuters.com`

Abstract

Legal litigation planning can benefit from statistics collected from past decisions made by judges. Information on the typical duration for a submitted motion, for example, can give valuable clues for developing a successful strategy. Such information is encoded in semi-structured documents called dockets. In order to extract and aggregate this information, we deployed various information extraction and machine learning techniques. The aggregated data can be queried in real time within the Westlaw Edge search engine. In addition to a keyword search for judges, lawyers, law firms, parties and courts, we also implemented a question answering interface that offers targeted questions in order to get to the respective answers quicker.

1 Introduction

Dockets contain valuable meta-data about the legal actions carried out by the parties, the lawyers and law firms representing their clients and the judges presiding over the cases. A detailed record of the activities by the parties involved is kept by the court's clerk and it provides indirect insights into litigation strategies.

The entries of a docket contain the motions filed and orders issued. Understanding those entries unlocks the information that fuels litigation analytics. A detailed manual analysis of a docket could provide valuable information for the suit and the respective judge, but reading through hundreds of dockets would be very time-consuming.

Applying machine learning and NLP capabilities to all federal dockets allowed us to collect this information for 8 million past dockets and also enables us to keep up with all newly closed dockets. The information is being extracted automatically and extractions that are of low confidence identified by the machine are then manually reviewed

in order to ensure the quality of the analytics. We extracted about 300,000 parties, 500,000 lawyers, 125,000 law firms and 6,700 judges from 90 million state and federal dockets combined. Approximately 18 million motion and orders were extracted from 8 million federal dockets processed.

This demonstration paper describes in more detail the underlying problems we solved and provides an overview of how we utilized machine learning and manual review in combination with rules (that are designed based on expert knowledge). The remainder of this paper is organized as follows: Section 2 describes previous work followed by Section 3 detailing the way we extracted the information on motions and orders from federal dockets. We briefly describe the annotation study we carried out and how the motions and orders and the chains between them were extracted from the docket. Section 5 shows how users can use natural language questions to directly query judges and how they ruled on various motions (e.g., motion for summary judgment). Section 4 will run through the various steps of the demo showing how a legal researcher would interact with the system and Section 6 concludes.

2 Problem description and previous work

2.1 Motions and orders in the US Federal court

All dockets for the US federal courts are recorded by the PACER (Public Access to Court Records) system. PACER is a US government computer system that provides a front-end to the CM/ECF (Case Management/Electronic Court Filing) system in use in most Federal District Courts. CM/ECF allows counsel, clerks, and judges to quickly access case documents and the documents with the court electronically.

Proceedings of NAACL-HLT 2019: Demonstrations, pages 116–121
Minneapolis, Minnesota, June 2 - June 7, 2019. ©2019 Association for Computational Linguistics

A litigation normally starts with the claims filed by the plaintiff and the dockets keep track of the various court actions by the participating parties and the judge. Lawyers may file various motions (e.g., motion to dismiss, motion in limine). The following docket entries show a motion to dismiss in entry 9 and later denied by the judge via an order in entry 25. Note that there are entries in between related to the original motion that could be confused as motions to dismiss.

9 MOTION to dismiss Party Alamo Rent-A-Car

15 REQUEST/STATEMENT of Oral Argument by Shannin Woody regarding [9] [11] motions to Dismiss.

16 RESPONSE/MEMORANDUM in Opposition to motion to dismiss filed by Shannin Woddy

25 ORDER granting [9] Motion to dismiss; granting [11] motion to dismiss

A simple keyword-based approach will fail to reliably extract the motions and orders because the language describing a motion filing is often very similar to filings of replies and sur-replies. In addition, linking the respective orders and motions is not always straight forward because links normally indicated by a number (e.g., [9]) may not be always present. Lastly, the language to indicate motions, although fairly standardized, differs sometimes in language and the details provided by the parties and judges:[1]

- MOTION in Limine by Amber Blackwell, Kevin Blackwell.

- MOTION to Exclude Any Evidence Relating to Recordings of Defendants or Their Agents by Keith Castilla, Uretek USA, Inc., filed. Motion Docket Date 6/7/2013.

2.2 Previous work

The task of automatically parsing docket documents is a relatively novel task and there are only a few approaches that have dealt with information extraction and classification tasks of legal court proceedings. Nallapati and Manning (2008) are

one of the few researchers who investigated machine learning approaches applied to classifying summary judgment motions only. Their findings indicated that rule-based approaches showed better results than a machine learning approach such as using a Support Vector machine (SVM). Their results indicated that a classification approach using an SVM achieves only an overall F1-value of about 80, while a specified rule-based approach is able to reach almost 90 F1-value.

More recent work by Branting (2017) addresses the issue of detecting errors in filing motions as well as the matching between motions and orders. They report a mean rank of 0.5-0.6 on this task.

The method for answering questions is described in more detail in previous work (Song et al., 2017, 2015). The capabilities of the parser, however, have been extended in order to answer specific questions on motion rulings and the time to rule. The previous parser version was restricted to case documents and was able to answer questions such as *who many cases has Judge John Tunheim ruled on in 2018*.

3 Motion analysis

We carried out an extensive annotation study for the problem at hand. Multiple domain experts annotated federal dockets with the motion information and detailed relationship information between the docket entries. Similar to Nallapati and Manning (2008), we found machine learning approaches not sufficient and only a combination of rules, ML approaches and editorial review could ensure high quality output.

Data collection Accurate gold data is necessary for hypothesis testing. Given that the editorial definitions have profound implications to the amenability of the task to automation and the significance of the results, we sought an expressive annotation scheme that would capture the language and structure of the text of each docket entry with respect to events that we were interested in. We developed a small set of token classes and structural dependencies for the annotation scheme. Dependencies only exist between these tokens and phrases, and the dependency relations are defined by the meaning of the underlying text, not necessarily its grammatical structure.

Domain experts were instructed to scan each entry of a docket to determine if any part should be annotated. We suspected that domain experts, be-

---

[1] Both motions are motions in limine, but the second motion does not explicitly use the term of art.

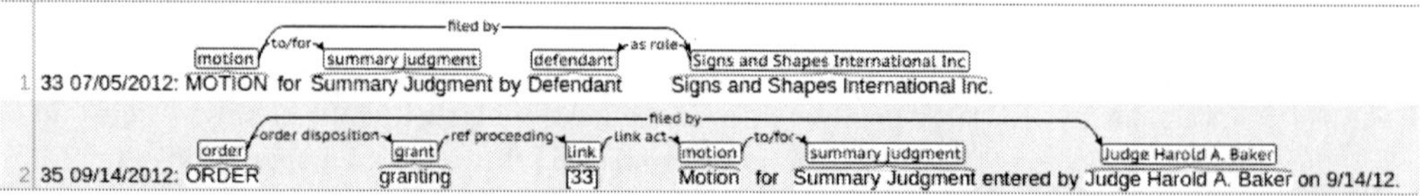

Figure 1: Example of an annotated motion order in the BRAT tool. The annotated tokens were seeded automatically, and domain experts used the drag-and-drop UI to place arcs. Annotations are based on the meaning of the sentence and tied to the most important tokens.

ing human, were susceptible to tunnel vision, i.e. putting a great deal of attention into accurately annotating one docket entry while completely missing another one. Since our token classes are only applicable to tokens related to high-level events in motion practice, more than 75% of docket entries are expected to have no annotations at all. We used the BRAT annotation tool (Stenetorp et al., 2012). Our distinction between token classes and dependencies maps perfectly into BRAT's taxonomy of entities and relations. We found that the token class annotations could be reliably seeded using regular-expression matching rules. The seeded token class annotations amounted to a keyword search, which focused the domain expert's attention on the parts of the document most likely in need of annotation. Seeding the token class annotations removed the most time consuming step of the annotation task, so that the remaining effort almost exclusively involved dragging and dropping relationship arcs. A screenshot of the tool is given at Figure 1.

Docket parsing The core component of the Litigation Analytics system focusses on motion and order detection. The overall system deploys a mix of high-precision and high-recall rules as well as some machine learning models to increase overall recall. First, motions and orders are tagged with high-precision rules. Then motions and orders are parsed in order to extract motion type, filer, order type, decision type, and judge names. Finally, the motions and orders are chained together.

High-precision rules that have very high confidence in identifying the motions in questions extract many of the motions that follow a clearly identifiable pattern. However, such rules may miss unusual language or motion/order description that contain typos or other additional material. In addition to the high-precision rules, we also adopt high-recall rules in order to capture as many motions/orders as possible and a machine learning module to learn the language variants associated with in limine motions, for example. The machine learning component is is a fall-back system for the high-precision rules system and it is triggered when the language variants in the data prevents the high-precision rules from finding a high confidence result. The learner used in this module is a regression SVM (Chang and Lin, 2011) that outputs a score that is fine-tuned for the required precision and recall numbers.

A second system that implements high-recall rules will also derive motions and linked orders. Eventually, the outputs of both components are merged to ensure overall high-precision output. The identified motions/orders are merged and cross-referenced with data we also have manually annotated for a smaller subset of dockets from past products. The merging process focusses on precision, but will also allow for higher recall and additional editorial process.

The output of all the motion analysis component is then ingested into the Litigation Analytics application of Westlaw Edge, demonstrating the analytics by judge, lawyer or law firm. Figure 2 shows how the analytics can be further explored by selecting different views. Users may be interested in specific motions, case types or parties. The app allows the user to explore the entire set of motions extracted from the federal court docket set.

Evaluation The performance of the docket parsing component was evaluated by using the annotated test data. The goal was to achieve high-precision results with acceptable recall. See Table 1 for precision and recall values we achieved. The experiments reported here are not directly comparable with (Nallapati and Manning, 2008), as their task is to detect a court order on summary judgment, whereas our task is to detect the filing of a motion.

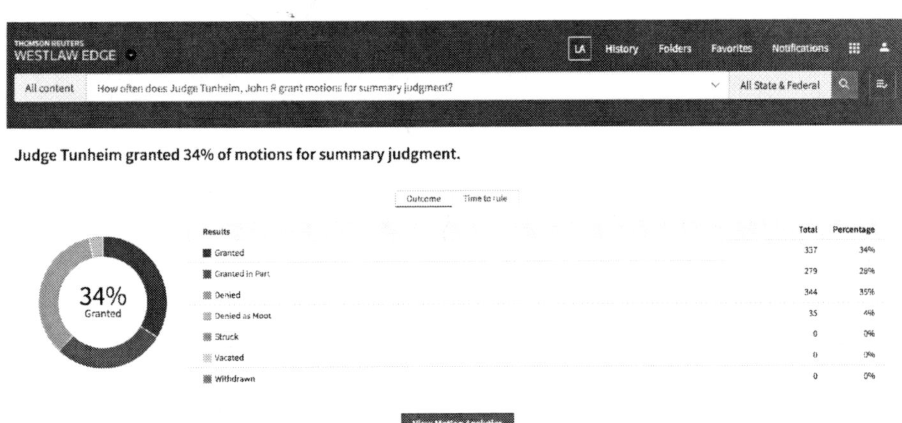

Figure 2: Natural language questions allow direct access to Litigation Analytics feature

Motion	Pecision	Recall
Dismiss	92.4	90.3
Summary Judgment	97.8	92.6
Pro Hac Vice	84.9	93.7
In Limine	94.7	91.5

Table 1: Precision and Recall values for the four most frequent motions

4 Demo

The demo of the Litigation Analytics feature will start with asking a natural language question. Typing in a name judge name into the search box will trigger multiple example questions to be asked.

- How often does Judge Tunheim, John R grant motions for summary judgment?

- How often does Judge Tunheim, John R deny motions for summary judgment?

- How long does it take Judge Tunheim, John R to rule on motions for summary judgment?

The default motion suggested is summary judgment, but the user can also specify other motions such as motion to dismiss or in limine. After selecting one of those questions, the meaning of the questions is computed and an answer in form of a generated sentence as well as a chart is generated (cf. Figure 2).

The user can link to the Litigation Analytics tool by clicking on the View Motion Analytics button. A more comprehensive view of the data collected for the respective judge will be displayed and the user can analyze the data and plan their litigation strategy. A bar chart, for example, will provide an overview of up to 23 different motions and the collected analytics. The user may drill down to another motion and is able to click through the actual docket for a particular motions or decision if desired. The overview page will also show a direct comparison between the judge's time to rule and their peers on the respective court (cf. 3).

5 Natural Language Interface

In order to enable our customers to easily find the exact information they are looking for, we developed a natural language interface *TR Discover*. Given a natural language question, we first parse it into its First Order Logic representation (FOL) via a feature-based context free grammar (FCFG). The grammar defines the options available to the user and implements the mapping from English into logic. A second translation step then maps from the FOL representation into a standard query language (e.g., a SQL or a Boolean query), allowing the translated query to rely on robust existing technology. Since all professionals can use natural language, we retain the accessibility advantages of keyword search, and since the mapping from the logical formalism to the query language is information-preserving, we retain the precision of query-based information access.

Our FCFG consists of phrase structure rules (i.e., grammar rules) and lexical entries (i.e., lexicon). The majority of our grammar rules are domain independent allowing the grammar to be portable to new domains (e.g., Tax). *G1* and *G2*

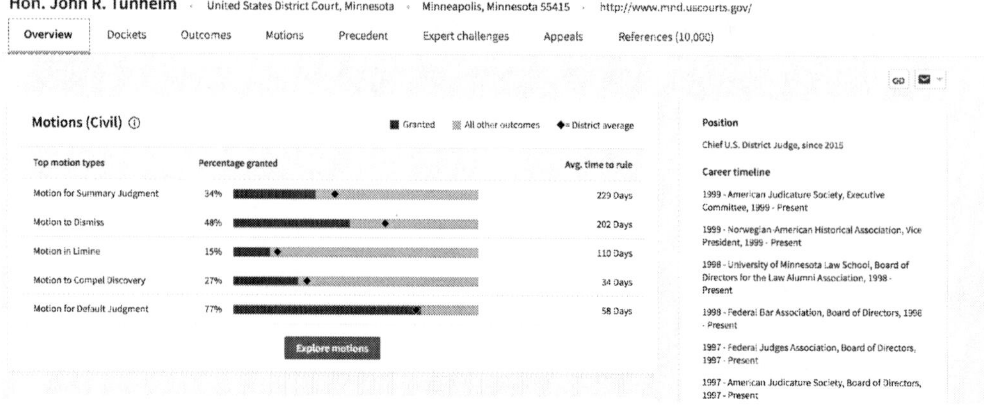

Figure 3: Average time to rule allows comparison with other judges

are two example grammar rules. Specifically, Rule *G2* indicates that a verb phrase (*VP*) contains a verb (*V*) and a noun phrase (*NP*).

- G1: NP → N

- G2: VP → V NP

Furthermore, each lexical entry in the FCFG contains a variety of domain-specific features that are used to constrain the number of parses computed by the parser preferably to a single, unambiguous parse. *L1* and *L2* are two examples of our lexical entries.

- L1:   N[TYPE=motion,   NUM=sg, SEM=$<\lambda x.\text{mtn}(x)>$] → 'motion'

- L2:   TV[TYPE=[judge,motion,grant], SEM=$<\lambda X\ x.X(\lambda y.\text{grant\_judge\_mtn}(x,y))>$, TNS=prog, NUM=?n, -PASS] → 'grant'

Here, *L1* is the lexical entry for the term *motion*, indicating that it is of TYPE *motion*, is single ("NUM=sg"), and has the semantic representation $\lambda x.mtn(x)$. Verbs (V) have additional features, such as tense (TNS) and TYPE, as shown in *L2*. The TYPE of verbs specify both the potential subject-TYPE and object-TYPE. A general form for specifying the subject and object types for verbs is as following: TYPE=[subject_constraint, object_constraint, predicate_name]. With such type constraints, we can then license the question *motion for summary judgment granted by Judge John R. Tunheim* while rejecting other questions like *motion for summary judgment granted by Attorney John R. Tunheim* on the basis of the mismatch in semantic type.

By using our FCFG, the question *How often does Judge Tunheim, John R grant motions for summary judgment?* can then be parsed into the following FOL representation:

$$count(user, P1)) \land$$
$$\forall P1.((((label(P1, summary\_judgment)) \land$$
$$(type(P1, motion))) \to$$
$$((\exists P2.(((grantedBy\_motion\_judge(P1, P2))$$
$$\land (label(P2, Tunheim, John, R, \_)) \land$$
$$(type(P2, judge)))))))$$

This FOL representation is further translated into a SQL or Boolean query in order to retrieve the search results.

6   Conclusions

This demo shows how various machine learning and NLP techniques can be used to (a) get access to analytical data more quickly via a natural language interface and (b) to create data from semistructured documents such as legal dockets. The Westlaw Edge product provides legal researchers access to this newly created analytics for judges and courts in order to formulate their litigation strategy. Motion Analytics has unlocked a large trove of data that up until now required painstaking manual review to glean useful insights. This product gives attorneys, clients, and the public a new level of insight into the litigation process.

Future research will focus on exploring machine learning methods and transfer learning techniques in order to apply our findings to other jurisdictions as well.

References

Luther Karl Branting. 2017. Automating judicial document analysis. In *Proceedings of the Second Workshop on Automated Semantic Analysis of Information in Legal Texts co-located with the 16th International Conference on Artificial Intelligence and Law (ICAIL 2017), London, UK, June 16, 2017*.

Chih-Chung Chang and Chih-Jen Lin. 2011. LIBSVM: A library for support vector machines. *ACM Transactions on Intelligent Systems and Technology*, 2:27:1–27:27. Software available at `http://www.csie.ntu.edu.tw/~cjlin/libsvm`.

Ramesh Nallapati and Christopher D Manning. 2008. Legal docket-entry classification: Where machine learning stumbles. In *Proceedings of the Conference on Empirical Methods in Natural Language Processing*, pages 438–446, Honolulu, Hawaii. Association for Computational Linguistics, Association for Computational Linguistics.

Dezhao Song, Frank Schilder, Shai Hertz, Giuseppe Saltini, Charese Smiley, Phani Nivarthi, Oren Hazai, Dudi Landau, Mike Zaharkin, Tom Zielund, et al. 2017. Building and querying an enterprise knowledge graph. *IEEE Transactions on Services Computing*.

Dezhao Song, Frank Schilder, Charese Smiley, Chris Brew, Tom Zielund, Hiroko Bretz, Robert Martin, Chris Dale, John Duprey, Tim Miller, and Johanna Harrison. 2015. TR Discover: A Natural Language Interface for Querying and Analyzing Interlinked Datasets. In *The Semantic Web - ISWC 2015*, volume 9367 of *Lecture Notes in Computer Science*, pages 21–37. Springer International Publishing.

Pontus Stenetorp, Sampo Pyysalo, Goran Topić, Tomoko Ohta, Sophia Ananiadou, and Jun'ichi Tsujii. 2012. Brat: A web-based tool for nlp-assisted text annotation. In *Proceedings of the Demonstrations at the 13th Conference of the European Chapter of the Association for Computational Linguistics*, EACL '12, pages 102–107, Stroudsburg, PA, USA. Association for Computational Linguistics.

Community lexical access for an endangered polysynthetic language:
An electronic dictionary for St. Lawrence Island Yupik

Benjamin Hunt
George Mason University
`bhunt6@gmu.edu`

Emily Chen
University of Illinois
at Urbana-Champaign
`echen41@illinois.edu`

Sylvia L.R. Schreiner
George Mason University
`sschrei2@gmu.edu`

Lane Schwartz
University of Illinois
at Urbana-Champaign
`lanes@illinois.edu`

Abstract

In this paper, we introduce a morphologically-aware electronic dictionary for St. Lawrence Island Yupik, an endangered language of the Bering Strait region. Implemented using HTML, Javascript, and CSS, the dictionary is set in an uncluttered interface and permits users to search in Yupik or in English for Yupik root words and Yupik derivational suffixes. For each matching result, our electronic dictionary presents the user with the corresponding entry from the Badten et al. (2008) Yupik-English paper dictionary. Because Yupik is a polysynthetic language, handling of multi-morphemic word forms is critical. If a user searches for an inflected Yupik word form, we perform a morphological analysis and return entries for the root word and for any derivational suffixes present in the word. This electronic dictionary should serve not only as a valuable resource for all students and speakers of Yupik, but also for field linguists working towards documentation and conservation of the language.

1 Introduction

St. Lawrence Island Yupik (hereafter *Yupik*) is an endangered, polysynthetic language of the Bering Strait region, spoken primarily on St. Lawrence Island, Alaska, and the Chukotka Peninsula of Russia.[1] It has undergone a radical language shift in the past few decades, with the youngest generation largely abandoning Yupik in favor of English (Koonooka, 2005) and Russian (Morgounova, 2007), respectively.

There is overt community interest on St. Lawrence Island in Yupik language revitalization, specifically in developing modern technologies to facilitate language-learning. We present one such technology resource: a morphologically-aware web-based version of the Badten et al. (2008) Yupik-English dictionary.[2]

2 Motivation & Prior Work

The electronic dictionary is part of a larger effort to digitize and develop resources for Yupik. A major goal of ours is to build an integrated (mobile-friendly) Yupik language portal to eventually provide St. Lawrence Island community members with an easy mechanism to access digitized Yupik print resources that are integrated with dictionary, morphological analysis, and concordance features.

Over the past two years, we have scanned, cleaned, and OCR'd several volumes of existing Yupik resources, including four anthologies of legends and folk tales (Apassingok et al., 1985, 1987, 1989; Koonooka, 2003) and three elementary readers (Apassingok et al., 1993, 1994, 1995), as well as the Yupik reference grammar of Jacobson (2001). We have also scanned (but not yet cleaned and OCR'd) nearly all of the Yupik language pre-primers, primers, and pedagogical materials present in the school library and Materials Development Center archive in Gambell, Alaska.

In addition to initiating this digital corpus for Yupik, we have also begun to implement a suite of computational systems with a wide range of utilities. To date, we have implemented a Yupik finite-state morphological analyzer (Chen and Schwartz, 2018) and a web utility (Schwartz and Chen, 2017) capable of performing orthotactic spell-checking, transliteration between Yupik's Latin and Cyrillic orthographies and IPA, syllabification, and stress-marking. A morphologically-aware web-based

---

[1]Special thanks to the Native Village of Gambell and the St. Lawrence Island Yupik speakers who have graciously shared their language and culture with us, the Gambell Schools, and the Alaska Native Language Center. This work was supported by NSF Awards 1761680 and 1760977, by a GMU Presidential Scholarship, and by a University of Illinois Graduate College Illinois Distinguished Fellowship.

[2]Demo at `https://youtu.be/quPyL3SXsdk`

Proceedings of NAACL-HLT 2019: Demonstrations, pages 122–126
Minneapolis, Minnesota, June 2 - June 7, 2019. ©2019 Association for Computational Linguistics

(1) **mangteghaghrugllangllaghyunghitunga**

mangteghagh-	-ghrugllag-	-ngllagh-	-yug-	-nghite-	-tu-	-nga
house-	-big-	-build-	-want.to-	-to.not-	-INTR.IND-	-1SG

'*I didn't want to make a huge house*'   (Jacobson, 2001, pg. 43)

(2) **angyasqughhalgunghitukung**

angyagh-	-squghhagh-	-leg-	-ngu-	-nghite-	-tu-	-kung
boat-	-small-	-one.that.has-	-to.be-	-to.not-	-INTR.IND-	-1DU

'*We$_2$ don't, or didn't, have a small boat*'   (Jacobson, 2001, pg. 43)

Figure 1: Examples of Yupik words and their component morphemes (shown as interlinear glosses).

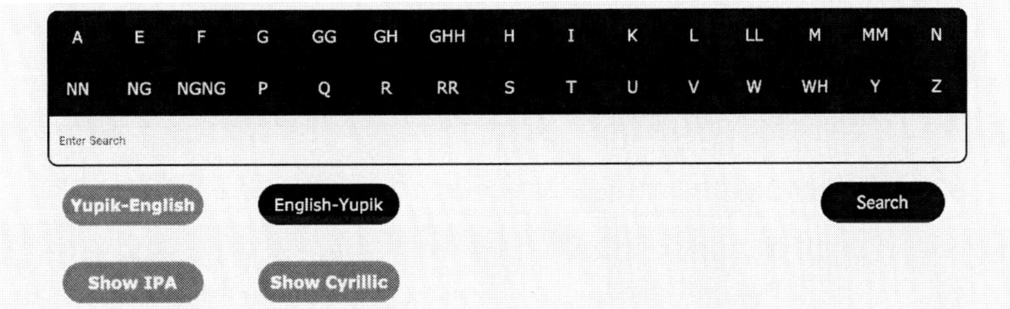

Figure 2: The primary search interface of the electronic dictionary.

dictionary represents a significant next step in supporting community language revitalization efforts.

3 Morphologically-aware searchable electronic Yupik dictionary

Yupik is a polysynthetic language with a relatively high average number of morphemes per word (Schwartz et al., 2019). Figure 1 shows examples where a single Yupik word containing multiple morphemes constitutes an entire sentence. Any Yupik electronic dictionary must be sensitive to both derivational and inflectional morphology.

Entries for the electronic dictionary were exported from the original FileMaker Pro database files used by the Alaska Native Language Center to create the Badten et al. (2008) print dictionary. Each entry in the print dictionary includes a Yupik morpheme (either a root or a derivational suffix) in both Latin and Cyrillic orthographies, an English definition, and (for many entries) example sentence(s) in which the morpheme appears and/or other notes about word origin or usage. We augment these entries by specifying the part of speech: each Yupik root is marked as noun, verb, particle, or demonstrative, and each Yupik derivational morpheme is marked for its derivation pattern (that is, as attaching to either a noun root or to a verb root, and as yielding either a noun or a verb). The pronunciation of a Yupik word is predictable from its spelling; we therefore also augment each dictionary entry with its predicted pronunciation in IPA to provide additional utility to linguists working with the language.

Our searchable Yupik electronic dictionary is implemented as a static HTML page and basic CSS style sheet, with dictionary search and morphology functions implemented in Javascript (see Figure 2 above). This provides the user access to all entries from the Badten et al. (2008) print dictionary, including roots and derivational morphemes. Internet access and mobile data coverage on St. Lawrence Island and Chukotka is relatively poor and sometimes unreliable; to support use in these environments the electronic dictionary does not require an internet connection to function.

Users can browse all dictionary entries that begin with a particular letter by selecting that letter from the Yupik alphabet displayed above the search box (Figure 3a), or search for Yupik substrings (Figure 3b), uninflected morphemes (Figure 3d), or fully inflected Yupik words (Figure 3e) including those with multiple morphemes (Figure 3f). The search results present all Yupik dictionary entries (both roots and derivational mor-

(a) After the user selects letter *S* from the search interface, all words beginning with that letter are displayed. The first three results are shown here.

sa (ся) [sɑ] *noun root* - what?; something; relative (kin)
*"sameng piyugsin? 'what do you want?'; sanguzin? 'what are you?'; sa tamaghhaan 'everything'; savut 'our relative', 'our thing(s)'; relative case is saam (rather than *sam); the expanded base sangaa- (underlyingly sangau-) rather than sangu- is used for asking what something (3rd person) is; thus: sangaawa? 'what is it?'; cf. sangwaa"*

saa (сӑ) [sɑː] *particle* - I don't know; it doesn't register in my mind; never mind
this exclamation is often pronounced with vowel as in English "hat"; = saami"

sa- (ся-) [sɑ] *verb root* - to do what?; to do something
"saa? 'what did he do?'; aatkaghten saat aghvingisafki 'what happened to your clothes when you didn't wash them?'; ayveq saa guusavgu? 'what did the walrus do when you shot it?'; saaqat? 'what's going on?, what are they doing?'"

(b) The user can enter a search term either in Yupik or in English. Here, partial results are shown for the incomplete Yupik search term *aghna*. Yupik words containing that substring are displayed.

aghnagan (аӷнаган) [ɑʁ.nɑ.ɣɑn] *particle* - hurry up
aghnagan uyuq emta 'hurry up you, knowing how you are'"

aghnagh- (аӷнаӷ-) [ɑʁ.nɑʁ] *verb root* - to wear a dress
aghnaghluni 'wearing a dress'; direct verbalization of aghnaq 'woman'

(c) The user may alternatively search in English. Here, partial results are shown for the search term *family*. Note that derivational suffixes containing the English search term are returned in addition to roots.

-nkuk / -nkut (-нкук -нкут) [nkuk.n.kut] *noun-elaborating postbase* - N and partner; N and associate(s); N and family
see %(e)nkuk / %(e)nkut

aalghaq (а̄лгак) [ɑːl.ʁɑq] *noun root* - another family in the same clan; the other of a pair of boats cooperating in a hunt; hunting partner; second wife

(d) Yupik searches may also return entries corresponding to Yupik derivational suffixes. Here, partial results are shown for the search term *nkut*.

-nkuk / -nkut (-нкук -нкут) [nkuk.n.kut] *noun-elaborating postbase* - N and partner; N and associate(s); N and family
see %(e)nkuk / %(e)nkut

kinkut (кинкут) [kin.kut] *noun root* - who? (plural)
look under kina

(e) The user may search for fully inflected Yupik words. Here, results are shown for the search term *nagatunga* 'I listened.'

nagate- (нагаты-) [nɑ.ɣɑ.tə] *verb root* - to listen
nagatuq 'he is listened'; nagataa 'he listened to her' /

(f) Preliminary support is included for multi-morphemic Yupik word searches. Here, partial results for the Yupik word *mangteghaghrugllangllaghyunghitunga* 'I didn't want to make a huge house' are shown.

mangteghagh- *verb root* - to make a house for; to reassemble a house (in fall after its parts have been aired out)
direct verbalization of mangteghaq 'house'

–ghrugllak *noun-elaborating postbase* - big N; large N
mangteghaghrugllak 'big house', mangteghaghrugllaget 'very big houses' (from mangteghaq 'house')

(g) Preliminary support is included for Yupik searches using the Cyrillic orthography. Here, partial results for the Yupik word *qikmiq* are shown. The search was performed in Cyrillic.

qikmighaq (кикмиӷак) [qik.m̩i.ʁɑq] *noun root* - puppy

qikmiq (кикмик) [qik.m̩iq] *noun root* - dog

124

Figure 3: Dictionary results for various types of searches.

phemes) that completely or partially match the Yupik search string. Users may also search in English. In that case, search results return any dictionary entries that contain the search term as a substring in the English definition (Figure 3c).

In order to facilitate use by Yupik speakers in Chukotka as well as Alaska, preliminary support is included for searches where the Yupik search term is input in the Yupik Cyrillic orthography. Figure 3g depicts results where the search term was written in Cyrillic. Currently, searches performed in Cyrillic return English entries only, as entries pull from the English-language Badten et al. (2008) dictionary. This may be useful for a user who does not speak Russian but who has come across a Yupik word written in Cyrillic and wishes to find out its meaning. However, it does not address the needs of Yupik speakers who also speak Russian, but not English. We intend future iterations to integrate entries from Russian-language dictionaries of Yupik, such that a search performed in Cyrillic will return Yupik or Russian entries, depending on the search term, just as a search performed in the Latin orthography returns Yupik or English entries.

4   Community & Research Impacts

The electronic dictionary with its existing functionalities has the ability to make a significant impact on the Yupik language community as well as researchers working on the language. The current version of the electronic dictionary includes preliminary support for multi-morphemic searches using the integrated morphological analyzer, and preliminary support for searches performed in Cyrillic. More robust implementations of these features are ongoing.

We anticipate that the electronic dictionary will greatly facilitate access to knowledge that was otherwise difficult to obtain, and make it readily available to all community members. Versions of the print dictionary have been available through the University of Alaska Press in various editions since 1983, with revisions in 1987 and 2008. However, the print edition is bulky and relatively expensive; while the school libraries in Gambell and Savoonga have copies, most community members (including some members of the Yupik Bible translation project) do not.

While the dictionary should impact all community members, regardless of age, we expect it to most positively shape the language experience of the younger generations, promoting language use among youth who may be unlikely (for social reasons) to ask elders about word-forms. Moreover, one of the most promising features of the dictionary with respect to language learning is the integration of the `foma` finite-state analyzer, which allows fully inflected word forms with multiple morphemes to be searched in order to either define parts of the word or to reconstruct its full meaning. This should be especially valuable for students who have not yet mastered the polysynthetic aspects of the Yupik language. For example, students could be allowed to use the dictionary in the classroom to help them read through Yupik texts that contain vocabulary that is at a higher level than they might otherwise be able to handle. Students would not need to be able to parse an unfamiliar word to be able to look up the meaning of the root.

The electronic dictionary is practical in much the same ways for linguists and researchers, allowing them to swiftly search for word forms and definitions via a resource that is significantly more portable than a two-volume paper dictionary. The integration of the `foma` finite-state analyzer is of particular note, however, since it can be used in the construction of morphological interlinear glosses (see Figure 1), which are critical for the processing and sharing of linguistic data. The electronic dictionary supplemented with the morphological analyzer greatly expedites this process, which must otherwise be done by hand.

We plan to conduct live user field testing of the electronic dictionary in the Gambell School during spring and summer 2019. User feedback will inform user-interface redesign decisions and will provide valuable feedback regarding which features are most valued by Yupik community members. We also plan to embed the dictionary in native mobile apps for Android and iOS, and to conduct field testing of those user interfaces as well.

While this electronic dictionary provides direct support for the language revitalization efforts of the Yupik community specifically, we hope that it might serve as a blueprint for similar tools for other endangered languages, particularly those of a polysynthetic nature. Such an analyzer-linked dictionary may be of use both to the language communities themselves, and to researchers working with the communities to reinforce their efforts.

References

Anders Apassingok, (Iyaaka), Jessie Uglowook, (Ayuqliq), Lorena Koonooka, (Inyiyngaawen), and Edward Tennant, (Tengutkalek), editors. 1993. *Kallagneghet / Drumbeats*. Bering Strait School District, Unalakleet, Alaska.

Anders Apassingok, (Iyaaka), Jessie Uglowook, (Ayuqliq), Lorena Koonooka, (Inyiyngaawen), and Edward Tennant, (Tengutkalek), editors. 1994. *Akiingqwaghneghet / Echoes*. Bering Strait School District, Unalakleet, Alaska.

Anders Apassingok, (Iyaaka), Jessie Uglowook, (Ayuqliq), Lorena Koonooka, (Inyiyngaawen), and Edward Tennant, (Tengutkalek), editors. 1995. *Suluwet / Whisperings*. Bering Strait School District, Unalakleet, Alaska.

Anders Apassingok, (Iyaaka), Willis Walunga, (Kepelgu), and Edward Tennant, (Tengutkalek), editors. 1985. *Sivuqam Nangaghnegha — Siivanllemta Ungipaqellghat / Lore of St. Lawrence Island — Echoes of our Eskimo Elders*, volume 1: Gambell. Bering Strait School District, Unalakleet, Alaska.

Anders Apassingok, (Iyaaka), Willis Walunga, (Kepelgu), and Edward Tennant, (Tengutkalek), editors. 1987. *Sivuqam Nangaghnegha — Siivanllemta Ungipaqellghat / Lore of St. Lawrence Island — Echoes of our Eskimo Elders*, volume 2: Savoonga. Bering Strait School District, Unalakleet, Alaska.

Anders Apassingok, (Iyaaka), Willis Walunga, (Kepelgu), and Edward Tennant, (Tengutkalek), editors. 1989. *Sivuqam Nangaghnegha — Siivanllemta Ungipaqellghat / Lore of St. Lawrence Island — Echoes of our Eskimo Elders*, volume 3: Southwest Cape. Bering Strait School District, Unalakleet, Alaska.

Adelinda W. (Aghnaghaghpik) Badten, Vera Oovi Kaneshiro, Marie Oovi, and Steven A. Jacobson, editors. 1983. *A Dictionary of the St. Lawrence Island / Siberian Yupik Eskimo Language*, 1st edition. Alaska Native Language Center, Fairbanks, Alaska. Alaska Native Language Archive Identifier SY975J1983b.

Adelinda W. (Aghnaghaghpik) Badten, Vera Oovi Kaneshiro, Marie Oovi, and Steven A. Jacobson, editors. 1987. *A Dictionary of the St. Lawrence Island / Siberian Yupik Eskimo Language*, 2nd edition. Alaska Native Language Center, Fairbanks, Alaska.

Linda Womkon Badten, (Aghnaghaghpik), Vera Oovi Kaneshiro, (Uqiitlek), Marie Oovi, (Uvegtu), and Christopher Koonooka, (Petuwaq). 2008. *St. Lawrence Island / Siberian Yupik Eskimo Dictionary*. Alaska Native Language Center, University of Alaska Fairbanks. Alaska Native Language Archive Identifier SY975J2008.

Emily Chen and Lane Schwartz. 2018. A morphological analyzer for St. Lawrence Island / Central Siberian Yupik. In *Proceedings of the 11th Language Resources and Evaluation Conference (LREC'18)*, Miyazaki, Japan.

Steven A. Jacobson. 2001. *A Practical Grammar of the St. Lawrence Island/Siberian Yupik Eskimo Language*, 2nd edition. Alaska Native Language Center, University of Alaska Fairbanks, Fairbanks, Alaska. Alaska Native Language Archive Identifier SY975J2001.

Christopher Koonooka, (Petuwaq). 2003. *Ungipaghaghlanga — Quutmiit Yupigita Ungipaghaatangit / Let Me Tell a Story — Legends of the Siberian Eskimos*. Alaska Native Language Center, University of Alaska Fairbanks, Fairbanks, Alaska. Transliterated and translated from the Chukotka collection of G.A. Menovshchikov. Stories told by Ayveghhaq, Tagikaq, Asuya, Alghalek, Nanughhaq, and Wiri. Alaska Native Language Archive Identifier SY003K2003.

Christopher Koonooka, (Petuwaq). 2005. Yupik language instruction in Gambell (St. Lawrence Island, Alaska). *Études/Inuit/Studies*, 29(1/2):251–266.

Daria Morgounova. 2007. Language, identities and ideologies of the past and present Chukotka. *Études/Inuit/Studies*, 31(1-2):183–200.

Lane Schwartz and Emily Chen. 2017. Liinnaqumalghiit: A web-based tool for addressing orthographic transparency in St. Lawrence Island/Central Siberian Yupik. *Language Documentation and Conservation*, 11:275–288.

Lane Schwartz, Sylvia L.R. Schreiner, and Emily Chen. 2019. Community-focused language documentation in support of language education and revitalization for St. Lawrence Island Yupik. *Études/Inuit/Studies*. Forthcoming.

Visualizing Inferred Morphotactic Systems

Haley Lepp
University of Washington
Department of Linguistics
hlepp@uw.edu

Olga Zamaraeva
University of Washington
Department of Linguistics
olzama@uw.edu

Emily M. Bender
University of Washington
Department of Linguistics
ebender@uw.edu

Abstract

We present a web-based system that facilitates the exploration of complex morphological patterns found in morphologically rich languages. The need for better understanding of such patterns is urgent for linguistics and important for cross-linguistically applicable natural language processing. We give an overview of the system architecture and describe a sample case study on Abui [abz], a Trans-New Guinea language spoken in Indonesia.

1 Introduction

Understanding and describing morphological patterns is a fundamental task in both documentary linguistics and the development of language technology. Many low-resource or underdescribed languages evince a high degree of morphological complexity, with large numbers of distinct affix types and many affix tokens possible within a single word. At the same time, building language technology for morphologically complex low-resource languages requires a rule-based morphological analyzer when datasets are not large enough for ML approaches (see Garrette et al. 2013; Erdmann and Habash 2018, *inter alia*). Our contribution is within the context of the AGGREGATION project, which aims to automatically infer broad typological characteristics and morphological patterns for understudied languages (Bender et al., 2013; Zamaraeva et al., 2017). We developed this visualization tool to help linguists to understand the morphological system implicit in large datasets and to refine automatically generated grammar specifications which model that morphological system. Thus we expect this tool to directly assist in language description. Because linguistic typology depends on accurate language description, and truly language-independent NLP depends on linguistic typology (see Bender 2011

and Gerz et al. 2018), we also anticipate long-term benefits for NLP.

We present a visualization component for the MOM morphological inference system (see §2.1) which takes as input a collection of morpheme-segmented, glossed text and produces a set of hypotheses about classes of stems and affixes, and the cooccurrence and ordering possibilities between them. This set of hypotheses is cast as a grammar specification that can be used by the Grammar Matrix customization system (Bender et al., 2010) to automatically create an implemented grammar capable of morphological parsing. Our system helps the linguist visualize and explore these hypotheses, facilitating both further linguistic theorizing of the dataset and the production of a more accurate implemented grammar. The grammar can be used to produce annotations for additional unglossed data, as in Zamaraeva et al. 2017, because the inferred system generalizes beyond the specific combinations of morphemes observed.[1]

2 System overview

2.1 Back-end

The morphological graph that our system visualizes comes from the MOM morphological inference software (Wax, 2014; Zamaraeva, 2016). MOM outputs a directed acyclic graph specified in DOT (Gansner et al., 1993) where nodes are inflectional classes of words and position classes of affixes, and edges reflect the ordering possibilities of those affixes. This graph is translated by the Grammar Matrix customization system to

---

[1] The (frequently updated) Alpha-version of the system can be accessed via http://uakari.ling.washington.edu/aggregation/. The demonstration video is at https://youtu.be/qn96Zg-6wkE. All of the code and sample data are available in the repository: https://git.ling.washington.edu/agg/mom

Proceedings of NAACL-HLT 2019: Demonstrations, pages 127–131
Minneapolis, Minnesota, June 2 - June 7, 2019. ©2019 Association for Computational Linguistics

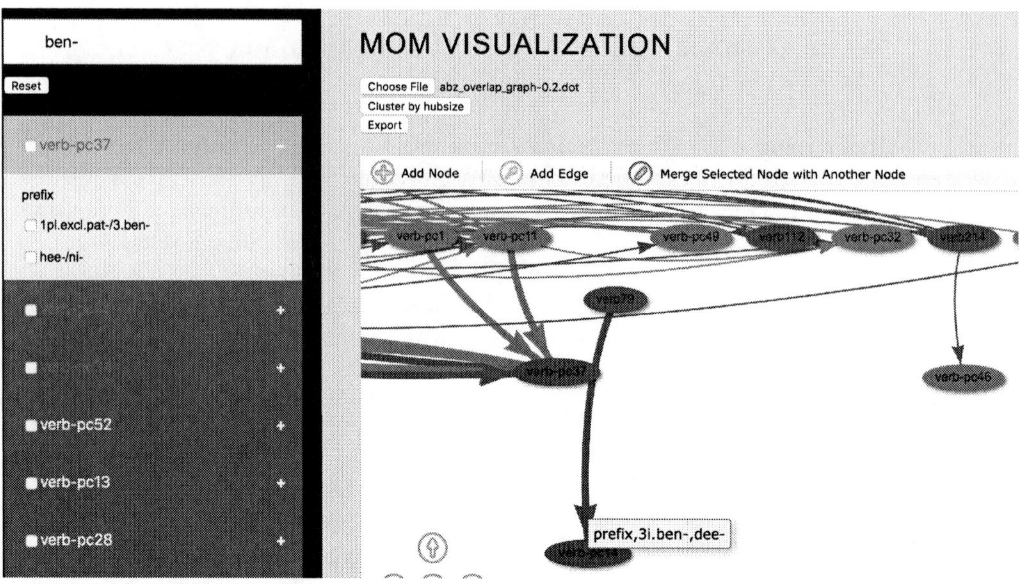

Figure 1: A portion of the visualization window, with two of the nodes selected. The contents of the nodes can also be explored via the sidebar which has a search field. Moving nodes around helps the user explore the denser parts of the graph.

a grammar that includes: (i) lexical types, each instantiated by (ii) lexical entries, and (iii) lexical rule types, defining position classes, and each instantiated by (iv) lexical rules, which each attach a specific affix. The position classes also define the possible order of attachment of morphemes, known as the morphotactics of the language.

These graphs tend to be quite large, because of the underlying complexity of the systems they describe and because of noise introduced by glossing inconsistencies and the inference process. For example, the graph we use in our case study (see §3) is the visualization of an analysis of a dataset consisting of 8609 glossed verb tokens and includes 65 nodes (20 for stems and 45 for affixes).

2.2 Visualization window

The first component of our visualization front-end, built using the Network library of vis.js,[2] is a visual network of all the morphological data that MOM outputs as a text (DOT) file. When a user imports a DOT file into the system, the gold, right-hand side of the webpage will load a visual representation of the graph.

Roots are represented as dark purple nodes, while prefixes are a medium purple, and suffixes are light purple. The morphemes are labeled with

a unique ID, such as "verb1", and hovering over a node with a cursor will bring up a truncated list of root and affix spellings assigned to that stem or position class in the inferred graph.

The relationships between these morphemes are represented by directed arrows, showing in what ways the roots and affixes in a language can be combined. The root will point to the first affix, such as a prefix, and that affix will point to whichever next affix is possible.[3]

There are a number of actions that the user can take within this visualization. When the user clicks on a node, the node and all its associated linkages become bold, to aid the user in viewing the relationships. The user can also drag nodes and arrows to examine particular linkages, and zoom in on specific relationships. A "cluster" button above the visualization will combine nodes with many linkages into one, allowing the user to better see the morphemes with fewer connections. Double-clicking on the cluster will reset the graph to a full view.

---

[3]On the analysis provided by the backend system, word construction starts with the root, prefixes are added from the root out, and suffixes are attached last, again from the root out. Thus the leftmost prefix is the input for the first suffix.

---

[2]http://visjs.org/docs/network/

2.3 Manipulation

The primary purpose of giving researchers a visual representation of a graph is to give a new perspective that may elicit the discovery of new patterns or possibly inconsistencies in the glossing of the underlying data. A secondary purpose is to help the user make improvements to the graph, so that the resulting grammar output by the Grammar Matrix customization system will also function better. For both purposes, it is important that the user be able to manipulate the analysis while looking at the visual representation. Thus the second component of the interface is the functionality for the user to manipulate the graph within the visualization. At the top of the network window, there is a purple button called "Edit". When clicked, the Add Edge button appears, with Remove Edge appearing once an edge is selected.

The simplest modification that the user is expected to make to the graph is adding and deleting edges. MOM typically infers lots of possibilities for morpheme orderings from the data (see Figure 1). Some of these orderings may reflect noise in either the underlying data or in the inference results; there may also be missing orderings that the linguist is aware of based on their expertise. Either way, the morphological hypothesis presented by the system will normally require revisions. To add an ordering possibility between a stem and an affix or between two affixes, the user may add a directed arrow by clicking on a node and dragging the new arrow to another node before releasing the click. If the user notices an incorrect linkage between the morphemes, they can select the arrow and click "remove edge".

When the user clicks on a node, two more options appear: Remove Edge (explained above) and Merge Nodes. "Merge" allows the user to combine two previously separate nodes. This is useful if the researcher notices that the MOM inference system has done insufficient generalization and failed to combine two sets of affixes into one position class or two sets of stems in one inflectional class. "Split", when implemented, will split a node into two if the visualization allows the researcher to see that the graph incorrectly combines two position or inflectional classes. With "Split", we will be adding the functionality to select subsets of node contents (e.g. some but not all of the stem spellings associated with a node). This will also add the functionality to merge a subset of a node with another node.

Once the user has made changes to the graph, they can click the "Export" button above the window. The system will save the adjusted analysis to a downloadable DOT file, which can be imported into MOM or reloaded into the visualization system at a later time.

2.4 Sidebar

The third component of the interface is the purple sidebar on the left-hand side of the page. When the user loads a graph, the sidebar populates with a list of every node in the graph. When the user clicks on a plus sign on a row in the list, the row will expand, listing every associated content item, such as stems for inflectional classes and affix spellings and glosses for position classes.

In a large graph, it can be difficult to find a specific morpheme in the visual representation. At the top of the sidebar, there is a search box in which the user can search for any node ID or spelling, or gloss. The user can reset the results by clicking the "Reset" button.

3 Case study

In this section we demonstrate how the system can be used to refine morphological hypotheses suggested automatically by the MOM system and in the process discover a glossing inconsistency in the underlying data.

We run the MOM system (the back end) on the Abui dataset (Kratochvíl, 2017, abz; Trans-New Guinea). The dataset comes from a multi-year fieldwork project which involves data collection, transcription, and linguistic analysis, including that of morphology. Our tool targets this last stage. Example 1 illustrates the original input.

(1) Na   aloba   he-mia
     1SG.AGT thorn.LOC 3UND.LOC-take.IPFV

     'I am taking out the thorn.'   [abz; N12.064]

Glossed examples like this one present an analysis of morphology on one particular sentence; the linguist will want to generalize to a set of hypotheses about the general morphological system in the language. For example, a question might be: Which prefixes occur with which verb stems (Zamaraeva et al., 2017) and is there any semantic coherence to the verb inflectional classes identified this way (Kratochvíl and Delpada, 2015)? In order to answer this kind of question more fully, linguists

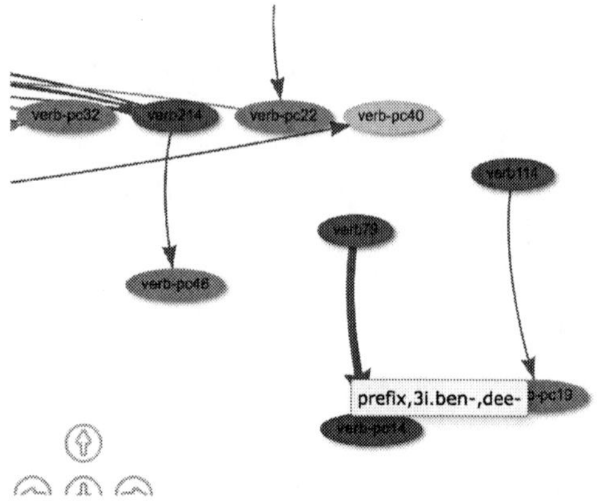

Figure 2: Some nodes ended up separate from the main portion of the morphological graph.

Figure 3: Two nodes for the benefactive prefix were merged in one.

may find it helpful not only to find all possible cooccurrences of, say, prefixes and verbs, but also to visualize them as a graph. The MOM system produces a DOT file which represents all possible cooccurrences, and our tool visualizes it. The morphological hypotheses that the DOT file represents are the result of all of the cooccurrence patterns found in the original data being compressed in such a way that nodes which share more than 20% of edges are combined (Wax, 2014).[4]

Examining the graph, we notice that, while most of it is connected, there are a couple of nodes on the right that stand alone. Upon inspection, it turns out that the node "verb79" contains only one stem, the serial verb l ('give'). The position class that it is linked to, "verb-pc14", contains prefixes which are glossed as 3rd person, benefactive. After we search for "ben-", we see that there are two more nodes in the graph which contain affixes with this gloss (see Figure 1). Now we can hypothesize that two or all three of them actually should be one position class and we can merge them in the graph as described above and the result shown in Figure 3. Furthermore, after we search for "give", we discover that the serial verb l is present in the graph both as a root and as a prefix (l-). In other words, the visualization helped us to discover that a single morpheme (pairing of form and meaning) was analyzed in two different ways in the annotations (as a stem and as a prefix). This could be the result of simple inconsistency in glossing in the dataset or it could be indicative of variation in the language meriting further attention by the linguist. Finally, recall that the graph is a specification of a morphological grammar, so any revisions of the hypotheses that we make in this fashion can be tested by creating a grammar automatically using the Grammar Matrix customization system and then parsing held-out data.

4 Future work

Among the technical improvements we envision are more manipulation functions, such as the ability to split a node in two. We also plan to allow the user to manipulate the graph from the sidebar in addition to from the visual representation. With these improvements in place, we plan to invite field linguists to try out the system and map out further features based on user feedback.

A second direction for future work is to update the back-end MOM system so it can run inference constrained by user-specified improvements to the graph. Our goal here will be to assist the linguist in discovering the further implications of split/merge decisions and more generally facilitate collaborative human-machine discovery of morphological systems.

5 Conclusion

We have presented a visualization tool that allows users to explore automatically inferred morphological grammar specifications based on linguistically annotated datasets. For the linguist-user, this tool has two purposes: (i) to help them better understand the systems inherent in their datasets and annotations and (ii) to help them refine the resulting morphological analyzer so as to produce better annotations of unglossed data. In the longer term, more thorough glossing of linguistic datasets and analyses of morphological systems benefits both linguistic typology and, ultimately, NLP.

---

[4]The compression rate is a configurable parameter.

Acknowledgments

This material is based upon work supported by the National Science Foundation under Grant No. BCS-1561833. Any opinions, findings, and conclusions or recommendations expressed in this material are those of the authors and do not necessarily reflect the views of the National Science Foundation.

We thank Swetha Ramaswamy for developing the prototype for our system; Russel Hugo and David Inman for participating in the prototype interviews; Tara Clark for contributing to the initial UI implementation discussion; and František Kratochvíl for motivating discussion and for sharing the Abui data.

References

Emily M Bender. 2011. On achieving and evaluating language-independence in NLP. *Linguistic Issues in Language Technology*, 6(3):1–26.

Emily M Bender, Scott Drellishak, Antske Fokkens, Laurie Poulson, and Safiyyah Saleem. 2010. Grammar customization. *Research on Language & Computation*, 8:1–50. ISSN 1570-7075.

Emily M Bender, Michael Wayne Goodman, Joshua Crowgey, and Fei Xia. August 2013. Towards creating precision grammars from interlinear glossed text: Inferring large-scale typological properties. In *Proceedings of the 7th Workshop on Language Technology for Cultural Heritage, Social Sciences, and Humanities*, pages 74–83, Sofia, Bulgaria, August 2013. Association for Computational Linguistics. URL http://www.aclweb. org/anthology/W13-2710.

Alexander Erdmann and Nizar Habash. 2018. Complementary strategies for low resourced morphological modeling. In *Proceedings of the Fifteenth Workshop on Computational Research in Phonetics, Phonology, and Morphology*, pages 54–65.

Emden R. Gansner, Eleftherios Koutsofios, Stephen C. North, and Kiem phong Vo. 1993. A technique for drawing directed graphs. *IEEE transactions on software engineering*, 19(3):214–230.

Dan Garrette, Jason Mielens, and Jason Baldridge. 2013. Real-world semi-supervised learning of postaggers for low-resource languages. In *Proceedings of the 51st Annual Meeting of the Association for Computational Linguistics (Volume 1: Long Papers)*, volume 1, pages 583–592.

Daniela Gerz, Ivan Vulić, Edoardo Maria Ponti, Roi Reichart, and Anna Korhonen. 2018. On the relation between linguistic typology and (limitations of) multilingual language modeling. In *Proceedings of the 2018 Conference on Empirical Methods in Natural Language Processing*, pages 316–327.

František Kratochvíl. 2017. Abui Corpus. Electronic Database: 162,000 words of natural speech, and 37,500 words of elicited material (February 2017). Nanyang Technological University, Singapore.

František Kratochvíl and Benidiktus Delpada. 2015. Degrees of affectedness and verbal prefixation in Abui (Papuan). In Stefan Müller, editor, *Proceedings of the 22nd International Conference on Head-Driven Phrase Structure Grammar, Nanyang Technological University (NTU), Singapore*, pages 216–233, Stanford, CA, 2015. CSLI Publications.

David Wax. 2014. Automated grammar engineering for verbal morphology. Master's thesis, University of Washington.

Olga Zamaraeva. 2016. Inferring morphotactics from interlinear glossed text: combining clustering and precision grammars. In *Proceedings of the 14th SIG-MORPHON Workshop on Computational Research in Phonetics, Phonology, and Morphology*, pages 141–150.

Olga Zamaraeva, František Kratochvíl, Emily M Bender, Fei Xia, and Kristen Howell. 2017. Computational support for finding word classes: A case study of Abui. In *Proceedings of the 2nd Workshop on the Use of Computational Methods in the Study of Endangered Languages*, pages 130–140.

A Research Platform for Multi-Robot Dialogue with Humans

Matthew Marge, Stephen Nogar, Cory J. Hayes, Stephanie M. Lukin,
Jesse Bloecker, Eric Holder, Clare Voss

U.S. Army Research Laboratory
Adelphi, MD 20783
`matthew.r.marge.civ@mail.mil`

Abstract

This paper presents a research platform that supports spoken dialogue interaction with multiple robots. The demonstration showcases our crafted MultiBot testing scenario in which users can verbally issue search, navigate, and follow instructions to two robotic teammates: a simulated ground robot and an aerial robot. This flexible language and robotic platform takes advantage of existing tools for speech recognition and dialogue management that are compatible with new domains, and implements an inter-agent communication protocol (tactical behavior specification), where verbal instructions are encoded for tasks assigned to the appropriate robot.

1 Introduction

We investigate dialogue dynamics between a human and multiple robotic teammates in scenarios that reflect the urgency of tasks, such as search and rescue. While multi-participant dialogue has long been studied (Sacks et al., 1978), human-robot communication remains an area that merits further investigation. Natural language offers human teammates a hands-free way to interact with multiple robots, unlike *direct teleoperation* where a robot is controlled with a hand-held device. Language also encourages human teammates to issue complex, abstract-level instructions, rather than lower-level command-and-control instructions.

This demonstration shows the completed integration of spoken dialogue with simulated robots in a simulated environment. A ground robot (Clearpath Husky) and a small, quadrotor aerial robot (Qualcomm Snapdragon Flight) work with a human teammate in a search and rescue scenario using a platform we call MultiBot. Spoken instructions are interpreted and independent tasks are delegated by a dialogue manager to

these robots, including waypoint navigation, exploration, and object detection, as well as joint tasks such as following one another. The robots adapt their behavior to meet human-specified conditions, e.g., moving quickly given an urgent task.

One contribution of this research is a software platform for exploring new aspects of multi-robot dialogue to explore language, robotics, and human-robot interaction research. Natural language serves as a single interface to consistently interact with multiple robots on a team, despite these robots having different capabilities. The robotic behaviors are built on top of the Robot Operating System (ROS), an open-source framework that uses the same communication protocols for physical platforms as in simulation, to explore how interaction dynamics change in new environments and tasks.

A second contribution of this research is methodological: the software components within our platform for dialogue management and robot navigation are "wizard-swappable", meaning that human operators (i.e., wizards) may stand-in functionally for software components yet to be developed, typically in the initial design stage of an autonomous system. This approach supports collecting training data for the underlying algorithms. The most immediate application of our research platform is for collecting natural language data from experiment participants to use in modeling how humans communicate with multiple robots in task-oriented dialogue.

2 Scenarios and Research Approach

Our platform allows for the testing and implementation of new testing scenarios for language, robotics, and human-robot interaction research. A testing scenario may vary the number and types of robots and robotic capabilities, language under-

Proceedings of NAACL-HLT 2019: Demonstrations, pages 132–137
Minneapolis, Minnesota, June 2 - June 7, 2019. ©2019 Association for Computational Linguistics

	Exp 1 (Marge et al., 2016)	Exp 2 (Bonial et al., 2017)	Exp 3 completed 2018	Exp 4 ongoing data collection	ScoutBot (Lukin et al., 2018)	MultiBot current
Dialogue Processing	wizard + typing	wizard + button presses	wizard + button presses	ASR + auto-DM	ASR + auto-DM	ASR + auto-DM
Robotic Behaviors	wizard + joystick	wizard + joystick	wizard + joystick	wizard + joystick	finite state machine	auto-assign via TBS
Robot(s)	1 physical	1 physical	1 simulated	1 simulated	1 simulated	2 simulated
Environment	indoors + real building	indoors + real building	indoors + sim building	indoors + sim building	indoors + sim building	outdoors + sim buildings

Table 1: Testing scenarios over time. Columns depict progression of testing scenario experimentation and development; rows represent scenario components (DM: Dialogue Management; TBS: tactical behavior specification)

standing and dialogue management capabilities, as well as the physical or simulated environment and user task. Scenarios can be crafted for the following interdisciplinary research objectives:

Language research, to test linguistically-challenging instructions that are situationally-relevant given different objects, structures, landmarks, and locations within the environment;

Robotics research, to demonstrate robotic behaviors on the ground and in the air, feasible for the physical robots and their simulated counterparts;

Human-robot interaction research, to track effective navigation and coordinated exploration in the environment by multiple autonomous robots as a result of spoken dialogue with human teammates.

The MultiBot Platform was built upon a foundation of prior research and development efforts in these areas of research. The columns of Table 1 show the temporal progression and development of various testing scenarios leading up to Multi-Bot. Technical details specific to MultiBot follow in Section 3.

Components supported by the MultiBot Platform are depicted as rows in Table 1. The key milestones in the progression included using human wizards through Experiments 1-4 (prior and ongoing work) with different methods of performing the task (typing or pressing buttons that have predefined text messages) to build up the databases of dialogue interactions, a dialogue manager, and robot behaviors. The data collected in these prior experiments was used to train the ScoutBot system as an end-to-end, fully autonomous dialogue management and autonomous robot implementation (Lukin et al., 2018) for control of a single simulated robot in an indoor simulated building.

The crafting of a new, realistic testing scenario for dialogue with more than one autonomous robot made evident new integration requirements in our research platform. We needed a testing scenario with a coherent, structured narrative involving a ground and an aerial robot demonstrating new behavior sequences as the software components were being developed. To develop MultiBot, we used a simulated outdoor environment that covers a complex region of roads and buildings. MultiBot also builds on the ScoutBot testing scenario with two other significant changes: (i) the human operator can now address these two robots, each of which may verbally respond with their own feedback, and (ii) the navigation commands to the robot from the dialogue manager are now adaptable, pivoting through an intermediary computational representation language that can in turn be mapped to robot-specific behaviors.

The MultiBot Platform supports targeted evaluation of the individual components (the rows in Table 1) as well as holistic, systematic evaluation. Possible measures of these components include evaluation of the robot behaviors (e.g., distance to goal), the performance of the robot itself (e.g., energy efficiency in performing tasks), and dialogue processing (e.g., coverage of utterances and appropriateness of recovery strategies). Holistic evaluation in human subject experiments can measure perceived task workload, success, and satisfaction, as well as overall task completion and efficiency both for individual robots and as a team in comparison to a system using direct teleoperation of the robots.

3 Architecture Overview

Figure 1 showcases a high-level view of the flow of information in our platform, depicting the MultiBot testing scenario as an example. The user visually observes the simulated environment, listens to audio feedback from the robots (lower left-hand corner of Figure 1), and speaks verbal instructions. A speech recognizer (top left-hand

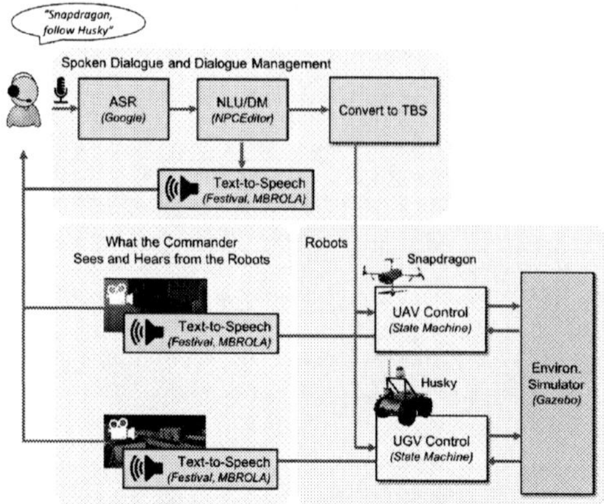

Figure 1: Platform Architecture, MultiBot Testing Scenario

corner of Figure 1) passes the user utterance to a Natural Language Understanding (NLU) and Dialogue Management (DM) process. The NLU/DM module ensures the utterance is well-formed and executable, and may prompt for additional information from the user. Well-formed instructions are then sent to a process that formats them into an unambiguous, structured command that triggers robot behaviors (lower right-hand corner) which work in tandem with the environment simulator to continuously update the status of the robot(s) within the simulated environment. The platform generates verbal feedback from the robots, and the visualization is updated based on the actions of the robot(s).

3.1 Spoken Dialogue and Dialogue Management

The MultiBot Platform is designed to support experimentation through the swapping of different language understanding and processing capabilities. The capabilities chosen for the MultiBot testing scenario leverage existing components of a spoken dialogue and dialogue management interface, extending these tools to support conversing with multiple robots. Speech recognition is supported by Google's Automatic Speech Recognition API. Dialogue processing utilizes the NPCEditor dialogue manager (Leuski and Traum, 2011; Hartholt et al., 2013). The NLU/DM module interprets dialogue instructions and produces responses using statistical retrieval algorithms from prior dialogue system implementations (Traum et al., 2015; Lukin et al., 2018) which allow for a range of unconstrained speech input. This testing sce-

nario uses a novel configuration with five categories of instructions: (1) wake (get a particular robot's attention), (2) waypoint navigation of one or more robots, (3) follow-behind commands, (4) inspection, and (5) patrol of a pre-defined area.

We use the simultaneous message generation that the ScoutBot system implements to support generating clarification responses to the human teammate and to the robotic platforms, the latter of which are converted into an instruction issued using a Tactical Behavior Specification (TBS) message (Oh et al., 2015) for MultiBot. This provides a common format for issuing a high level action with relevant location data and object information. When robot actions are completed, a text message signal is sent that may either be converted from text to speech, as depicted in Figure 1, or shown in a chat window if the environment is noisy or if stealth is desired. Text-to-speech synthesis of the robots and the NLU/DM module is performed using the Festival Speech Synthesis System[1] with MBROLA voices.[2]

3.2 Robotic Behaviors

Robotic behaviors tailored for a particular task may be substituted using the MultiBot Platform. For the teaming application supported by the MultiBot testing scenario, robots need the ability to make independent decisions once a verbal instruction has been issued. To support complex actions, we implement a behavior tree based on the open-source Smach library[3] within ROS.[4] The library is an implementation of a finite state machine that manages the robot's behavior, chaining simple actions into more complex actions or tasks. Each robot state (e.g., searching, following, landing) must terminate with one of multiple specific outcomes (e.g., succeeded, failed, interrupted). This outcome determines the next action according to the behavior tree. Once an instruction is implemented as a chain of actions, it can be used as a building block in other instruction, providing a framework for more advanced behaviors.

TBS messages are defined in ROS in coordination with the Smach-based behavior trees. The output of the behaviors are any discovered objects of interest and the resulting state of the robot, such as position, and are provided back to the human

---

[1] http://www.cstr.ed.ac.uk/projects/festival/
[2] http://tcts.fpms.ac.be/synthesis/mbrola.html
[3] http://wiki.ros.org/smach
[4] http://www.ros.org/

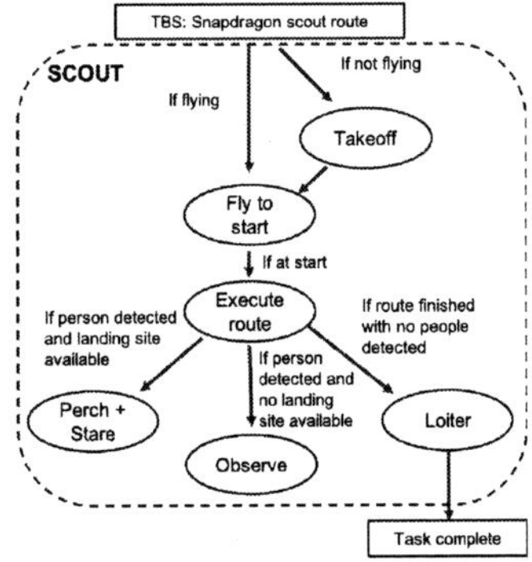

Figure 2: Behavior tree for "scout" instruction

operator through the speech synthesis previously described. Included behaviors are "go-to", "follow", "scout", "search", and (for the aerial robot) "takeoff/land". The "scout" instruction is presented in Figure 2. As the robot moves, it uses an onboard camera and an object classifier (Bjelonic, 2016–2018) to search for objects of interest. In the MultiBot testing scenario, if it recognizes an injured person it can consider multiple actions on how best to continue observation. If a suitable landing location is nearby, the robot will execute a "perch and stare" behavior, otherwise it will hover nearby and observe.

4 Demo Summary

A demonstration of the developed behaviors for the MultiBot testing scenario was performed in a software in the loop simulation (SITL). This simulates the robotic sensors and actuators, allowing for verification of the developed language comprehension, perception algorithms, and behavior trees by maximizing the similarity of the code between the robot and the simulator. The demonstration showcases the natural language interface and robot capabilities in a search scenario in which the ground and aerial robotic teammates, named Husky and Snapdragon respectively, are given verbal instructions from a Commander to explore the environment and identify injured individuals. A video recording of the testing scenario can be found at `https://youtu.be/5kVvj9xEK3E`.

In the live demonstration, visitors will engage with the two simulated robots in a game scenario to coordinate and navigate both robots to a designated zone along a route with injured individuals. Visitors will be given a 2D map of the environment as well as a set of navigation functions and robot names. The robots will follow the visitor's instructions autonomously, allowing the visitor to analyze the entire map and plan the best route for the robots while simultaneously overcoming several challenges in the task and environment.

5 Ongoing Research

This research platform has been used to investigate multi-participant dialogue, with a particular focus on interaction between one human and multiple robots. The testing scenario presented in this demo utilizes an *explicit addressee* approach, where tasks require first getting an individual robot's attention before issuing a task. In our ongoing research, we explore an *implicit addressee* approach by leveraging the NPCEditor dialogue retrieval algorithm, which matches responses to instructions using a word co-occurrence metric. This required creating a synthetic dataset of possible instructions. By associating tasks to robots directly in the training data, the dialogue retrieval algorithm can automatically match tasks specific to one robot without requiring mention of that robot's name. For example, tasks related to flying, such as *"Scout route bravo"*, will be automatically bound to the aerial robot when the instruction is passed as a TBS. No commonsense reasoning is required for this capability. In this research, robot capabilities have been shown to disambiguate which robot performs which task implicitly, an improvement over the explicit addressee approach and allows further research on multi-participant dialogue.

Another application of this platform is to categorize user preferences in instructed robot navigation behavior to reduce user workload and improve task efficiency (Hayes et al., 2018). The aim is to reflect individual user preferences by automatically fine-tuning robot movements as the interaction history between the user and robot grows, thereby reducing the need for users to verbally provide instruction clarifications or corrections. The first stage of this research implements inverse reinforcement learning to train a general, automated navigation model from manual human demonstrations. The second stage will use speech as part of a reward signal to modify the general navigation model on a per-user basis using traditional reinforcement learning techniques.

6 Related Work

Several other architectures have explored dialogue with robots. TeamTalk (Marge and Rudnicky, 2019) for example, controls multiple ground robots by way of a predefined grammar, while DIARC (Scheutz et al., 2019) also supports dialogue with multiple robots, and has been implemented on ground, aerial, and social robots. Open-source architectures such as OpenDial (Lison and Kennington, 2016), IrisTK (Skantze and Al Moubayed, 2012), and Microsoft's PSI (Bohus et al., 2017) can be used to build many situated dialogue agents, including robots. Compared to similar architectures, MultiBot leverages wizard-swappable components from ScoutBot and extends the mode of interaction to multi-participant dialogue. Training data for a MultiBot-based system can be collected from Wizard-of-Oz studies or synthetically derived and easily incorporated into MultiBot to accommodate a new domain, feature, or capability, as Table 1 details.

7 Summary and Future Work

This paper presents a platform to conduct spoken dialogue interaction with robots in a flexible, scenario-based architecture. The demonstrated testing scenario, MultiBot, is an implementation of autonomous dialogue management and navigation of two simulated robots in a large, outdoor simulated environment. This platform enables the crafting of various testing scenarios to perform language, robotics, and human-robot interaction research in a physical or simulated environment with multiple robots, while testing various language and robotic behavior capabilities. The platform provides the opportunity to study human-robot communication and behaviors in competitive and cooperative teaming and train future human-robot teams for a variety of challenging environments. Additionally, the platform may be used to experiment with new tasks in simulation as new autonomous robot navigation capabilities emerge.

Acknowledgments

This work was supported by the U.S. Army Research Laboratory. The authors thank the anonymous reviewers for their feedback, as well as Judith Klavans, Chris Kroninger, and Garrett Warnell for their contributions to this project.

References

Marko Bjelonic. 2016–2018. YOLO ROS: Real-Time Object Detection for ROS. `https://github.com/leggedrobotics/darknet_ros`.

Dan Bohus, Sean Andrist, and Mihai Jalobeanu. 2017. Rapid Development of Multimodal Interactive Systems: A Demonstration of Platform for Situated Intelligence. In *Proceedings of the 19th ACM International Conference on Multimodal Interaction*.

Claire Bonial, Matthew Marge, Ron Artstein, Ashley Foots, Felix Gervits, Cory J. Hayes, Cassidy Henry, Susan G. Hill, Anton Leuski, Stephanie M. Lukin, Pooja Moolchandani, Kimberly A. Pollard, David Traum, and Clare R. Voss. 2017. Laying Down the Yellow Brick Road: Development of a Wizard-of-Oz Interface for Collecting Human-Robot Dialogue. In *Proceedings of the AAAI Fall Symposium Series: Natural Communication for Human-Robot Collaboration*.

Arno Hartholt, David Traum, Stacy C Marsella, Ari Shapiro, Giota Stratou, Anton Leuski, Louis-Philippe Morency, and Jonathan Gratch. 2013. All Together Now: Introducing the Virtual Human Toolkit. In *Proceedings of the International Conference on Intelligent Virtual Agents*.

Cory J. Hayes, Matthew Marge, Ethan Stump, Claire Bonial, Clare Voss, and Susan G. Hill. 2018. Towards Learning User Preferences for Remote Robot Navigation. In *Proceedings of the RSS 2018 Workshop on Models and Representations for Human-Robot Communication*.

Anton Leuski and David Traum. 2011. NPCEditor: Creating Virtual Human Dialogue Using Information Retrieval Techniques. *AI Magazine*, 32(2).

Pierre Lison and Casey Kennington. 2016. OpenDial: A Toolkit for Developing Spoken Dialogue Systems with Probabilistic Rules. In *Proceedings of the Annual Meeting of the Association for Computational Linguistics - System Demonstrations*.

Stephanie M. Lukin, Felix Gervits, Cory J. Hayes, Anton Leuski, Pooja Moolchandani, John G. Rogers, Carlos Sanchez Amaro, Matthew Marge, Clare Voss, and David Traum. 2018. ScoutBot: A Dialogue System for Collaborative Navigation. In *Proceedings of the Annual Meeting of the Association for Computational Linguistics - System Demonstrations*.

Matthew Marge, Claire Bonial, Kimberly A. Pollard, Ron Artstein, Brendan Byrne, Susan G Hill, Clare Voss, and David Traum. 2016. Assessing Agreement in Human-Robot Dialogue Strategies: A Tale of Two Wizards. In *Proceedings of the International Conference on Intelligent Virtual Agents*.

Matthew Marge and Alexander I. Rudnicky. 2019. Miscommunication Detection and Recovery in Situated Human-Robot Dialogue. *ACM Transactions on Interactive Intelligent Systems*, 9(1).

Jean Oh, Arne Suppe, Felix Duvallet, Abdeslam Boularias, Jerry Vinokurov, Luis Ernesto Navarro-Serment, Oscar Romero, Robert Dean, Christian Lebiere, Martial Hebert, and Anthony (Tony) Stentz. 2015. Toward Mobile Robots Reasoning Like Humans. In *Proceedings of the Twenty-Ninth AAAI Conference on Artificial Intelligence.*

Harvey Sacks, Emanuel A Schegloff, and Gail Jefferson. 1978. A Simplest Systematics for the Organization of Turn-Taking for Conversation. *Langauge*, 50(4).

Matthias Scheutz, Thomas Williams, Evan Krause, Bradley Oosterveld, Vasanth Sarathy, and Tyler Frasca. 2019. An Overview of the Distributed Integrated Cognition Affect and Reflection DIARC Architecture. In *Cognitive Architectures.*

Gabriel Skantze and Samer Al Moubayed. 2012. IrisTK: A Statechart-Based Toolkit for Multi-Party Face-to-Face Interaction. In *Proceedings of the 14th ACM International Conference on Multimodal Interaction.*

David Traum, Andrew Jones, Kia Hays, Heather Maio, Oleg Alexander, Ron Artstein, Paul Debevec, Alesia Gainer, Kallirroi Georgila, Kathleen Haase, Karen Jungblut, Anton Leuski, Stephen Smith, and William Swartout. 2015. New Dimensions in Testimony: Digitally Preserving a Holocaust Survivor's Interactive Storytelling. In *International Conference on Interactive Digital Storytelling.*

Chat-crowd: A Dialog-based Platform for Visual Layout Composition

Paola Cascante-Bonilla[1]   **Xuwang Yin**[1]   **Vicente Ordonez**[1]   **Song Feng**[2]
[1]University of Virginia, [2]IBM Thomas J. Watson Research Center.
`[pc9za, xy4cm, vicente]@virginia.edu, sfeng@us.ibm.com`

Abstract

In this paper we introduce Chat-crowd, an interactive environment for visual layout composition via conversational interactions. Chat-crowd supports multiple agents with two conversational roles: agents who play the role of a *designer* are in charge of placing objects in an editable canvas according to instructions or commands issued by agents with a *director* role. The system can be integrated with crowd-sourcing platforms for both synchronous and asynchronous data collection and is equipped with comprehensive quality controls on the performance of both types of agents. We expect that this system will be useful to build multimodal goal-oriented dialog tasks that require spatial and geometric reasoning.

1 Introduction

There has been growing interest in building visually grounded dialog systems (Ren et al., 2015; Bisk et al., 2016; Das et al., 2017; Chen et al., 2018; El-Nouby et al., 2018; Shridhar and Hsu, 2018). Building interactive agents that can complete goal-oriented tasks in a situated environment using natural language is a challenging problem that requires both robust natural language understanding (NLU) and natural language generation (NLG). Datasets for visually grounded dialog tasks have started to emerge but more general and effective tools for data collection are still missing.

We introduce an interactive data collection and annotation tool[1] for the collaborative tasks of visual layout composition through natural language dialogs (see Figure 1). In this work, we refer to layouts to the spatial distribution of objects in a 2D canvas as well as their attributes such as name, shape, or color. More specifically, Chat-crowd is designed to support a basic model task consisting

---

[1] `chatcrowd.github.io`

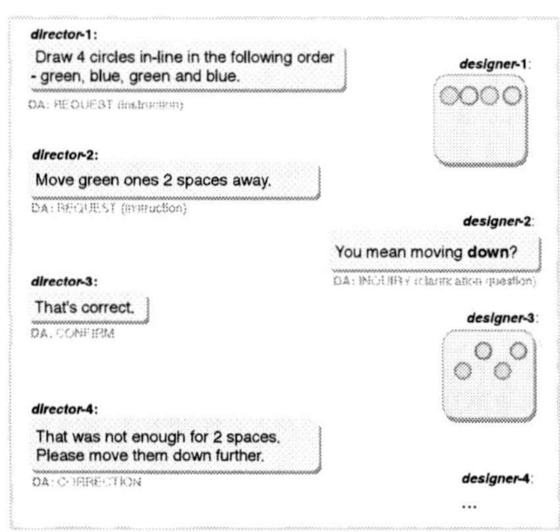

Figure 1: An illustration of the interactions and dialog acts (DA) between a *director* and a *designer* for one of our sample tasks. In asynchronous mode, the role of an agent can be taken by a different user in each round.

of dialogs between a *director* agent that is provided with a visual layout as a reference, and a *designer* agent that is provided with a canvas where one can add, remove, resize, or relocate visual elements. The two agents can communicate using natural language within the context of various dialog acts ("DA") as illustrated in Figure 1. The *director* provides instructions to modify elements in the canvas, and the *designer* optionally writes clarifying questions or modifies the canvas. While the *director* can see the progress of the *designer* as the dialog proceeds, the *designer* only sees the instructions from the *director*. The dialog ends when the visual layout composed by the *designer* matches the given visual layout to the *director*.

One key feature of our system is that it allows asynchronous conversations, i.e. the *director* and *designer* do not need to be online at the same time, or be persistent throughout the task. This means that different users can pick up the task where it was left off in the previous interaction, thus simplifying the overall collection process. Furthermore,

138

Proceedings of NAACL-HLT 2019: Demonstrations, pages 138–142
Minneapolis, Minnesota, June 2 - June 7, 2019. ©2019 Association for Computational Linguistics

it enables a process for data validation and job distribution at a finer level. Additionally, our system optionally employs a bot agent to inject synthetic utterances that trigger diversified or less represented dialog activities. Such injections can also be used for evaluating the responses from human agents since the optimal responses to the synthetic utterances are already given. We show that under this asynchronous mode, crowdsourced contributors are still able to converse based on the dialog history and complete the tasks.

To validate our system, we first apply the system on a task with more controllable visual layouts consisting of visual primitives (e.g., circles, rectangles, triangles); we also test our system on grounding for visual layouts corresponding to objects in real-images from an object recognition dataset (Lin et al., 2014). Separating the pattern recognition task from the visual understanding task through visual layouts allows us to explore richer language for spatial reasoning yet still connects to real-world images.

Our contributions are the following: (1) a new multi-modal dialog simulation system with a focus on spatial reasoning; (2) an asynchronous dialog collection platform that can trigger more diverse dialog activities and evaluate the performance of crowdsourced contributors in ongoing tasks; (3) an analysis of the difficulty and the type of language used by people to accomplish the proposed collaborative task of re-constructing visual layouts from asynchronous dialogs.

2 Visual Layout Dialog Collection

This work aims to demonstrate the usage of Chatcrowd for obtaining dialog data for geometric and spatial reasoning, ranging from abstract to more complex scenes. To this end, we explore two types of visual layouts: layouts in a shape-world with automatically generated simple 2D shape primitives, and layouts of objects from real images.

2D-shape Layouts We propose a synthetic layout world where objects of different shapes (circle, square, triangle) and colors (blue, red, green) are pinned to a set of 5×5 grid locations on a canvas. This setup allows us to focus on the language, and the accurate reconstruction of the visual layouts by discarding the additional complexities of real-world scenes. We generate two types of 2D-shape layouts: (1) `2d-shape-random`: consisting of scenes with 4 to 6 objects with shapes,

color, and locations selected randomly, and `2d-shape-pattern`: consisting of objects generated by following a set of customizable production rules that encourage adjacent objects. Figure 3 presents our user interface for the data collection tasks of 2D-shape layouts. For the real-image layouts, the interface includes additional features for resizing, moving, and naming objects.

COCO Layouts We use as reference and test bed of the object layouts of real-world images from the COCO dataset (Lin et al., 2014). The layout of an image includes objects and their locations. All objects are represented by a set of rectangles (proportional to the size of the corresponding object) and the object class (e.g., `people`, `dog` and `surfboard`). We also experiment with two types of scenarios: (1) `COCO-simple`: corresponding to images with simple layouts with 3 to 4 object instances belonging to 3 distinct classes, and (2) `COCO-complex`: corresponding to images consisting of layouts with 6 to 8 object instances belonging to 6 distinct object classes.

2.1 Crowdsourcing Task Design

In our task, crowd agents interact under two roles: *director* and *designer*. In the *director* mode, agents direct the drawing in the following ways: (1) providing instructions for how layouts should be modified; (2) giving suggestions for correcting or improving the current layout; (3) answering questions from the *designer* agents. In the *designer* mode, the agents either follow the instructions to draw on the canvas by specifying the attributes and locations for 2D-shapes/COCO, or ask clarifying questions if needed.

Data Collection One challenge for such multi-model dialog collection via crowdsourcing is that it could be very complicated and expensive to pair two qualified contributors to converse in real time (Lasecki and Bigham, 2013). Our system is designed to support both synchronous as well as asynchronous interactions. In the asynchronous mode, the agents are asked to review and understand a chat history before taking an action. Thus, we design quizzes to assist agents in learning how to examine the chat history to determine what actions are helpful for reconstructing the layouts.

Quality Control The most common quality assurance provided by crowdsourcing platforms is to evaluate the performance with gold standard data,

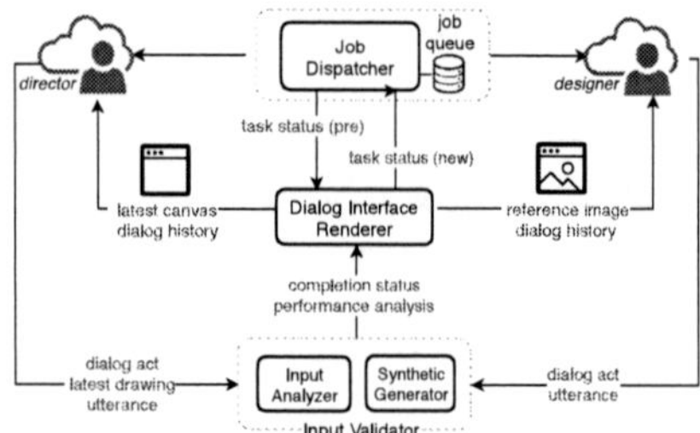

Figure 2: Overview of the Chat-crowd System

which is not applicable in our case. We propose to verify and ensure the success of the task using the following criteria: a task is considered successful if a layout is reconstructed with high similarity with respect to the reference layout. For 2D shape layouts, a layout similarity is tested by computing an exact match; For COCO layouts the matching is confirmed by the *director* agents who determines when the task should end.

Output Data The output includes free-form textual utterances from *director* and *designer* agents annotated with dialog acts, a sequence of drawings on the canvas and the final layouts of images. In our task setting, the dialog data can be potentially divided into sub-dialogs or atomic dialog interactions accordingly.

3 Experiment Results and Analysis

3.1 System Overview

Figure 2 presents an overview of our system. In synchronous mode, it allows the agents to converse in real time to perform a given task. In asynchronous mode, the automated Job Dispatcher determines a job of a role for next turn to interface with the crowdsourcing platforms. The latest canvas and dialog history of a given job are dynamically generated by Dialog Interface Renderer. Once an input (e.g, dialog act, utterance, or latest canvas) is submitted, Input Validator first examine the content via its sub-module Input Analyzer. It identifies the modification to the previous canvas; object features and locations in the utterance[2] and the dialog acts etc.. Additionally, Synthetic Generator is applied to inject certain responses: (1) to intrigue more diverse dialog activities such as designer asking clarification questions; (2) to inspect the performance of the contributors, for instance, when a *designer* submits a canvas given a non-viable instruction by Synthetic Generator.

___
[2]We employ NLP tools by `spacy.io`

3.2 Experimental Settings

We post the jobs on the FigureEight crowdsourcing platform. We collected dialogs for 100 `2d-shape-random` layouts, 100 `2d-shape-pattern` layouts, and additionally run a pilot study on 10 `COCO-simple` layouts and 10 `COCO-complex` layouts, leading to $2,520$ individual user interactions for 2d-shapes and 595 for real scene COCO layouts.

3.3 Quantitative and Qualitative Analysis

Director Word Usage Analysis We first analyzed the types of words that people in the *director* agent role used to provide instructions to the *designers*. We found that people mention location, color, and shape words in over 90% of the total of instructions and often all three with a slight preference for mentioning shape over color information. For the `2d-shape-pattern` task there was slightly lower preference to mention shape and color, than in `2d-shape-random`. This is because when each object is placed randomly, then people have to more often refer to each object individually on each round.

Designer Reactions Analyzing the interactions by *designer* agents we found that about 60% of the times they modify the canvas without necessarily asking clarification questions. Here is a set of example responses: "I did not understand instructions from instructor ...", "please give instruction", examples of questions are: "where to put circle?", "do the boxes mean squares", "where exactly, in the middle, left or right?", "It is done?".

Task Duration We additionally analyze the difficulty of each task by the number of rounds that it takes to complete a layout, and the average length (in words) for the instructions issued by the *director*. Table 1 shows these statistics for our four type of layouts. We found, unsurprisingly, that for `2d-shape-pattern` layouts, the average number of rounds is significantly lower than for `2d-shape-random`, indicating that the pattern in the distribution of objects in the canvas is indeed being exploited by the agents. Additionally, we can gauge the difference in difficulty between `COCO-complex` and `COCO-simple`, where the number of rounds is more than double even when the average instruction is only two words larger.

Instruction Efficiency In terms of single instruction efficiency, we found that for 2d-

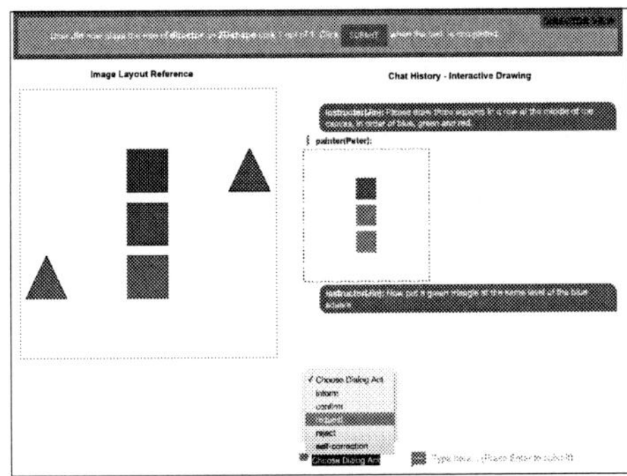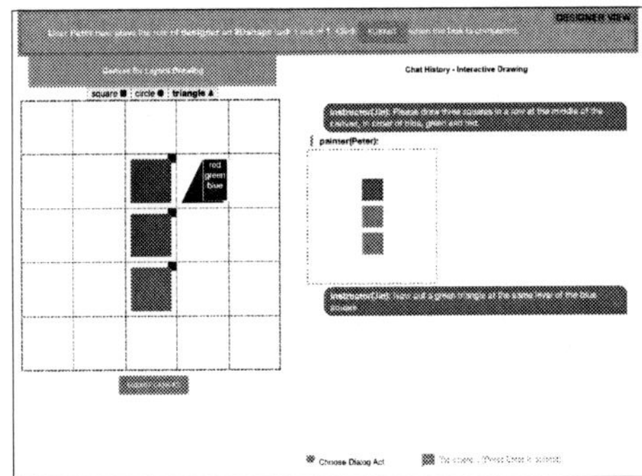

Figure 3: UI for *director* (left) and *designer* (right) agents for 2D-shape layout task.

LAYOUT-TYPE	#ROUNDS	AVG-WORDS
2d-shape-random	7.23	18.0 ± 14.3
2d-shape-pattern	5.37	19.4 ± 15.8
COCO-simple	7.6	18.7 ± 13.9
COCO-complex	22.1	20.9 ± 28.2

Table 1: Statistics for task duration for each type of layout based on the number of rounds needed and average number of words in the instructions.

shape-random layouts, *designer* agents were able to modify more than three objects per turn only 14% of the times, while this number was 20% for 2d-shape-pattern layouts. Thus, it further confirms that people are effective at using the patterns to optimize language for the task. We also notice how the COCO layouts elicit semantic relations that are not present in the 2D-shape layouts, so while we expect that some of the language from 2D-shape layouts will translate to real-world scenes, such as references to locations, and shapes, the realm of semantic relations might need a separate treatment.

4 Related Work

Given some of the limitations of tasks such as human-robot interactions, text-to-scene conversion or visual question answering, there has been recent interest on building more complex multimodal datasets of visually grounded dialogs (Geman et al., 2015; Mostafazadeh et al., 2017; Das et al., 2017; Kim et al., 2017). Our goal oriented task of re-constructing the spatial distribution of objects in a canvas through conversational interactions sets our task apart from these previous works. In our work, we additionally explore re-construction of layouts corresponding to real-world images with a focus on the inclusion of spatial and geometric reasoning and more dynamic dialog activities while completing the tasks.

Another aspect that sets our work apart from previous efforts in this domain is that we leverage asynchronous dialog interactions. However, there have been important previous works studying this type of dialogs in the more general setting (e.g. Blaylock et al. (2002); Joty et al. (2011); Tavafi et al. (2013)). We similarly show that our proposed visually grounded task is feasible under asynchronous dialogs.

Finally, object layouts, and visual grounding on geometric primitives has generally been of interest to study the compositionality of language. The work of Mitchell et al. (2013); FitzGerald et al. (2013) used synthetic object layouts and simple scenes to study referring expressions, while Yin and Ordonez (2017) used layouts from real images for image captioning. Andreas et al. (2016), and Johnson et al. (2017) introduced synthetic abstract scene datasets to test visual question answering. Our work is instead focused on visually grounded dialogs for spatial reasoning.

5 Conclusions

We developed Chat-crowd, a framework and associated platform to collect dialogs for goal-oriented tasks involving visual reasoning. Our platform incorporates mechanisms to encourage diverse dialog activities and provides a new way of evaluating the performance of crowdsourcing agents during the task. Our system demonstrated the feasibility of a *director-designer* agent interaction to reconstruct input visual layouts based only on asynchronous dialog interactions.

Acknowledgment This project was funded in part by an IBM Faculty Award to V.O.

References

Jacob Andreas, Marcus Rohrbach, Trevor Darrell, and Dan Klein. 2016. Neural module networks. In *Proceedings of the IEEE Conference on Computer Vision and Pattern Recognition*, pages 39–48.

Yonatan Bisk, Deniz Yuret, and Daniel Marcu. 2016. Natural language communication with robots. In *Proceedings of the 2016 Conference of the North American Chapter of the Association for Computational Linguistics: Human Language Technologies*, pages 751–761.

Nate Blaylock, James Allen, and George Ferguson. 2002. Synchronization in an asynchronous agent-based architecture for dialogue systems. In *Proceedings of the 3rd SIGdial workshop on Discourse and dialogue-Volume 2*, pages 1–10. Association for Computational Linguistics.

Howard Chen, Alane Shur, Dipendra Misra, Noah Snavely, and Yoav Artzi. 2018. Touchdown: Natural language navigation and spatial reasoning in visual street environments. *arXiv preprint arXiv:1811.12354*.

Abhishek Das, Satwik Kottur, Khushi Gupta, Avi Singh, Deshraj Yadav, José MF Moura, Devi Parikh, and Dhruv Batra. 2017. Visual dialog. In *Proceedings of the IEEE Conference on Computer Vision and Pattern Recognition*, volume 2.

Alaaeldin El-Nouby, Shikhar Sharma, Hannes Schulz, Devon Hjelm, Layla El Asri, Samira Ebrahimi Kahou, Yoshua Bengio, and Graham W Taylor. 2018. Keep drawing it: Iterative language-based image generation and editing. *arXiv preprint arXiv:1811.09845*.

Nicholas FitzGerald, Yoav Artzi, and Luke Zettlemoyer. 2013. Learning distributions over logical forms for referring expression generation. In *Proceedings of the 2013 conference on empirical methods in natural language processing*, pages 1914–1925.

Donald Geman, Stuart Geman, Neil Hallonquist, and Laurent Younes. 2015. Visual turing test for computer vision systems. *Proceedings of the National Academy of Sciences*, 112(12):3618–3623.

Justin Johnson, Bharath Hariharan, Laurens van der Maaten, Li Fei-Fei, C Lawrence Zitnick, and Ross Girshick. 2017. Clevr: A diagnostic dataset for compositional language and elementary visual reasoning. In *Computer Vision and Pattern Recognition (CVPR), 2017 IEEE Conference on*, pages 1988–1997. IEEE.

Shafiq Joty, Giuseppe Carenini, and Chin-Yew Lin. 2011. Unsupervised modeling of dialog acts in asynchronous conversations. In *IJCAI Proceedings-International Joint Conference on Artificial Intelligence*, volume 22, page 1807.

Jin-Hwa Kim, Devi Parikh, Dhruv Batra, Byoung-Tak Zhang, and Yuandong Tian. 2017. Codraw: Visual dialog for collaborative drawing. *arXiv preprint arXiv:1712.05558*.

Walter S Lasecki and Jeffrey P Bigham. 2013. Interactive crowds: Real-time crowdsourcing and crowd agents. In *Handbook of human computation*, pages 509–521. Springer.

Tsung-Yi Lin, Michael Maire, Serge Belongie, James Hays, Pietro Perona, Deva Ramanan, Piotr Dollár, and C Lawrence Zitnick. 2014. Microsoft coco: Common objects in context. In *European conference on computer vision*, pages 740–755. Springer.

Margaret Mitchell, Kees Van Deemter, and Ehud Reiter. 2013. Generating expressions that refer to visible objects. In *Proceedings of the 2013 Conference of the North American Chapter of the Association for Computational Linguistics: Human Language Technologies*, pages 1174–1184.

Nasrin Mostafazadeh, Chris Brockett, Bill Dolan, Michel Galley, Jianfeng Gao, Georgios P Spithourakis, and Lucy Vanderwende. 2017. Image-grounded conversations: Multimodal context for natural question and response generation. *arXiv preprint arXiv:1701.08251*.

Mengye Ren, Ryan Kiros, and Richard Zemel. 2015. Exploring models and data for image question answering. In *Advances in neural information processing systems*, pages 2953–2961.

Mohit Shridhar and David Hsu. 2018. Interactive visual grounding of referring expressions for human-robot interaction. *arXiv preprint arXiv:1806.03831*.

Maryam Tavafi, Yashar Mehdad, Shafiq Joty, Giuseppe Carenini, and Raymond Ng. 2013. Dialogue act recognition in synchronous and asynchronous conversations. In *Proceedings of the SIGDIAL 2013 Conference*, pages 117–121.

Xuwang Yin and Vicente Ordonez. 2017. Obj2text: Generating visually descriptive language from object layouts. In *Conference on Empirical Methods in Natural Language Processing (EMNLP)*.

Author Index

Association for Computational Linguistics
209 N. Eighth Street
Stroudsburg, Pennsylvania 18360

ISBN 978-1-5108-8757-2